PORNOGRAPHY

BY THE SAME AUTHOR

NONFICTION

Woman Hating

Our Blood: Prophecies and Discourses on Sexual Politics

Right-wing Women

Intercourse

Letters from a War Zone: Writings 1976–1989

Pornography and Civil Rights (with Catharine A. MacKinnon)

FICTION

the new womans broken heart: short stories

Ice and Fire

ANDREA DWORKIN

PORNOGRAPHY

MEN POSSESSING WOMEN

A PLUME BOOK

PLUME
Published by the Penguin Group
Penguin Books USA Inc., 375 Hudson Street, New York, New York 10014, U.S.A.
Penguin Books Ltd, 27 Wrights Lane, London W8 5TZ, England
Penguin Books Australia Ltd, Ringwood, Victoria, Australia
Penguin Books Canada Ltd, 10 Alcorn Avenue, Toronto, Ontario, Canada, M4V 3B2
Penguin Books (N.Z.) Ltd, 182-190 Wairau Road, Auckland 10, New Zealand

Penguin Books Ltd, Registered Offices: Harmondsworth, Middlesex, England

Published by Plume, an imprint of New American Library, a division of Penguin Books USA Inc.

This paperback edition of *Pornography* first published in 1989 by Dutton, an imprint of New American Library, a division of Penguin Books USA Inc. Published simultaneously in Canada by Fitzhenry and Whiteside, Limited, Toronto.

Library of Congress Catalog Card Number: 89-51147

ISBN: 0-452-26793-5

10 9 8 7 6 5 4 3 2 1

The author gratefully acknowledges permission from the following sources to reprint material in this book:

Gena Corea for an unpublished interview with Dr. Herbert Ratner, September 20, 1979.

Alex de Jonge for his translation of four lines from *Journaux Completes* by Charles Baudelaire, cited in *Baudelaire: Prince of Clouds* by Alex de Jonge, copyright © 1976 by Alex de Jonge.

Grove Press, Inc., for *Justine* from *The Complete Marquis de Sade* by Marquis de Sade, translated by Richard Seaver and Austryn Wainhouse, copyright © 1965 by Richard Seaver and Austryn Wainhouse.

The Institute for Sex Research, Indiana University, for *Sex Offenders: An Analysis of Types* by Paul H. Gebhard, John H. Gagnon, Wardell B. Pomeroy, and Cornelia V. Christenson, published by Harper & Row, Publishers, and Paul B. Hoeber, Inc., Medical Books © 1965 by The Institute for Sex Research. And for *Sexual Behavior in the Human Male* by Alfred C. Kinsey, Wardell B. Pomeroy, and Clyde E. Martin, published by W. B. Saunders Company, copyright © 1948 by W. B. Saunders Company.

Robin Morgan for "The Network of the Imaginary Mother" in *Lady of the Beasts: Poems*, published by Random House, copyright © 1976 by Robin Morgan.

New Directions for two lines from *A Season in Hell* by Arthur Rimbaud, translated by Louise Varese, copyright © 1945, 1952, 1961 by New Directions.

W. W. Norton & Company, Inc. for "Poem I" from "21 Love Poems" in *Dream of a Common Language* by Adrienne Rich, copyright © 1978 by W. W. Norton & Company, Inc.

Portions of this book have appeared in slightly altered form in *New Political Science, Sinister Wisdom, Mother Jones*, and *Ms.*

For John Stoltenberg
In Memory of Rose Keller

Troubles walk in long lines.

Russian proverb

No two of us think alike about it, and yet it is clear to me, that question underlies the whole movement, and all our little skirmishing for better laws, and the right to vote, will yet be swallowed up in the real question, viz: Has woman a right to herself? It is very little to me to have the right to vote, to own property, etc., if I may not keep my body, and its uses, in my absolute right. Not one wife in a thousand can do that now.

Lucy Stone, in a letter to Antoinette Brown,
July 11, 1855

Sexual freedom, then, means the abolition of prostitution both in and out of marriage; means the emancipation of woman from sexual slavery and her coming into ownership and control of her own body; means the end of her pecuniary dependence upon man, so that she may never even seemingly have to procure whatever she may desire or need by sexual favors .

Victoria Woodhull, "Tried As By Fire;
or, The True and The False, Socially," 1874

He said that life is very expensive. Even women are more expensive. That when he wants to f—— a woman they want so much money that he gives up the idea.

I pretended I didn't hear, because I don't speak pornography.

Carolina Maria de Jesus, *Child of the Dark*

Contents

Introduction

1

> I did not hesitate to let it be known of me, that the white man who expected to succeed in whipping, must also succeed in killing me.
>
> Frederick Douglass, *Narrative of the Life of Frederick Douglass An American Slave Written by Himself*

In 1838, at the age of 21, Frederick Douglass became a runaway slave, a hunted fugitive. Though later renowned as a powerful political orator, he spoke his first public words with trepidation at an abolitionist meeting—a meeting of white people—in Massachusetts in 1841. Abolitionist leader William Lloyd Garrison recalled the event:

> He came forward to the platform with a hesitancy and embarrassment, necessarily the attendants of a sensitive mind in such a novel position. After apologizing for his ignorance, and reminding the audience that slavery was a poor school for the human intellect and heart, he proceeded to narrate some of the facts in his own history as a slave. . . . As soon as he had taken his seat, filled with hope and admiration, I rose . . . [and] . . . reminded the audience of the peril which surrounded this self-emancipated young man at the North,—even in Massachusetts, on the soil of the Pilgrim Fathers, among the descendants of revolutionary

> sires; and I appealed to them, whether they would ever allow him to be carried back into slavery—law or no law, constitution or no constitution.[1]

Always in danger as a fugitive, Douglass became an organizer for the abolitionists; the editor of his own newspaper, which advocated both abolition and women's rights; a station chief for the underground railroad; a close comrade of John Brown's; and the only person willing, at the Seneca Falls Convention in 1848, to second Elizabeth Cady Stanton's resolution demanding the vote for women. To me, he has been a political hero: someone whose passion for human rights was both visionary and rooted in action; whose risk was real, not rhetorical; whose endurance in pursuing equality set a standard for political honor. In his writings, which were as eloquent as his orations, his repudiation of subjugation was uncompromising. His political intelligence, which was both analytical and strategic, was suffused with emotion: indignation at human pain, grief at degradation, anguish over suffering, fury at apathy and collusion. He hated oppression. He had an empathy for those hurt by inequality that crossed lines of race, gender, and class because it was an empathy animated by his own experience—his own experience of humiliation and his own experience of dignity.

To put it simply, Frederick Douglass was a serious man—a man serious in the pursuit of freedom. Well, you see the problem. Surely it is self-evident. What can any such thing have to do with us—with women in our time? Imagine—in present time—a woman saying, and meaning, that a man who expected to succeed in whipping, must also succeed in killing her. Suppose there were a politics of liberation premised on that assertion—an assertion not of ideology but of deep and stubborn outrage at being mis-

1. William Lloyd Garrison, Preface, *Narrative of the Life of Frederick Douglass An American Slave Written by Himself*, Frederick Douglass, ed. Benjamin Quarles (Cambridge, Mass.: The Belknap Press of Harvard University Press, 1960), p. 5.

used, a resolute assertion, a serious assertion by serious women. What are serious women; are there any; isn't serousness about freedom by women for women grotesquely comic; we don't want to be laughed at, do we? What would this politics of liberation be like? Where would we find it? What would we have to do? Would we have to do something other than dress for success? Would we have to stop the people who are hurting us from hurting us? Not debate them; stop them. Would we have to stop slavery? Not discuss it; stop it. Would we have to stop pretending that our rights are protected in this society? Would we have to be so grandiose, so arrogant, so unfeminine, as to believe that the streets we walk on, the homes we live in, the beds we sleep in, are *ours*—belong to us—really belong to us: we decide what is right and what is wrong and if something hurts us, it stops. It is, of course, gauche to be too sincere about these things, and it is downright ridiculous to be serious. Intelligent people are well mannered and moderate, even in pursuing freedom. Smart women whisper and say please.

Now imagine Cherry Tart or Bunny or Pet or Beaver saying, and meaning, that a man who expected to succeed in whipping must also succeed in killing her. She says it; she means it. It is not a pornographic scenario in which she is the dummy forced by the pimp-ventriloquist to say the ubiquitous No-That-Means-Yes. It is not the usual sexual provocation created by pornographers using a woman's body, the subtext of which is: I refuse to be whipped so whip me harder, whip me more; I refuse to be whipped, what I really want is for you to kill me; whip me, then kill me; kill me, then whip me; whatever you want, however you want it—was it good for you? Instead, the piece on the page or in the film steps down and steps out: I'm real, she says. Like Frederick Douglass, she will be hesitant and embarrassed. She will feel ignorant. She will tell a first-person story about her own experience in prostitution, in pornography, as a victim of incest, as a victim of rape, as someone who has been beaten or tortured, as someone who has been bought and sold. She may not remind her audience that sexual servitude is a poor school for the human intellect and heart—sexually violated, often since childhood, she may not know the value of her human intellect or her human heart—and the audience cannot be counted on to know that she deserved better than she got. Will there be someone there to implore the audience to help her escape the pornography—law or no law, constitution or no constitution; will the audience understand that as long as the pornography of her exists she is a captive of it, a fugitive from it? Will the audience be willing to fight for her freedom by fighting against the pornography of her, because, as Linda Marchiano said of *Deep Throat*, "every time someone watches that film, they are watching me being raped"[2]? Will the audience understand that she is standing in for those who didn't get away; will the audience understand that those who didn't get away were *someone*—each one was someone? Will the audience understand what stepping down from the page or out of the film cost her—what it took for her to survive, for her to escape, for her to dare to speak now about what happened to her then?

"I'm an incest survivor, ex–pornography model, and ex-prostitute," the woman says. "My incest story begins before preschool and ends many years later—this was with my father. I was also molested by an uncle and a minister . . . my father forced me to perform sexual acts with men at a stag party when I was a teenager. . . . My father was my pimp in pornography. There were three occasions from ages nine to sixteen when he forced me to be a pornography model . . . in Nebraska, so, yes, it does happen here."[3]

I was thirteen when I was forced into prostitution and

2. Public Hearings on Ordinances to Add Pornography as Discrimination Against Women, Minneapolis City Council, Government Operations Committee, December 12 and 13, 1983, in transcript available from Organizing Against Pornography, 734 East Lake Street, Minneapolis, Mn. 55407, p. 16.
3. Name withheld, manuscript.

pornography, the woman says. I was drugged, raped, gang-raped, imprisoned, beaten, sold from one pimp to another, photographed by pimps, photographed by tricks; I was used in pornography and they used pornography on me; "[t]hey knew a child's face when they looked into it. It was clear that I was not acting of my own free will. I was always covered with welts and bruises. . . . It was even clearer that I was sexually inexperienced. I literally didn't know what to do. So they showed me pornography to teach me about sex and then they would ignore my tears as they positioned my body like the women in the pictures and used me."[4]

"As I speak about pornography, here, today," the woman says, "I am talking about my life." I was raped by my uncle when I was ten, by my stepbrother and stepfather by the time I was twelve. My stepbrother was making pornography of me by the time I was fourteen. "I was not even sixteen years old and my life reality consisted of sucking cocks, posing nude, performing sexual acts and actively being repeatedly raped."[5]

These are the women in the pictures; they have stepped out, though the pictures may still exist. They have become very serious women; serious in the pursuit of freedom. There are many thousands of them in the United States, not all first put in pornography as children though most were sexually molested as children, raped or otherwise abused again later, eventually becoming homeless and poor. They are feminists in the antipornography movement, and they don't want to debate "free speech." Like Frederick Douglass, they are fugitives from the men who made a profit off of them. They live in jeopardy, always more or less in hiding. They organize to help others escape. They write—in blood, their own. They publish sometimes, including their own newsletters. They demonstrate; they

4. Sarah Wynter, pseudonym, manuscript, June 19, 1985.

5. Name withheld, manuscript; also testimony before the Subcommittee on Juvenile Justice of the Committee on the Judiciary, United States Senate, September 12, 1984.

resist; they disappear when the danger gets too close. The Constitution has nothing for them—no help, no protection, no dignity, no solace, no justice. The law has nothing for them—no recognition of the injuries done them by pornography, no reparations for what has been taken from them. They are real, and even though this society will do nothing for them, they are women who have resolved that the man who expects to succeed in whipping must also succeed in killing them. This changes the nature of the women's movement. It must stop slavery. The runaway slave is now part of it.

2

> One new indulgence was to go out evenings alone. This I worked out carefully in my mind, as not only a right but a duty. Why should a woman be deprived of her only free time, the time allotted to recreation? Why must she be dependent on some man, and thus forced to please him if she wished to go anywhere at night?
>
> A stalwart man once sharply contested my claim to this freedom to go alone. "Any true man," he said with fervor, "is always ready to go with a woman at night. He is her natural protector." "Against what?" I inquired. As a matter of fact, the thing a woman is most afraid to meet on a dark street is her natural protector. Singular.
>
> Charlotte Perkins Gilman,
> *The Living of Charlotte Perkins Gilman: An Autobiography*

She was thirteen. She was at a Girl Scout camp in northern Wisconsin. She went for a long walk in the woods alone during the day. She had long blond hair. She saw three hunters reading magazines, talking, joking. One looked up and said: "There's a live one." She thought they meant a deer. She ducked and started to run away. They meant her. They chased her, caught her, dragged her back to where they were camped. The magazines were pornography of women she physically resembled: blond, childlike. They called her names from the pornography: Little Godiva, Golden Girl, also bitch and slut. They threatened to kill her. They made her undress. It was November and cold. One held a rifle to her head; another beat her breasts with his rifle. All three raped her—penile penetration into the vagina. The third one couldn't get hard at first so he demanded a blow job. She didn't know what that was. The third man forced his penis into her mouth; one of the others cocked the trigger on his rifle. She was told she had better do it right. She tried. When they were done with her they kicked her: they kicked her naked body and they kicked leaves and pine needles on her. "[T]hey told me that if I wanted more, that I could come back the next day."[6]

She was sexually abused when she was three by a boy who was fourteen—it was a "game" he had learned from pornography. "[I]t seems really bizarre to me to use the word 'boy' because the only memory I have of this person is as a three year old. And as a three year old he seemed like a really big man." When she was a young adult she was drugged by men who made and sold pornography. She remembers flashing lights, being forced onto a stage, being undressed by two men and sexually touched by a third. Men were waving money at her: "one of them shoved it in my stomach and essentially punched me. I kept wondering how it was possible that they couldn't see that I didn't want to be there, that I wasn't there willingly."[7]

She had a boyfriend. She was twenty-one. One night he went to a stag party and watched pornography films. He called her up to ask if he could have sex with her. She felt obligated to make him happy. "I also felt that the refusal would be indicative of sexual quote unquote hang-ups on my part and that I was not quote unquote liberal enough.

6. See Public Hearings, Minneapolis, pp. 38–39.
7. See Public Hearings, Minneapolis, pp. 39–41.

When he arrived, he informed me that the other men at the party were envious that he had a girlfriend to fuck. They wanted to fuck too after watching the pornography. He informed me of this as he was taking his coat off." He had her perform oral sex on him: "I did not do this of my own volition. He put his genitals in my face and he said 'Take it all.' " He fucked her. The whole encounter took about five minutes. Then he dressed and went back to the party. "I felt ashamed and numb and I also felt very used."[8]

She was seventeen, he was nineteen. He was an art student. He used her body for photography assignments by putting her body in contorted positions and telling her rape stories to get the expression he wanted on her face: fear. About a year later he had an assignment to do body casts in plaster. He couldn't get models because the plaster was heavy and caused fainting. She was a premed student. She tried to explain to him how deleterious the effects of the plaster were. "When you put plaster on your body, it sets up, it draws the blood to the skin and the more area it covers on your body, the more blood is drawn to your skin. You become dizzy and nauseous and sick to your stomach and finally faint." He needed his work to be exhibited, so he needed her to model. She tried. She couldn't stand the heat and the weight of the plaster. "He wanted me to be in poses where I had to hold my hands up over my head, and they would be numb and they would fall. He eventually tied my hands over my head." They got married. During the course of their marriage he began to consume more and more pornography. He would read excerpts to her from the magazines about group sex, wife swapping, anal intercourse, and bondage. They would go to pornography films and wet T-shirt contests with friends. "I felt devastated and disgusted watching it. I was told by those men that if I wasn't as smart as I was and if I would be more sexually liberated and more sexy that I would get along a lot better in the world and that they and a lot of

8. See Public Hearings, Minneapolis, p. 41.

other men would like me more. About this time I started feeling very terrified. I realized that this wasn't a joke anymore." She asked her mother for help but was told that divorce was a disgrace and it was her responsibility to make the marriage work. He brought his friends home to act out the scenarios from the pornography. She found the group sex humiliating and disgusting, and to prevent it she agreed to act out the pornography in private with her husband. She began feeling suicidal. He was transferred to an Asian country in connection with his job. The pornography in the country where they now lived was more violent. He took her to live sex shows where women had sex with animals, especially snakes. Increasingly, when she was asleep he would force intercourse on her. Then he started traveling a lot, and she used his absence to learn karate. "One night when I was in one of those pornographic institutions, I was sitting with a couple of people that I had known, watching the women on stage and watching the different transactions and the sales of the women and the different acts going on, and I realized that my life wasn't any different than these women except that it was done in the name of marriage. I could see how I was being seasoned to the use of pornography and I could see what was coming next. I could see more violence and I could see more humiliation and I knew at that point I was either going to die from it, I was going to kill myself, or I was going to leave. And I was feeling strong enough that I left. . . . Pornography is not a fantasy, it was my life, reality."[9]

At the time she made this statement, she couldn't have been older than twenty-two. She was terrified that the people would be identifiable, and so she spoke in only the most general terms, never specifying their relationship to her. She said she had lived in a house with a divorced woman, that woman's children, and the ex-husband, who refused to leave. She had lived there for eighteen years. During

9. See Public Hearings, Minneapolis, pp. 42–46.

that time, "the woman was regularly raped by this man. He would bring pornographic magazines, books, and paraphernalia into the bedroom with him and tell her that if she did not perform the sexual acts that were being done in the 'dirty' books and magazines he would beat and kill her. I know about this because my bedroom was right next to hers. I could hear everything they said. I could hear her screams and cries. In addition, since I did most of the cleaning in the house, I would often come across the books, magazines, and paraphernalia that were in the bedroom and other rooms of the house. . . . Not only did I suffer through the torture of listening to the rapes and tortures of a woman, but I could see what grotesque acts this man was performing on her from the pictures in the pornographic materials. I was also able to see the systematic destruction of a human being taking place before my eyes. At the time I lived with the woman, I was completely helpless, powerless in regard to helping this woman and her children in getting away from this man." As a child, she was told by the man that if she ever told or tried to run away he would break her arms and legs and cut up her face. He whipped her with belts and electrical cords. He made her pull her pants down to beat her. "I was touched and grabbed where I did not want him to touch me." She was also locked in dark closets and in the basement for long periods of time.[10]

She was raped by two men. They were acting out the pornographic video game "Custer's Revenge." She was American Indian; they were white. "They held me down and as one was running the tip of his knife across my face and throat he said, 'Do you want to play Custer's Last Stand? It's great. You lose but you don't care, do you? You like a little pain, don't you, squaw.' They both laughed and then he said, 'There is a lot of cock in Custer's Last Stand. You should be grateful, squaw, that all-American boys like

10. See Public Hearings, Minneapolis, pp. 65–66.

us want you. Maybe we will tie you to a tree and start a fire around you.' "[11]

Her name is Jayne Stamen. She is currently in jail. In 1986, she hired three men to beat up her husband. She wanted him to know what a beating felt like. He died. She was charged with second-degree murder; convicted of first-degree manslaughter; sentenced to eight-and-a-half to twenty-five years. She was also convicted of criminal solicitation: in 1984 she asked some men to kill her husband for her, then reneged; she was sentenced on the criminal solicitation charge to two-and-a-third to seven years. The sentences are to run consecutively. She was tortured in her marriage by a man consumed by acting out pornography. He tied her up when he raped her; he broke bones; he forced anal intercourse; he beat her mercilessly; he penetrated her vagina with objects, "his rifle, or a long-necked wine decanter, or twelve-inch artificial rubber penises." He shaved the hair off her pubic area because he wanted, in his words, to "screw a baby's cunt." He slept with a rifle and kept a knife by the bed; he would threaten to cut her face with the knife if she didn't act out the pornography, and he would use the knife again if she wasn't showing pleasure. He called her all the names: whore, slut, cunt, bitch. "He used to jerk himself off on my chest while I was sleeping, or I would get woke up with him coming in my face and then he'd urinate on me." She tried to escape several times. He came after her armed with his rifle. She became addicted to alcohol and pills. "The papers stated that I didn't report [the violence] to the police. I did have the police at my home on several occasions. Twice on Long Island was for the gun threats, and once in Starrett City was also for the gun. The rest of the times were for the beatings and throwing me out of the house. A few times the police helped me get away from him with my clothes and the boys. I went home to my

11. See Public Hearings, Minneapolis, pp. 66–67.

mom's. [He came after her with a rifle.] I went to the doctor's and hospitals on several occasions, too, but I could not tell the truth on how I 'hurt myself.' I always covered up for him, as I knew my life depended on that." The judge wouldn't admit testimony on the torture because he said the husband wasn't on trial. The defense lawyer said in private that he thought she probably enjoyed the abusive sex. Jayne's case will be appealed, but she may well have to stay in jail at Bedford Hills, a New York State prison for women, for the duration of the appeal because Women Against Pornography, a group that established the Defense Fund for Jayne Stamen, has not been able to raise bail money for her. Neither have I or others who care. It isn't chic to help such women; they aren't the Black Panthers. Ironically, there are many women—and recently a teenage girl, a victim of incest—who have hired others to kill the men—husbands, fathers—who were torturing them because they could not bear to do it themselves. Or the woman pours gasoline on the bed when he sleeps and lights the fire. Jayne didn't hire the men to kill her husband; the real question may be, why not? why didn't she? Women don't understand self-defense the way men do—perhaps because sexual abuse destroys the self. We don't feel we have a right to kill just because we are being beaten, raped, tortured, and terrorized. We are hurt for a long time before we fight back. Then, usually, we are punished: "I have lived in a prison for ten years, meaning my marriage," says Jayne Stamen, ". . . and now they have me in a real prison."[12]

I've quoted from statements, all made in public forums, by women I know well (except for Jayne Stamen; I've talked with her but I haven't met her). I can vouch for them; I know the stories are true. The women who made these particular statements are only a few of the thousands of women I have met, talked with, questioned: women who

12. Direct quotations are from the Statement of Jayne Stamen, issued by Women Against Pornography, February 14, 1988.

have been hurt by pornography. The women are real to me. I know what they look like standing tall; I've seen the fear; I've watched them remember; I've talked with them about other things, all sorts of things: intellectual issues, the weather, politics, school, children, cooking. I have some idea of their aspirations as individuals, the ones they lost during the course of sexual abuse, the ones they cherish now. I know them. Each one, for me, has a face, a voice, a whole life behind her face and her voice. Each is more eloquent and more hurt than I know how to convey. Since 1974, when my book *Woman Hating* was first published, women have been seeking me out to tell me that they have been hurt by pornography; they have told me how they have been hurt in detail, how much, how long, by how many. They thought I might believe them, initially, I think, because I took pornography seriously in *Woman Hating*. I said it was cruel, violent, basic to the way our culture sees and treats women—and I said the hate in it was real. Well, they knew that the hate in it was real because they had been sexually assaulted by that hate. One does not make the first tentative efforts to communicate about this abuse to those who will almost certainly ridicule one. Some women took a chance on me; and it was a chance, because I often did not want to listen. I had my limits and my reasons, like everyone else. For many years, I heard the same stories I have tried to encapsulate here: the same stories, sometimes more complicated, sometimes more savage, from thousands of women, most of whom hadn't dared to tell anyone. No part of the country was exempt; no age group; no racial or ethnic group; no "life-style" however "normal" or "alternative." The statements I have paraphrased here are not special: not more sadistic, not chosen by me because they are particularly sickening or offensive. In fact, they are not particularly sickening or offensive. They simply are what happens to women who are brutalized by the use of pornography on them.

Such first-person stories from women are dismissed by defenders of pornography as "anecdotal"; they misuse the word to make it denote a story, probably fictive, that is small, trivial, inconsequential, proof only of some defect in the woman herself—the story tells us nothing about pornography but it tells us all we need to know about the woman. She's probably lying; maybe she really liked it; and if it did happen, how could anyone (sometimes referred to as "a smart girl like you") be stupid enough, simple-minded enough, to think that pornography had anything to do with it? Wasn't there, as one grinning adversary always asks, also coffee in the house? The coffee, he suggests, is more likely to be a factor in the abuse than the pornography—after all, the bad effects of coffee have been proven in the laboratory. What does one do when women's lives are worth so little—worth arrogant, self-satisfied ridicule and nothing else, not even the appearance, however false, of charity or concern? Alas, one answers: the man (the husband, the boyfriend, the rapist, the torturer—you or your colleague or your best friend or your buddy) wasn't reading the coffee label when he tied the knots; the directions he followed are found in pornography, and, frankly, they are not found anywhere else. The first-person stories are human experience, raw and true, not mediated by dogma or ideology *or* social convention; "human" is the trick word in the sentence. If one values women as human beings, one cannot turn away or refuse to hear so that one can refuse to care without bearing responsibility for the refusal. One cannot turn one's back on the women or on the burden of memory they carry. If one values women as human beings, one will not turn one's back on the women who are being hurt today and the women who will be hurt tomorrow.

Most of what we know about the experience of punishment, the experience of torture, the experience of socially sanctioned sadism, comes from the first-person testimony of individuals—"anecdotal" material. We have the first-person stories of Frederick Douglass and Sojourner Truth, of Primo Levy and Elie Wiesel, of Nadezhda Mandelstam and Aleksandr Solzhenitsyn. Others in the same or different circumstances of torture and terror have spoken out to bear witness. Often, they were not believed. They were shamed, not honored. We smelled the humiliation, the degradation, on them; we turned away. At the same time, their stories were too horrible, too impossible, too unpleasant; their stories indicted those who stood by and did nothing—most of us, most of the time. Respectfully, I suggest that the women who have experienced the sadism of pornography on their bodies—the women in the pornography and the women on whom the pornography is used—are also survivors; they bear witness, now, for themselves, on behalf of others. "Survivors," wrote Terrence Des Pres, "are not individuals in the bourgeois sense. They are living remnants of the general struggle, and certainly they know it."[13] Of these women hurt by pornography, we must say that they know it now. Before, each was alone, unspeakably alone, isolated in terror and humiliated even by the will to live—it was the will to live, after all, that carried each woman from rape to rape, from beating to beating. Each had never heard another's voice saying the words of what had happened, telling the same story; because it is the same story, over and over—and none of those who escaped, survived, endured, are individuals in the bourgeois sense. These women will not abandon the meaning of their own experience. That meaning is: pornography is the orchestrated destruction of women's bodies and souls; rape, battery, incest, and prostitution animate it; dehumanization and sadism characterize it; it is war on women, serial assaults on dignity, identity, and human worth; it is tyranny. Each woman who has survived knows from the experience of her own life that pornography is captivity—the woman trapped in the picture used on the woman trapped wherever he's got her.

13. Terrence Des Pres, *The Survivor: An Anatomy of Life in the Death Camps* (New York: Pocket Books, 1977), p. 39.

3

> The burden of proof will be on those of us who have been victimized. If I [any woman] am able to prove that the picture you are holding, the one where the knife is stuffed up my vagina, was taken when my pimp forced me at gunpoint and photographed it without my consent, if my existence is proved real, I am coming to take what is mine. If I can prove that the movie you are looking at called *Black Bondage*, the one where my black skin is synonymous with filth and my bondage and my slavery is encouraged, caused me harm and discrimination, if my existence is proved real, I am coming to take what is mine. Whether you like it or not, the time is coming when you will have to get your fantasy *off my ass*.
>
> Therese Stanton, "Fighting for Our Existence" in *Changing Men* #15, Fall 1985

In the fall of 1983, something changed. The speech of women hurt by pornography became public and real. It, they, began to exist in the sphere of public reality. Constitutional lawyer Catharine A. MacKinnon and I were hired by the City of Minneapolis to draft an amendment to the city's civil rights law: an amendment that would recognize pornography as a violation of the civil rights of women, as a form of sex discrimination, an abuse of human rights. We were also asked to organize hearings that would provide a legislative record showing the need for such a law. Essentially, the legislators needed to know that these violations were systematic and pervasive in the population they represented, not rare, peculiar anomalies.

The years of listening to the private stories had been years of despair for me. It was hopeless. I could not help. There was no help. I listened; I went on my way; nothing changed. Now, all the years of listening were knowledge, real knowledge that could be mined: a resource, not a burden and a curse. I knew how women were hurt by pornography. My knowledge was concrete, not abstract: I knew the ways it was used; I knew how it was made; I knew the scenes of exploitation and abuse in real life—the lives of prostitutes, daughters, girlfriends, wives; I knew the words the women said when they dared to whisper what had happened to them; I could hear their voices in my mind, in my heart. I didn't know that there were such women all around me, everywhere, in Minneapolis that fall. I was heartbroken as women I knew came forward to testify: though I listened with an outer detachment to the stories of rape, incest, prostitution, battery, and torture, each in the service of pornography, inside I wanted to die.

The women who came forward to testify at the hearings held by the Minneapolis City Council on December 12 and 13, 1983, gave their names and specified the area of the city in which they lived. They spoke on the record before a governmental body in the city where they lived; there they were, for family, neighbors, friends, employers, teachers, and strangers to see, to remember. They described in detail sexual abuse through pornography as it had happened to them. They were questioned on their testimony by Catharine MacKinnon and myself and also by members of the city council and sometimes the city attorney. There were photographers and television cameras. There were a couple of hundred people in the room. There was no safety, no privacy, no retreat, no protection; only a net of validation provided by the testimony of experts—clinical psychologists, prosecutors, experimental psychologists, social scientists, experts in sexual abuse from rape crisis centers and battered women's shelters, and those who worked with sex offenders. The testimony of these experts was not abstract or theoretical; it brought the lives of more women, more children, into the room: more rape, more violation through pornography. They too were talking about real people who had been hurt, sometimes killed; they had seen, known, treated, interviewed, numbers of them. A new social truth emerged, one that had been buried in fear, shame, and the silence of the socially powerless: no woman hurt by pornography was alone—she never had been; no woman hurt by pornography would ever be alone again because each was—truly—a "living remnant of the general struggle." What the survivors said was speech; the pornography had been, throughout their lives, a means of actively suppressing their speech. They had been turned into pornography in life and made mute; terrorized by it and made mute. Now, the mute spoke; the socially invisible were seen; the women were real; they mattered. This speech—their speech—was new in the world of public discourse, and it was made possible by the development of a law that some called censorship. The women came forward because they thought that the new civil rights law recognized what had happened to them, gave them recourse and redress, enhanced their civil dignity and human worth. The law itself gave them *existence*: I am real; they believed me; I count; social policy at last will take my life into account, validate my worth—me, the woman who was forced to fuck a dog; me, the woman he urinated on; me, the woman he tied up for his friends to use; me, the woman he masturbated in; me, the woman he branded or maimed; me, the woman he prostituted; me, the woman they gang-raped.

The law was passed twice in Minneapolis in 1983 and 1984 by two different city councils; it was vetoed each time by the same mayor, a man active in Amnesty International, opposing torture outside of Minneapolis. The law was passed in 1984 in Indianapolis with a redrafted definition that targeted violent pornography—the kind "everyone" opposes. The city was sued for passing it; the courts found it unconstitutional. The appeals judge said that pornography did all the harm we claimed—it promoted insult and injury, rape and assault, even caused women to have lower wages—and that these effects proved its power as speech; therefore, it had to be protected. In 1985, the law was put on the ballot by popular petition in Cambridge,

Massachusetts. The city council refused to allow it on the ballot; we had to sue for ballot access; the civil liberties people opposed our having that access; we won the court case and the city was ordered to put the law on the ballot. We got 42 percent of the vote, a higher percentage than feminists got on the first women's suffrage referendum. In 1988, the law was on the ballot in Bellingham, Washington, in the presidential election; we got 62 percent of the vote. The city had tried to keep us off the ballot; again we had to get a court order to gain ballot access. The City of Bellingham was sued by the ACLU in federal court for having the law, however unwillingly; a federal district judge found the law unconstitutional, simply reiterating the previous appeals court decision in the Indianapolis case—indeed, there was a statement that the harms of pornography were recognized and not in dispute.

We have not been able to get the courts to confront a real woman plaintiff suing a real pornographer for depriving her of real rights through sexual exploitation or sexual abuse. This is because the challenges to the civil rights law have been abstract arguments about speech, as if women's lives are abstract, as if the harms are abstract, conceded but not real. The women trapped in the pictures continue to be perceived as the free speech of the pimps who exploit them. No judge seems willing to look such a woman, three-dimensional and breathing, in the face and tell her that the pimp's use of her is his constitutionally protected right of speech; that he has a right to express himself by violating her. The women on whom the pornography is used in assault remain invisible and speechless in these court cases. No judge has had to try to sleep at night having heard a real woman's voice describing what happened to her, the incest, the rape, the gang rape, the battery, the forced prostitution. Keeping these women silent in courts of law is the main strategy of the free speech laywers who defend the pornography industry. Hey, they love literature; they deplore sexism. If some women get hurt, that's the price we pay for freedom. Who are the "we"? What is the "freedom"? These speech-loving lawyers keep the women from speaking in court so that no judge will actually be able to listen to them.

Women continue speaking out in public forums, even though we are formally and purposefully silenced in actual courts of law. Hearings were held by a subcommittee of the Senate Judiciary Committee on the effects of pornography on women and children; the Attorney General's Commission on Pornography listened to the testimony of women hurt by pornography; women are demanding to speak at conferences, debates, on television, radio. This civil rights law is taught in law schools all over the country; it is written about in law journals, often favorably; increasingly, it has academic support; and its passage has been cited as precedent in at least one judicial decision finding that pornography in the workplace can be legally recognized as sexual harassment. The time of silence—at least the time of absolute silence—is over. And the civil rights law developed in Minneapolis has had an impact around the world. It is on the agenda of legislators in England, Ireland, West Germany, New Zealand, Tasmania, and Canada; it is on the agenda of political activists all over the world.

The law itself is civil, not criminal. It allows people who have been hurt by pornography to sue for sex discrimination. Under this law, it is sex discrimination to coerce, intimidate, or fraudulently induce anyone into pornography; it is sex discrimination to force pornography on a person in any place of employment, education, home, or any public place; it is sex discrimination to assault, physically attack, or injure any person in a way that is directly caused by a specific piece of pornography—the pornographers share responsibility for the assault; in the Bellingham version, it is also sex discrimination to defame any person through the unauthorized use in pornography of their name, image, and/or recognizable personal likeness; and it is sex discrimination to produce, sell, exhibit, or distribute pornography—to traffic in the exploitation of women, to traffic in material that provably causes aggression against and lower civil status for women in society.

The law's definition of pornography is concrete, not abstract. Pornography is defined as the graphic, sexually explicit subordination of women in pictures and/or words that also includes women presented dehumanized as sexual objects, things, or commodities; or women presented as sexual objects who enjoy pain or humiliation; or women presented as sexual objects who experience sexual pleasure in being raped; or women presented as sexual objects tied up or cut up or mutilated or bruised or physically hurt; or women presented in postures or positions of sexual submission, servility, or display; or women's body parts—including but not limited to vaginas, breasts, buttocks—exhibited such that women are reduced to those parts; or women presented as whores by nature; or women presented being penetrated by objects or animals; or women presented in scenarios of degradation, injury, torture, shown as filthy or inferior, bleeding, bruised, or hurt in a context that makes these conditions sexual. If men, children, or transsexuals are used in any of the same ways, the material also meets the definition of pornography.

For women hurt by pornography, this law simply describes reality; it is a map of a real world. Because the law allows them to sue those who have imposed this reality on them—especially the makers, sellers, exhibitors, and distributors of pornography—they have a way of redrawing the map. The courts now protect the pornography; they recognize the harm to women in judicial decisions—or they use words that say they recognize the harm—and then tell women that the Constitution protects the harm; profit is real to them and they make sure the pimps stay rich, even as women and their children are this country's poor. The civil rights law is designed to confront both the courts and the pornographers with a demand for substantive, not theoretical, equality. This law says: we have the right to stop them from doing this to us because we are human beings. "If my existence is proved real, I am coming to take what is mine," Therese Stanton wrote for every woman who wants to use this law. How terrifying that thought must be to those who have been using women with impunity.

Initially an amendment to a city ordinance, this law has had a global impact because: (1) it tells the truth about what pornography is and does; (2) it tells the truth about how women are exploited and hurt by the use of pornography; (3) it seeks to expand the speech of women by taking the pornographers' gags out of our mouths; (4) it seeks to expand the speech and enhance the civil status of women by giving us the courts as a forum in which we will have standing and authority; (5) it is a mechanism for redistributing power, taking it from pimps, giving it to those they have been exploiting for profit, injuring for pleasure; (6) it says that women matter, including the women in the pornography. This law and the political vision and experience that inform it are not going to go away. We are going to stop the pornographers. We are going to claim our human dignity under law. One ex-prostitute, who is an organizer for the passage of this civil rights law, wrote: "Confronting how I've been hurt is the hardest thing that I've ever had to do in my life. A hard life, if I may say so."[14] She is right. Confronting the pornographers is easier—their threats, their violence, their power. Confronting the courts is easier—their indifference, their contempt for women, their plain stupidity. Confronting the status quo is easier. Patience is easier and so is every form of political activism, however dangerous. Beaver is real, all right. A serious woman—formidable even—she is coming to take what is hers.

4

> That same night [July 20, 1944, the attempt by the generals to assassinate Hitler] he [Goebbels] turned

14. Toby Summer, pseudonym, "Women, Lesbians and Prostitution: A Workingclass Dyke Speaks Out Against Buying Women for Sex," *Lesbian Ethics*, vol. 2, no. 3, Summer 1987, p. 37.

> his house into "a prison, headquarters and court rolled into one"; Goebbels himself headed a commission of investigation; and he and Himmler cross-examined the arrested generals throughout the night. Those condemned, then or thereafter, were executed with revolting cruelty. They were hanged from meat-hooks and slowly strangled. Goebbels ordered a film to be made of their trial and execution: it was to be shown, *in terrorem* to Wehrmacht audiences. However, the reaction of the first audience was so hostile that it had to be suppressed.
>
> Hugh Trevor-Roper in his introduction to *Final Entries 1945: The Diaries of Joseph Goebbels*

As far as I can determine, Goebbels' film of the generals slowly, horribly dying—their innards caving in from the force of gravity on their hung bodies, the slow strangulation pushing out their tongues and eyes and causing erection (which strangulation invariably does in the male)—was the first snuff film. The master of hate propaganda didn't get it right though—a rare lapse. Audiences became physically sick. These were Nazi audiences watching Nazi generals, men of power, the society's patriarchs, so white they were Aryan; rulers, not slaves. It only works when the torture is done on those who have been dehumanized, made inferior—not just in the eyes of the beholder but in his real world. Goebbels started out with cartoons of Jews before the Nazis came to power; he could have moved on to the films made in Dachau in 1942, for instance, of "the reactions of the men placed in the Luftwaffe's low-pressure chambers"[15]; desensitizing his Nazi audiences to the humiliation, the torture, of Jews, he could have made a film that would have worked—of Jews hanging from meat hooks, slowly strangled. But never of power, never of those

15. Roger Manvell and Heinrich Fraenkel, *Himmler* (New York: G. P. Putnam's Sons, 1965), p. 105.

who were the same, never of those who had been fully human to the audience the day before, never of those who had been respected. Never.

Des Pres says it is easier to kill if "the victim exhibits self-disgust; if he cannot lift his eyes for humiliation, or if lifted they show only emptiness . . ."[16] There is some pornography in which women are that abject, that easy to kill, that close to being dead already. There is quite a lot of it; and it is highly prized, expensive. There is still more pornography in which the woman wets her lips and pushes out her ass and says hurt me. She is painted so that the man cannot miss the mark: her lips are bright red so that he can find the way into her throat; her vaginal lips are pink or purple so that he can't miss; her anus is darkened while her buttocks are flooded with light. Her eyes glisten. She smiles. Sticking knives up her own vagina, she smiles. She comes. The Jews didn't do it to themselves and they didn't orgasm. In contemporary American pornography, of course, the Jews do do it to themselves—they, usually female, seek out the Nazis, go voluntarily to concentration camps, beg a domineering Nazi to hurt them, cut them, burn them—and they do climax, stupendously, to both sadism and death. But in life, the Jews didn't orgasm. Of course, neither do women; not in life. But no one, not even Goebbels, said the Jews liked it. The society agreed that the Jews deserved it, but not that they wanted it and not that it gave them sexual pleasure. There were no photographs from Ravensbruck concentration camp of the prostitutes who were incarcerated there along with other women gasping for breath in pleasure; the gypsies didn't orgasm either. There were no photographs—real or simulated—of the Jews smiling and waving the Nazis closer, getting on the trains with their hands happily fingering their exposed genitals or using Nazi guns, swastikas, or Iron Crosses for sexual penetration. Such behaviors would not have been credible even in a society that believed the

16. Des Pres, *The Survivor*, p. 68.

Jews were both subhuman and intensely sexual in the racist sense—the men rapists, the women whores. The questions now really are: why is pornography credible in our society? how can anyone believe it? And then: how subhuman would women have to be for the pornography to be true? To the men who use pornography, how subhuman are women? If men believe the pornography because it makes them come—them, not the women—what is sex to men and how will women survive it?

This book—written from 1977 through 1980, published in 1981 after two separate publishers reneged on contractual agreements to publish it (and a dozen more refused outright), out of print in the United States for the last several years—takes power, sadism, and dehumanization seriously. I am one of those serious women. This book asks how power, sadism, and dehumanization work in pornography—against women, for men—to establish the sexual and social subordination of women to men. This book is distinguished from most other books on pornography by its bedrock conviction that the power is real, the cruelty is real, the sadism is real, the subordination is real: the political crime against women is real. This book says that power used to destroy women is atrocity. *Pornography: Men Possessing Women* is not, and was never intended to be, an effete intellectual exercise. I want real change, an end to the social power of men over women; more starkly, his boot off my neck. In this book, I wanted to dissect male dominance; do an autopsy on it, but it wasn't dead. Instead, there were artifacts—films, photographs, books—an archive of evidence and documentation of crimes against women. This was a living archive, commercially alive, carnivorous in its use of women, saturating the environment of daily life, explosive and expanding, vital because it was synonymous with sex for the men who made it and the men who used it—men so arrogant in their power over us that they published the pictures of what they did to us, how they used us, expecting submission from us, compliance; we were supposed to follow the orders implicit in the pictures. Instead, some of us understood that we could look at those pictures and see them—see the men. Know thyself, if you are lucky enough to have a self that hasn't been destroyed by rape in its many forms; and then, know the bastard on top of you. This book is about him, the collective him: who he is; what he wants; what he needs (the key to both his rage and his political vulnerability); how he's diddling you and why it feels so bad and hurts so much; what's keeping him in place on you; why he won't move off of you; what it's going to take to blow him loose. A different kind of blow job. Is he scared? You bet.

Pornography: Men Possessing Women also puts pornography, finally, into its appropriate context. A system of dominance and submission, pornography has the weight and significance of any other historically real torture or punishment of a group of people because of a condition of birth; it has the weight and significance of any other historically real exile of human beings from human dignity, the purging of them from a shared community of care and rights and respect. Pornography happens. It is not outside the world of material reality because it happens to women, and it is not outside the world of material reality because it makes men come. The man's ejaculation is real. The woman on whom his semen is spread, a typical use in pornography, is real. Men characterize pornography as something mental because their minds, their thoughts, their dreams, their fantasies, are more real to them than women's bodies or lives; in fact, men have used their social power to characterize a $10-billion-a-year trade in women as fantasy. This is a spectacular example of how those in power cannibalize not only people but language. "We do not know," wrote George Steiner, "whether the study of the humanities, of the noblest that has been said and thought, can do very much to humanize. We do not know; and surely there is something rather terrible in our doubt whether the study and delight a man finds in Shakespeare make him any less capable of organizing a concentration camp."[17] As long as language is a weapon of power—used to destroy the expressive abilities of the powerless by destroying their sense of reality—we do know. Beaver knows.

Some have said that pornography is a superficial target; but, truly, this is wrong. Pornography incarnates male supremacy. It is the DNA of male dominance. Every rule of sexual abuse, every nuance of sexual sadism, every highway and byway of sexual exploitation, is encoded in it. It's what men want us to be, think we are, make us into; how men use us; not because biologically they are men but because this is how their social power is organized. From the perspective of the political activist, pornography is the blueprint of male supremacy; it shows how male supremacy is built. The political activist needs to know the blueprint. In cultural terms, pornography is the fundamentalism of male dominance. Its absolutism on women and sexuality, its dogma, is merciless. Women are consigned to rape and prostitution; heretics are disappeared and destroyed. Pornography is the essential sexuality of male power: of hate, of ownership, of hierarchy; of sadism, of dominance. The premises of pornography are controlling in every rape and every rape case, whenever a woman is battered or prostituted, in incest, including in incest that occurs before a child can even speak, and in murder—murders of women by husbands, lovers, and serial killers. If this is superficial, what's deep?

5

When I first wrote this book, I was going to use these lines from Elizabeth Barrett Browning's letters as an epigraph: "If a woman ignores these wrongs, then may women as a sex continue to suffer them; there is no help for any of

17. George Steiner, *Language and Silence* (New York: Atheneum, 1977), pp. 65–66.

us—let us be dumb and die."[18] I changed my mind, because I decided that no woman deserved what pornography does to women: no woman, however stupid or evil, treacherous or cowardly, venal or corrupt; no woman. I also decided that even if some women did, I didn't. I also remembered the brave women, the women who had survived, escaped; in the late 1970s, they were still silent, but I had heard them. I don't want them, ever, to be dumb and die; and certainly not because some other woman somewhere is a coward or a fool or a cynic or a Kapo. There are women who will defend pornography, who don't give a damn. There are women who will use pornography, including on other women. There are women who will work for pornographers—not as so-called models but as managers, lawyers, publicists, and paid writers of "opinion" and "journalism." There are women of every kind, all the time; there are always women who will ignore egregious wrongs. My aspirations for dignity and equality do not hinge on perfection in myself or in any other woman; only on the humanity we share, fragile as that appears to be. I understand Elizabeth Barrett Browning's desperation and the rage behind it, but I'm removing her curse. No woman's betrayal will make us dumb and dead—no more and never again. Beaver's endured too much to turn back now.

—Andrea Dworkin
New York City
March 1989

18. Elizabeth Barrett Browning, *Letters of Elizabeth Barrett Browning* in Mary Daly, *Gyn/Ecology: The Metaethics of Radical Feminism* (Boston: Beacon Press, 1978), p. 153.

Preface

THIS IS A BOOK about the meaning of pornography and the system of power in which pornography exists. Its particular theme is the power of men in pornography.

This is not a book about the First Amendment. By definition the First Amendment protects only those who can exercise the rights it protects. Pornography by definition—"the graphic depiction of whores"—is trade in a class of persons who have been systematically denied the rights protected by the First Amendment and the rest of the Bill of Rights. The question this book raises is not whether the First Amendment protects pornography or should, but whether pornography keeps women from exercising the rights protected by the First Amendment.

This is not a book about obscenity. For something to be obscene, a judgment must be made that it is not fit to be shown or displayed. One possible (though not generally accepted) root meaning of the word *obscene* is the ancient Greek for "off stage"—in effect that which should not be shown, probably for aesthetic reasons. Another possible, more likely root meaning of the word *obscene* is the Latin for "against filth." This suggests our own contemporary legal usage: is a given work filth and are we, the people, against it? If so, it is obscene. Obscenity is not a synonym for pornography. Obscenity is an idea; it requires a judgment of value. Pornography is concrete, "the graphic depiction of whores."

With respect to both obscenity and the First Amendment: this is not a book about what should or should not be shown; it is a book about the meaning of what is being shown.

This book is not about the difference between pornography and erotica. Feminists have made honorable efforts to define the difference, in general asserting that erotica involves mutuality and reciprocity, whereas pornography involves dominance and violence. But in the male sexual lexicon, which is the vocabulary of power, erotica is simply high-class pornography: better produced, better conceived, better executed, better packaged, designed for a better class of consumer. As with the call girl and the streetwalker, one is turned out better but both are produced by the same system of sexual values and both perform the same sexual service. Intellectuals, especially, call what they themselves produce or like "erotica," which means simply that a very bright person made or likes whatever it is. The pornography industry, larger than the record and film industries combined, sells pornography, "the graphic depiction of whores." In the male system, erotica is a subcategory of pornography.

Finally, this is not a liberal book about how pornography hurts all of us. As militant feminist Christabel Pankhurst wrote concerning the trade in women in 1913: "Men have a simple remedy for this state of things. They can alter their way of life."[1]

PORNOGRAPHY

1

Power

For freedom is always relative to power, and the kind of freedom which at any moment it is most urgent to affirm depends on the nature of the power which is prevalent and established.

R. H. Tawney, *Equality*

The power of men is first a metaphysical assertion of self, an *I am* that exists a priori, bedrock, absolute, no embellishment or apology required, indifferent to denial or challenge. It expresses intrinsic authority. It never ceases to exist no matter how or on what grounds it is attacked; and some assert that it survives physical death. This self is not merely subjectively felt. It is protected by laws and customs, proclaimed in art and in literature, documented in history, upheld in the distribution of wealth. This self cannot be eradicated or reduced to nothing. It is. When the subjective sense of self falters, institutions devoted to its maintenance buoy it up.

The first tenet of male-supremacist ideology is that men have this self and that women must, by definition, lack it. Male self seems to be a contradiction. On the one hand, it hangs suspended in thin air; it is magically perpetual; it requires nothing to sustain or support it. On the other hand, it is entitled to take what it wants to sustain or improve itself, to have anything, to requite any need at any cost. In fact, there is no contradiction, just a simple circle: the nature of the male self is that it takes, so that, by definition, the absolute self is expressed in the absolute right to take what it needs to sustain itself. The immutable self of the male boils down to an utterly unselfconscious parasitism. The self is the conviction, beyond reason or scrutiny, that there is an equation between what one wants and the fact that one is. Going Descartes one better, this conviction might be expressed: I want and I am entitled to have, therefore I am.

Self is incrementally expanded as the parasite drains self from those not entitled to it. To him it is given, by faith and action, from birth. To her it is denied, by faith and action, from birth. His is never big enough; hers is always too big, however small. As a child, the first self he drains is that of his mother—whatever she has of it is reserved for him. He feeds off her labor and her qualities. He uses them up. She is devoted, more or less; but the more is as much insult as the less; and nothing is ever enough unless it has been too much; all of this regardless of what or how much it has actually been. As the boy matures, he is encouraged to make the treacherous and apparently devastating "normal adjustment," that is, to transfer his parasitism of the mother to other females, who have more succulent selves to which they are not entitled. In the course of his life, he reenacts this grand transition as often as he wishes. He finds the qualities and services he needs and he takes them. Especially he uses women, as Virginia Woolf described in *A Room of One's Own*, to enlarge himself. He is always in a panic, never large enough. But still, his self is immutable however much he may fear its ebbing away, because he keeps taking, and it is taking that is his immutable right and his immutable self. Even when he is obsessed with his need to be more and to have more, he is convinced of his right to be and to have.

Second, power is physical strength used over and against others less strong or without the sanction to use strength as power. If physical strength is not used over and against others—for instance, if a slave is strong—it is not power. The right to physical strength as power, in a male-supremacist system, is vouchsafed to men. The second tenet of male supremacy is that men are physically stronger than women and, for that reason, have dominion over them. Physical strength in women that is not directly harnessed to "women's work" becomes an abomination, and its use against men, that is, as power, is anathema, forbidden, horribly punished. The reality of male physical strength in an absolute sense is less important than the ideology that sacralizes and celebrates it. In part, the physical strength of men over women is realized because men keep women physically weak. Men choose women who are weak as mates (unless heavy labor is part of the female role); and systematically in the raising of women, physical strength is undermined and sabotaged. Women are physically weaker the higher their economic class (as defined by men); the closer they are to power, the weaker they are. Even women who are physically strong must pretend to be weak to underline not only their femininity but also their upwardly mobile aesthetic and economic aspirations. Physical incapacity is a form of feminine beauty and a symbol of male wealth: he is rich enough to keep her unable to labor, useless, ornamental. Women are also often mutilated, physically or by fashion and custom, so that whatever physical strength they may have is meaningless. Male physical strength, regardless of its absolute measure, is meaningful. Male physical strength expressed as power, like male self, is not a subjective phenomenon; its significance is not whimsical. Laws and customs protect it; art and literature adore it; history depends on it; the distribution of wealth maintains it. Its absolute value is mythologized and mystified so that women are cowed by its legend as well as its reality. The power of physical strength combines with the power of self so that he not only is, he is stronger; he not only takes, he takes by force.

Third, power is the capacity to terrorize, to use self and strength to inculcate fear, fear *in* a whole class of persons *of* a whole class of persons. The acts of terror run the gamut from rape to battery to sexual abuse of children to war to murder to maiming to torture to enslaving to kidnapping to verbal assault to cultural assault to threats of death to threats of harm backed up by the ability and sanction to deliver. The symbols of terror are commonplace and utterly familiar: the gun, the knife, the bomb, the fist, and so on. Even more significant is the hidden symbol of terror, the penis. The acts and the symbols meet up in all combinations, so that terror is the outstanding theme and consequence of male history and male culture, though it is smothered in euphemism, called glory or heroism. Even when it is villainous, it is huge and awesome. Terror issues forth from the male, illuminates his essential nature and his basic purpose. He chooses how much to terrorize, whether terror will be a dalliance or an obsession, whether he will use it brutally or subtly. But first, there is the legend of terror, and this legend is cultivated by men with sublime attention. In epics, dramas, tragedies, great books, slight books, television, films, history both documented and invented, men are giants who soak the earth in blood. Within the legend men have great chances and are the carriers of values. Within the legend, women are booty, along with gold and jewels and territory and raw materials. The legend of male violence is the most celebrated legend of mankind and from it emerges the character of man: he is dangerous. With the rise of social Darwinism in the nineteenth century and now in the pseudoscience of sociobiology, Man-the-Aggressor is at the apex of the evolutionary struggle, king of the earth because he is the most aggressive, the cruelest. Male-supremacist biology, which now suffuses the social sciences, is, in fact, an essential element in the modern legend of terror that man spews forth celebrating himself: he is biologically ordained (where before he was God's warrior) to terrorize women and other creatures into submission and conformity. Failing that, terror will fulfill its promise; the male will wipe out whatever terror does not control. The third tenet of male-supremacist ideology, in a secular society where biology has replaced God (and is used to buttress anachronistic theology whenever necessary), is that men are biologically aggressive, inherently combative, eternally antagonistic, genetically cruel, hormonally prone to conflict, irredeemably hostile and warring. For those who remain devout, God endowed man with what, by any standard, must be considered a universally bad disposition, fortunately put to good use in subduing women. The acts of terror, the symbols of terror, and the legend of terror all spread terror. This terror is not a psychological event as that phrase is commonly understood: it does not originate in the mind of the one experiencing it, though it fiercely resonates there. Instead, it is generated by cruel acts widely sanctioned and encouraged. It is also generated by its own enduring reputation, whether exquisite as in Homer, Genet, or Kafka; or fiendish as in Hitler, the real Count Dracula, or Manson. Rotting meat smells; violence produces terror. Men are dangerous; men are feared.

Fourth, men have the power of naming, a great and sublime power. This power of naming enables men to define experience, to articulate boundaries and values, to designate to each thing its realm and qualities, to determine what can and cannot be expressed, to control perception itself. As Mary Daly, who first isolated this power, wrote in *Beyond God the Father:* ". . . it is necessary to grasp the fundamental fact that women have had the power of naming stolen from us."[1] Male supremacy is fused into the language, so that every sentence both heralds and affirms it. Thought, experienced primarily as language, is permeated by the linguistic and perceptual values developed expressly to subordinate women. Men have defined the parameters of every subject. All feminist arguments, however radical in intent or consequence, are with or against assertions or premises implicit in the male system, which is made credible or authentic by the power of men to name. No transcendence of the male system is possible as long as men have the power of naming. Their names resonate wherever there is human life. As Prometheus stole fire from the gods, so feminists will have to steal the power of naming from men, hopefully to better effect. As with fire when it belonged to the gods, the power of naming appears magical: he gives the name, the name endures; she gives the name, the name is lost. But this magic is illusion. The male power of naming is upheld by force, pure and simple. On its own, without force to back it, measured against reality, it is not power; it is process, a more humble thing. "The old naming," Mary Daly wrote, "was not the product of dialogue—a fact inadvertently admitted in the Genesis story of Adam's naming the animals and the woman."[2] It is the naming by decree that is power over and against those who are forbidden to name their own experience; it is the decree backed up by violence that writes the name indelibly in blood in male-dominated culture. The male does not merely name women evil; he exterminates nine million women as witches because he has named women evil. He does not merely name women weak; he mutilates the female body, binds it up so that it cannot move freely, uses it as toy or ornament, keeps it caged and stunted because he has named women weak. He says that the female wants to be raped; he rapes. She resists rape; he must beat her, threaten her with death, forcibly carry her off, attack her in the night, use knife or fist; and still he says she wants it, they all do. She says no; he claims it means yes. He names her ignorant, then forbids her education. He does not allow her to use her mind or body rigorously, then names her intuitive and emotional. He defines femininity and when she does not conform he names her deviant, sick, beats her up, slices off her clitoris (repository of pathological masculinity), tears out her womb (source of her personality), lobotomizes or narcotizes her (perverse recognition that she can think, though thinking in a woman is named deviant). He names antagonism and violence, mixed in varying degrees, "sex"; he beats her and names it variously "proof of love" (if she is wife) or "eroticism" (if she is mistress). If she wants him sexually he names her slut; if she does not want him he rapes her and says she does; if she would rather study or paint he names her repressed and brags he can cure her pathological interests with the apocryphal "good fuck." He names her housewife, fit only for the house, keeps her poor and utterly dependent, only to buy her with his money should she leave the house and then he calls her whore. He names her whatever suits him. He does what he wants and calls it what he likes. He actively maintains the power of naming through force and he justifies force through the power of naming. The world is his because he has named everything in it, including her. She uses this language against herself because it cannot be used any other way. The fourth tenet of male supremacy is that men, because they are intellectually and creatively existent, name things authentically. Whatever contradicts or subverts male naming is defamed out of existence; the power of naming itself, in the male system, is a form of force.

Fifth, men have the power of owning. Historically, this power has been absolute; denied to some men by other men in times of slavery and other persecution, but in the main upheld by armed force and law. In many parts of the world, the male right to own women and all that issues from them (children and labor) is still absolute, and no human rights considerations seem to apply to captive populations of women. In the United States in the last 140 years, this right has been legally modified, but the letter of the law, even where somewhat enlightened, is not its spirit. Wife beating and marital rape, pervasive here as elsewhere, are predicated on the conviction that a man's ownership of his wife licenses whatever he wishes to do to her: her body belongs to him to use for his own sexual release, to beat, to impregnate. The male power of owning, by virtue of its historical centrality, is barely constrained by the modest legal restrictions put on it. True: a married woman in the United States today can own her own hairbrush and clothes, as she could not through most of the nineteenth century; should she run away from home, she is not likely to be hunted down like a runaway slave, as she would have been through most of the nineteenth century, nor will she be publicly flogged though in private she may still be beaten for her effrontery. But the power of male owning, like all male power, is not hindered by or confined to specifics. This power, like the others, is bigger than any of its discrete manifestations. The fifth tenet of male supremacy is the presumption that the male's right to own the female and her issue is natural, predating history, postdating progress. Whatever he does to effect or maintain ownership is also natural; it is action originating in an ethic that is in no sense relative. The power of owning comes from the power of self defined as one who takes. Here the taking is elevated in significance: he takes, he keeps; once he has had, it is his. This relationship between the self that takes and ownership is precisely mirrored, for instance, in the relationship between rape and marriage. Marriage as an institution developed from rape as a practice. Rape, originally defined as abduction, became marriage by capture. Marriage meant the taking was to extend in time, to be not only use of but lifelong possession of, or ownership.

Sixth, the power of money is a distinctly male power. Money speaks, but it speaks with a male voice. In the hands of women, money stays literal; count it out, it buys what it is worth or less. In the hands of men, money buys women, sex, status, dignity, esteem, recognition, loyalty, all manner of possibility. In the hands of men, money does not only buy; it brings with it qualities, achievements, honor, respect. On every economic level, the meaning of money is significantly different for men than for women. Enough money, amassed by men, becomes clean even when it is dirty. Women are cursed for succeeding relative to their peer group of men. Poor women, in general, use money for the basic survival of themselves and their children. Poor men, in general, use money to an astonishing degree for pleasure. Rich women use money especially for adornment so that they will be desirable to men: money does not free them from the dicta of men. Rich men use money for pleasure and to make money. Money in the hands of a man signifies worth and accomplishment; in the hands of a woman, it is evidence of something foul, unwomanly ambition or greed. The sixth tenet of male supremacy is that money properly expresses masculinity. Men keep money for themselves. They dole it out to women and children. Men keep the marketplace for themselves: women earn less than men for doing equivalent work, despite the fact that *everyone* believes in equal pay for equal work; working women with college degrees on the average earn less than men with an eighth-grade education; job segregation and just plain exclusion from the labor force, through outright discrimination in hiring and also through forced pregnancy, keep women as a class poor, away from money as such, unable to earn adequate amounts of money or to accumulate it.

Money has an extreme sexual component. As Phyllis Chesler and Emily Jane Goodman wrote in *Women, Money and Power:* "The male touch signifies economic dominance."[3] When a poor man seduces or rapes a richer woman, his touch signifies economic rebellion. Money is primary in the acquisition of sex and sex is primary in the making of money: it is tied into every industry through advertising (this car will bring you women, see that slinky thing draped over the hood), or items are eroticized in and of themselves because of what they cost. In the realm of money, sex and women are the same commodity. Wealth of any kind, to any degree, is an expression of male sexual power.

The sexual meaning of money is acted out by men on a wide scale, but it is also internalized, applied to the interior functioning of male sexual processes. Men are supposed to hoard sperm as they are supposed to hoard money. A central religious imperative (in both Western and Eastern religions) discourages expenditures of sperm not instrumental in effecting impregnation, because wealth wasted instead of invested is wealth lost. The phrase "spermatic economy" expressed this same idea in the secular realm, particularly in the nineteenth century. The idea that when a man spends sperm he uses up his most significant natural resource—that he spills his sons into nonexistence—both precedes and survives specific religious dogma and quasi-scientific theorizing. One meaning of the verb *to spend* is "to ejaculate." One meaning of the verb *to husband* is "to conserve or save"; its archaic meaning is "to plow for the purpose of growing crops." A husband, in this sense, is one who conserves or saves his sperm except to fuck for the purpose of impregnating. In the male system, control of money means sexual maturity, as does the ability to control ejaculation. The valuing and conserving of money, using money to make wealth—like the valuing and conserving of sperm, using sperm to make wealth—demonstrates a conformity to adult male values, both sexual and economic. A boy spends his sperm and his money on women. A man uses his sperm and his women to produce wealth. A boy spends; a man produces. Spending indicates an immature valuing of immediate gratification. Producing signifies an enduring commitment to self-control and to the control of others, both crucial in the perpetuation of male supremacy. The owning and impregnating of a woman in marriage or in some form of concubinage (however informal) are seen as mastery of spending without purpose, the first clear proof that masculinity is established as an irrefutable fact, adult, impervious to the ambivalences of youth still contaminated by female eroticism in which the penis has no intrinsic significance. A commitment to money as such follows as an obvious and public commitment to the display of masculinity as an aggressive and an aggrandizing drive. While poor or deprived men struggle for money to survive, all men, including poor or deprived men, struggle for money because it expresses masculinity, power over and against women. Having less money than a woman in one's field of perception is shameful: it means that one has less masculinity than she. Other male powers, such as the power of terror (violence) or the power of naming (defamation), must be called on to compensate.

Seventh, men have the power of sex. They assert the opposite: that this power resides in women, whom they view as synonymous with sex. The carnality of women, even when experienced as monstrous, is held to be the defining quality of women. Reduced to its most explicit and absurd detail by its most sexually explicit proponents, the argument is that women have sexual power because erection is involuntary; a woman is the presumed cause; therefore, the man is helpless, the woman is powerful. The male reacts to a stimulation for which he is not responsible; it is his very nature to do so; whatever he does he does because of a provocation that inheres in the female. Even on this most reductive level—she causes penile erection, therefore she is sexually powerful—the argument is willfully naive and self-serving. The male, through each and every one of his institutions, forces the female to conform to his supremely ridiculous definition of her as sexual object. He fetishizes her body as a whole and in its parts. He exiles her from every realm of expression outside the strictly male-defined sexual or male-defined maternal. He forces her to become that thing that causes erection, then holds himself helpless and powerless when he is aroused by her. His fury when she is not that thing, when she is either more or less than that thing, is intense and punishing.

More coherently defined—that is, defined outside the boundaries of male experience—the power of sex manifested in action, attitude, culture, and attribute is the exclusive province of the male, his domain, inviolate and sacred. Sex, a word potentially so inclusive and evocative, is whittled down by the male so that, in fact, it means penile intromission. Commonly referred to as "it," sex is defined in action only by what the male does with his penis. Fucking—the penis thrusting—is the magical, hidden meaning of "it," the reason for sex, the expansive experience through which the male realizes his sexual power. In practice, fucking is an act of possession—simultaneously an act of ownership, taking, force; it is conquering; it expresses in intimacy power over and against, body to body, person to thing. "The sex act" means penile intromission followed by penile thrusting, or fucking. The woman is acted on; the man acts and through action expresses sexual power, the power of masculinity. Fucking requires that the male act on one who has less power and this valuation is so deep, so completely implicit in the act, that the one who is fucked is stigmatized as feminine during the act even when not anatomically female. In the male system, sex is the penis, the penis is sexual power, its use in fucking is manhood.

Male sexual power is also expressed through an attitude or quality: virility. Defined first as manhood itself, virility in its secondary meaning is vigor, dynamism (in the patriarchal dictionary inevitably also called force). The vitality inherent in virility as a quality is held to be an exclusive masculine expression of energy, in its basic character sexual, in its origin biological, traceable to the penis itself. It is, in fact, an expression of energy, strength, ambition, and assertion. Defined by men and experienced by women as a form of male sexual power, virility is a dimension of energy and self-realization forbidden to women.

Male sexual power is the substance of culture. It resonates everywhere. The celebration of rape in story, song, and science is the paradigmatic articulation of male sexual power as a cultural absolute. The conquering of the woman acted out in fucking, her possession, her use as a thing, is the scenario endlessly repeated, with or without direct reference to fucking, throughout the culture. In fucking, he is enlarged. As Woolf wrote, she is his mirror; by diminishing her in his use of her he becomes twice his size. In the culture, he is a giant, enlarged by his conquest of her, implied or explicit. She remains his mirror and, as Woolf postulated, ". . . mirrors are essential to all violent and heroic action."[4] In culture, his sexual power is his theme. In culture, the male uses the female to explicate his theme.

Sexual power is also an attribute of the male, something that inheres in him as a taker of what he wants and needs, especially as one who uses his penis to take women, but more generally as a taker of land, of money. As an attribute, his sexual power illuminates his very nature.

The seventh tenet of male supremacy is that sexual power authentically originates in the penis. Masculinity in action, narrowly in the act of sex as men define it or more widely in any act of taking, is sexual power fulfilling itself, being true to its own nature. The male conceit that women have sexual power (cause erections) conveniently protects men from responsibility for the consequences of their acts, especially their acts of sexual conquest. Most of the time, after all, the used bodies do survive. Often they speak or scream or cry. Nowadays the uppity things even prosecute and sue. Ruthless blame—"you provoked me"—is used to encourage the individual and social silence which is the most hospitable environment for the continuation of conquest.

THE MAJOR THEME of pornography as a genre is male power, its nature, its magnitude, its use, its meaning. Male power, as expressed in and through pornography, is discernible in discrete but interwoven, reinforcing strains: the power of self, physical power over and against others, the power of terror, the power of naming, the power of owning, the power of money, and the power of sex. These strains of male power are intrinsic to both the substance and production of pornography; and the ways and means of pornography are the ways and means of male power. The harmony and coherence of hateful values, perceived by men as normal and neutral values when applied to women, distinguish pornography as message, thing, and experience. The strains of male power are embodied in pornography's form and content, in economic control of and distribution of wealth within the industry, in the picture or story as thing, in the photographer or writer as aggressor, in the critic or intellectual who through naming assigns value, in the actual use of models, in the application of the material in what is called real life (which women are commanded to regard as distinct from fantasy). A saber penetrating a vagina is a weapon; so is the camera or pen that renders it; so is the penis for which it substitutes (*vagina* literally means "sheath"). The persons who produce the image are also weapons as men deployed in war become in their persons weapons. Those who defend or protect the image are, in this same sense, weapons. The values in the pornographic work are also manifest in everything surrounding the work. The valuation of women in pornography is a secondary theme in that the degradation of women exists in order to postulate, exercise, and celebrate male power. Male power, in degrading women, is first concerned with itself, its perpetuation, expansion, intensification, and elevation. In her essay on the Marquis de Sade, Simone de Beauvoir describes Sade's sexuality as autistic. Her use of the word is figurative, since an autistic child does not require an object of violence outside of himself (most autistic children are male). Male power expressed in pornography is autistic as de Beauvoir uses the word in reference to Sade: it is violent and self-obsessed; no perception of another being ever modifies its behavior or persuades it to abandon violence as a form of self-pleasuring. Male power is the raison d'être of pornography; the degradation of the female is the means of achieving this power.

The photograph is captioned "BEAVER HUNTERS." Two white men, dressed as hunters, sit in a black Jeep. The Jeep occupies almost the whole frame of the picture. The two men carry rifles. The rifles extend above the frame of the photograph into the white space surrounding it. The men and the Jeep face into the camera. Tied onto the hood of the black Jeep is a white woman. She is tied with thick rope. She is spread-eagle. Her pubic hair and crotch are the dead center of the car hood and the photograph. Her head is turned to one side, tied down by rope that is pulled taut across her neck, extended to and wrapped several times around her wrists, tied around the rearview mirrors of the Jeep, brought back around her arms, crisscrossed under her breasts and over her thighs, drawn down and wrapped around the bumper of the Jeep, tied around her ankles. Between her feet on the car bumper, in orange with black print, is a sticker that reads: I brake for Billy Carter. The text under the photograph reads: "Western sportsmen report beaver hunting was particularly good throughout the Rocky Mountain region during the past season. These two hunters easily bagged their limit in the high country. They told HUSTLER that they stuffed and mounted their trophy as soon as they got her home."

The men in the photograph are self-possessed; that is, they possess the power of self. This power radiates from the photograph. They are armed: first, in the sense that they are fully clothed; second, because they carry rifles, which are made more prominent, suggesting erection, by extending outside the frame of the photograph; third, because they are shielded by being inside the vehicle, framed by the windshield; fourth, because only the top parts of their bodies are shown. The woman is possessed; that is, she has no self. A captured animal, she is naked, bound, exposed on the hood of the car outdoors, her features not distinguishable because of the way her head is twisted and tied down. The men sit, supremely still and confident, displaying the captured prey for the camera. The stillness of the woman is like the stillness of death, underlined by the evocation of taxidermy in the caption. He is, he takes; she is not, she is taken.

The photograph celebrates the physical power of men over women. They are hunters, use guns. They have captured and bound a woman. They will stuff and mount her. She is a trophy. While one could argue that the victory of two armed men over a woman is no evidence of physical superiority, the argument is impossible as one experiences (or remembers) the photograph. The superior strength of men is irrefutably established by the fact of the photograph and the knowledge that one brings to it: that it expresses an authentic and commonplace relationship of the male strong to the female weak, wherein the hunt—the targeting, tracking down, pursuing, the chase, the overpowering of, the immobilizing of, even the wounding of—is common practice, whether called sexual pursuit, seduction, or romance. The photograph exists in an immediate context that supports the assertion of this physical power; and in the society that is the larger context, there is no viable and meaningful reality to contradict the physical power of male over female expressed in the photograph.

In the photograph, the power of terror is basic. The men are hunters with guns. Their prey is women. They have caught a woman and tied her onto the hood of a car. The terror is implicit in the content of the photograph, but beyond that the photograph strikes the female viewer dumb with fear. One perceives that the bound woman must be in pain. The very power to make the photograph (to use the model, to tie her in that way) and the fact of the photograph (the fact that someone did use the model, did tie her in that way, that the photograph is published in a magazine and seen by millions of men who buy it specifically to see such photographs) evoke fear in the female observer unless she entirely dissociates herself from the photograph: refuses to believe or understand that real persons posed for it, refuses to see the bound person as a woman like herself. Terror is finally the content of the photograph, and it is also its effect on the female observer. That men have the power and desire to make, publish, and profit from the photograph engenders fear. That millions more men enjoy the photograph makes the fear palpable. That men who in general champion civil rights defend the photograph without experiencing it as an assault on women intensifies the fear, because if the horror of the photograph does not resonate with these men, that horror is not validated as horror in male culture, and women are left without apparent recourse. Rimbaud's devastating verse comes to mind: "One evening I seated Beauty on my knees. And I found her bitter. And I cursed her. / I armed myself against justice."[5]

The threat in the language accompanying the photograph is also fierce and frightening. She is an animal, think of deer fleeing the hunter, think of seals clubbed to death, think of species nearly extinct. The men will stuff and mount her as a trophy: think of killing displayed proudly as triumph.

Here is the power of naming. Here she is named beaver. In the naming she is diminished to the point of annihilation; her humanity is canceled out. Instead of turning to the American Civil Liberties Union for help, she should perhaps turn to a group that tries to prevent cruelty to animals—beaver, bird, chick, bitch, dog, pussy, and so forth. The words that transform her into an animal have permanence: the male has done the naming. The power of naming includes the freedom to joke. The hunters will brake for Billy Carter. The ridicule is not deadly; they will let him live. The real target of the ridicule is the fool who brakes for animals, here equated with women. The language on the bumper sticker suggests the idea of the car in motion, which would otherwise be lacking. The car becomes a weapon, a source of death, its actual character as males use it. One is reminded of the animal run over on the road, a haunting image of blood and death. One visualizes the car, with the woman tied onto its hood, in motion crashing into something or someone.

Owning is expressed in every aspect of the photograph. These hunters are sportsmen, wealth suggested in hunting as a leisure-time pursuit of pleasure. They are equipped and outfitted. Their car shines. They have weapons: guns, a car. They have a woman, bound and powerless, to do with as they like. They will stuff and mount her. Their possession of her extends over time, even into (her) death. She is owned as a thing, a trophy, or as something dead, a dead bird, a dead deer; she is dead beaver. The camera and the photographer behind it also own the woman. The camera uses and keeps her. The photographer uses her and keeps the image of her. The publisher of the photograph can also claim her as a trophy. He has already mounted her and put her on display. Hunting as a sport suggests that these hunters have hunted before and will hunt again, that each captured woman will be used and owned, stuffed and mounted, that this right to own inheres in man's relationship to nature, that this right to own is so natural and basic that it can be taken entirely for granted, that is, expressed as play or sport.

Wealth is implicit in owning. The woman is likened to food (a dead animal), the hunter's most immediate form of wealth. As a trophy, she is wealth displayed. She is a commodity, part of the measure of male wealth. Man as hunter owns the earth, the things of it, its natural resources. She is part of the wildlife to be plundered for profit and pleasure, collected, used. That they "bagged their limit," then used what they had caught, is congruent with the idea of economy as a sign of mature masculinity.

The fact of the photograph signifies the wealth of men as a class. One class simply does not so use another class unless that usage is maintained in the distribution of wealth. The female model's job is the job of one who is economically imperiled, a sign of economic degradation. The relationship of the men to the woman in the photograph is not fantasy; it is symbol, meaningful because it is rooted in reality. The photograph shows a relationship of rich to poor that is actual in the larger society. The fact of the photograph in relation to its context—an industry that generates wealth by producing images of women abjectly used, a society in which women cannot adequately earn money because women are valued precisely as the woman in the photograph is valued—both proves and perpetuates the real connection between masculinity and wealth. The sexual-economic significance of the photograph is so simple that it is easily overlooked: the photograph could not exist as a type of photograph that produces wealth without the wealth of men to produce and consume it.

Sex as power is the most explicit meaning of the photograph. The power of sex unambiguously resides in the male, though the characterization of the female as a wild animal suggests that the sexuality of the untamed female is dangerous to men. But the triumph of the hunters is the nearly universal triumph of men over women, a triumph ultimately expressed in the stuffing and mounting. The hunters are figures of virility. Their penises are hidden but their guns are emphasized. The car, beloved ally of men in the larger culture, also indicates virility, especially when a woman is tied to it naked instead of draped over it wearing an evening gown. The pornographic image explicates the advertising image, and the advertising image echoes the pornographic image.

The power of sex is ultimately defined as the power of conquest. They hunted her down, captured, tied, stuffed, and mounted her. The excitement is precisely in the nonconsensual character of the event. The hunt, the ropes, the guns, show that anything done to her was or will be done against her will. Here again, the valuation of conquest as being natural—of nature, of man in nature, of natural man—is implicit in the visual and linguistic imagery.

The power of sex, in male terms, is also funereal. Death permeates it. The male erotic trinity—sex, violence, and death—reigns supreme. She will be or is dead. They did or will kill her. Everything that they do to or with her is violence. Especially evocative is the phrase "stuffed and mounted her," suggesting as it does both sexual violation and embalming.

Whip Chick, a book, has as its central conceit that power defined as cruelty resides in the woman, especially the feminist woman. Called variously "amazon" and "liberated woman," she says "You male chauvinist pig" as she grinds her spiked heels into his balls. She is as dangerous as anyone can be, her malice directed at the genitals of the male, which she threatens to tear off with her bare hands. She is a fantasy, as opposed to a symbol: the power attributed to her nowhere resonates in the real world.

In *Whip Chick*, Scott Healy, who has a big cock and is a superstud, fucks Mrs. Alice Waverly in a motel. She thanks him. Alice and Scott are seen at the motel by Cora Hertzell, a professor at a local college. Alice is outraged that Cora, a teacher, is at the motel. She determines to rid the town of Cora. Scott's nephew Chris has a crush on Cora, his teacher. He thinks about how she moves like a stripper, then he masturbates. He thinks he is too old to masturbate but his image in a mirror seems to tell him that he cannot help it. Scott comes home and makes a TV dinner. Sandra Waverly, Alice's daughter, telephones for Chris. Sandra invites

Chris to do what he will to her. Chris says he is busy. Scott says: "The little faggot." Scott talks Chris into seeing Sandra. Sandra seduces Chris, who has a big cock. He goes home and telephones her. She wants him to come back. He says that he will only return if he is her master, if she will do anything he says: "His dick was beginning to grow now. He felt the urge to ram it down her throat." He orders her to put the telephone receiver up her cunt and use it to masturbate while she waits for him. Then he goes to her house to check up on her. He rips her clothes and slaps her. He keeps hitting her. She screams. Then she says: "Ooh master. Hurt me. Punish me." She also says: "I want my man to punish me." She calls him Daddy. William, Sandra's boyfriend, finds a letter Chris has written to Cora that expresses adoration. Sandra suggests that Chris intercept William with the letter before he can show it to Cora. Chris is grateful. Sandra ties his hands, then his balls, then emerges in black stockings with a whip and beats him. In a restaurant, Sandra's parents, Alice and Pete Waverly, are having dinner. Alice wants Cora removed from teaching. Cora is also in the restaurant. A bum brags about his masculinity. Cora picks him up. Alice makes Pete follow Cora and the bum to get evidence against Cora. Scott goes to speak with Alice, they argue about Cora, then Scott begins fingering Alice under the table and Alice begins fingering Scott, then they get into a car and start fucking. Cora jacks off the bum in the car. Cora takes him to a motel. Cora is characterized as "the amazon." She holds him by the cock and makes him walk around the room following her. He cannot get loose. She commands him to eat her. She says: "This is all a man is good for." She allows him to fuck her but he fails so she starts crushing his balls until he becomes "happily unconscious." Leaving the motel Cora sees Pete Waverly. She seduces him. He has a huge cock. They go back to her motel room. The bum is taking a shower. Pete fucks Cora. She has the bum suck her ass, then her cunt while Pete fucks her in the ass. After all have come, Cora orders the bum to clean Pete's genitals. Pete refuses to allow it, Cora senses repression and fear of an ultimate truth, Pete goes to take a shower, Cora sends the bum in after him, sounds of lust and pleasure eventually come from the shower. The next day, Chris fucks and is generally mauled by Sandra on campus, then another liberated woman named Carol joins in. Cora gets Chris's letter. She seduces him and insists that he ejaculate in her vagina: "I want those seeds planted in me." Carol follows Chris home and seduces him. Carol, liberated woman that she is, tries to make Chris lose his erection: "Her tone shifted to the pedantic style of the liberated woman." He fucks her on the kitchen table and sticks a glass saltshaker up her ass. The kitchen table collapses as they come. Scott has seen the whole thing. He says to Chris: "That's the best way to catch one of these liberated birds. You have to salt their tails." Scott is home alone. Sandra comes looking for Chris. Chris is at Cora's. Sandra throws her arms around Scott and seduces him. She keeps calling him "motherfucker," since she knows that he has fucked her mother. Chris is with Cora. She makes him undress. She sees the whip marks made by Sandra. These marks reveal that he is not the young lion she had thought so she keeps kicking him in the balls. She becomes his master. Meanwhile as Scott and Sandra are fucking, Sandra's mother telephones them. Everyone is to converge at Cora's house, even as Scott is using his "mammoth probing pole!" Cora asks Chris: "Are you a man?" His answer: "No!" He is "beside himself with lust and pain, and joy." Cora asks: "And are you mommy's little boy?" He answers: "Oh yes! Fuck me mommy! Tear me up!!" In the midst of all this, Cora, speaking to Chris, calls Scott a "loathsome chauvinist." Cora keeps battering Chris's penis with her leg. Cora sticks her fingers in his ear, her fist down his throat, while saying: "I know what you're thinking and you are right! Every hole, every nook and cranny. You are going to be fucked for your disobedience!" She strangles his balls in her fist and keeps slapping him across the face. She says: "Mommy's going to punish you now." She sticks a fountain pen up his ass, he falls to the floor, she pushes the pen up his rectum with her foot, then she pushes her foot up his ass. She says that she wants to see his uncle. The Waverlys arrive at Cora's house. They say they are looking for Sandra. Cora begins undressing. Alice says she put a drug in the water reservoir to cause weird behavior and expose Cora for what she is. Alice tells Cora she has always loved her. Cora gets her dildo and fucks Alice. Alice is afraid that the dildo is too big, then wants it in her ass. Pete watches. Sandra and Scott enter. Cora rises and unfastens the dildo. Sandra goes looking for Chris. Alice and Pete quarrel. Alice says she did not put a drug in the water reservoir. She says that Pete raped her on their wedding night and has been raping her for years, that all he ever thinks about is sex. Alice says: "You big chauvinist pig!" Then she straps on the dildo and fucks him in the ass. Pete and Alice agree that now their marriage is as it should be. Scott and Cora, her hand gently on his cock, no threat or possibility of threat in the gesture, only the promise of service, enter the room and watch. They announce that they are going to be married. Chris's screams of lust and pain, interwoven with cries of "Sandra, oh Sandra, please Sandra," fill the room. Finis.

In *Whip Chick*, male power is characterized as precarious at best, easily transformed into its opposite by women who are more ambitious in their masculinity than the anatomical males. Scott is the exception. His masculinity is so assured, so free of homosexual taint, so thoroughly uncontaminated by any longing for the mother, that he wins Cora's heart. Her quest has been for a real man, the ultimate fucker whom she cannot dominate. Pete's final fate—to be fucked by his wife in the ass with a dildo until death do them part—is foreshadowed by the homosexual pleasure he experienced with the bum Cora set upon him in the motel. Similarly, Chris's fate is also foreshadowed by Scott's description of him as "the little faggot."

Whip Chick was supposedly written by a woman, a conceit common enough in the kind of pornography that is written fast and sold to a publisher for a flat fee. The easy money for the author is in turning out the largest possible number of books in the shortest possible time. All the books produced by a single author may be published under different names. In general, arguments about the real gender of authors of pornography—from *Whip Chick* to *Story of O*—are meaningless, since the goal is to please the male consumer whose tastes are entirely predictable, existing as they do within the limited framework of male sexual values and ideas. Anaïs Nin tried to conform to the rules of the pornography-for-fast-money game, but dripped sensibility helplessly and foolishly. Most writers of pornography are male. The female name on the cover of the book is part of the package, an element of the fiction. It confirms men in their fantasy that the eroticism of the female exists within the bounds of male sexual imperatives.

How is male power served by *Whip Chick?* One would think that most of the sexual action in *Whip Chick* would be abhorrent to men who presumably have everything to lose and nothing to gain by the portrayal of a woman driving her spiked heel into a man's balls as being pleasurable for both male and female. But the resources of male power need not be thoroughly obvious to be effective. *Whip Chick* is not a mistake.

First of all, *Whip Chick* is not believable. The prose, the story, the action, the dialogue, all are absurd and ridiculous. The portrayal of men as sexual victims is distinctly unreal, ludicrous in part because it scarcely has an analogue in the real world. The woman tied on the hood of the car had a symbolic reality: that valuation of women is commonplace. *Whip Chick* is male fantasy, not rooted in reality, not rooted in the distribution of power as a social fact.

Second, the men in *Whip Chick* are punished by women for failures of masculinity: for being faggots or boys who want Mommy. Any loss of control by men over women will result in the loss of everything, all the kinds of male power that men should and must have. The dangerous female, now called an amazon or liberated woman, is ever present, ready to take over if the male lets up in his cruelty at all. Should the purity of his fuck—its absolute masculine integrity—be less than perfect, the bitch underneath will become castrator. A moment of immaturity, indecision, or gratitude (as when Chris thanks Sandra for suggesting that he intercept his letter to Cora before it reaches her) will mean total and absolute humiliation, not to mention penile mutilation.

Third, all the sexual action takes place in the realm of male-defined sexuality. Cruelty is the essence of sexual action; fucking is the most significant masculine act; the penis is the source and symbol of real manhood; punishment is the prerogative of the man unless he loses that prerogative by failing, in which case the female, as the most masculine, usurps the prerogative; force is integral to fucking; and dominance is the ultimate purpose of sexual behavior. These are the values embodied in *Whip Chick*. This is the house that Jack built.

Fourth, *Whip Chick* warns specifically that the feminist wants to castrate the male, use his sexuality as her own against him. It warns that if men do not keep male power sacrosanct, the dangerous, uppity women will take it from them and use it against them. It postulates that women will do to men what men have done to women. This presentation of women as vicious castrators if given the chance suggests that men's only protection is an unambiguous commitment on the part of men to sexual conquest of women.

Fifth, if men do experience guilt over what they do to women, the specter of women punishing them in ways they can understand, given their limited frame of reference, might provide some release from guilt with no loss of self-esteem (since the book is ludicrous in its style and since a man, Scott, triumphs over the amazon in the end).

Sixth, *Whip Chick* postulates that all any woman really wants—however shrewish or dangerous she is—is a man who can fuck or dominate her. Any bitch can be tamed by a man who is manly enough.

The ultimate impact of *Whip Chick* is to clarify the nature of male power and demonstrate how to hold onto it. In fantasy, the male can experiment with the consequences as he imagines them of loss of power over women. He can expect that what he has done to women will be done to him. He can view his own devastation in his imagination, experience it as a self-induced, self-contained, masturbatory sexual reality and, when the book is closed, as a result of having read it, be armed more thoroughly against any vulnerability that might imperil him. He will be convinced that male power can only be maintained by an absolutely cruel and ruthless subjugation of women. And not coincidentally, "liberated women," "amazons," will be the most dangerous women, most in need of subjugation, the greatest and best test of masculinity in action. *Whip Chick* targets feminists as the subgroup of women most threatening to male power, most in need of abusive, humiliating sexual treatment. *Whip Chick*—spiked heel in the groin notwithstanding—is a cunning and effective argument for male dominance.

I Love a Laddie, a book, consists of three short vignettes and a preface by a man whose name is followed by "M.A.," which one can only presume means Master of Arts. This person's introduction warns that "the constant practice of sexually perverse acts may very well lead to the point where an undesirable practice may become completely habitual in one *[sic]* body and mind. Awareness of the wide extent of sexual perversion and its pitfalls should be helpful in stopping these wrges *[sic]* . . ." Informed that one is being educated against vice, one is prepared to begin enjoying it.

In the first vignette, Dave the sailor is going on leave to London to have a ball. "Cunt desires" are raging. He has half a hard-on. When he leaves the train, all the porters ignore him because he is big and strong, except for one effeminate porter whose offer to carry Dave's bag had "a sort of carressing *[sic]* solicitude . . ." It was "like an invitation from a girl to slip into her pussy!" Dave has half a hard-on. A cabbie, assuming that Dave's inclinations are the same as the porter's, takes him to a hotel where the manager has a voice like the porter's. The manager hands him a pen with a caressing motion. Dave realizes that his leave will be a "feast of 'navy-cake'" and claims that "one hole [is] as good as another!" Dave undresses and admires himself and his hard prick in the mirror. Dave takes a bath. The carpet in his room reminds him of a man he slept with in India. His prick hardens and this time swells to "a deep, shiny red!" Dave masturbates on the carpet. Dave puts on his only suit. The manager offers to iron it. Dave takes off his only suit. Garry, the manager, makes subtle advances. Dave determines to "give him all the cock he could cope with" but only when Garry makes the first move. Garry brings in liquor and glasses. They undress. Soon "Dave's finger was throughly *[sic]* raping [Garry's] asshole." Dave fucks Garry who is called his victim. Garry comes, but remains "complacent to any whim of his master." Dave moves his victim to the carpet where he pinions him spread-eagle. Garry "shuddered and quiverred *[sic]* under the frantic assult *[sic]* on his prone body." Dave goes cruising in bars. He is excited by women in miniskirts. A middle-aged man tries to pick him up. He walks out. Someone follows him, a young hustler; Dave is insulted. Dave returns to the hotel, where the key to Garry's room, number 69, and a jar of Vaseline await him. Garry is dressed in a negligee. They bathe together, then go to Garry's seven-by-seven bed, which is dressed in satin. Dave fucks Garry. Garry sucks Dave. Next morning, Dave goes to a tailor recommended by Garry. Then he goes to a bar where he meets Harry, the middle-aged man who tried to pick him up the previous night. They go to a strip place (female strippers). Dave gets a hard-on. Harry jerks him off. Dave returns to the hotel. Garry fucks Dave. Dave comes. Garry keeps fucking. Dave discovers new dimensions of himself as "the intensity of the thrusts up into his rectum, and their violence was *[sic]* increasing every second and with every forwards *[sic]* drive of the other man's hip *[sic]* and loins!" They go to Garry's room. They look at each other. Dave sucks Garry's cock. Garry places Dave on his back "like a girl" and fucks him. Dave returns to his own room, his rectum sore, and takes a bath. He goes back to the bars, ends up in a homosexual bar, finds a young innocent from out of town, goes to the young innocent's room. Dave tells the boy about all kinds of girls and the "bizare *[sic]* things that he had seen them do." Innocent boy gets a hard-on. They jerk each other off, then Dave fucks him, despite his cries of pain, which change to cries of lust. Dave returns to the hotel and sleeps. Garry brings breakfast. Dave tells him about having initiated a virgin the previous night. Garry fucks Dave. Dave goes to the tailor, then to a bar. A stranger offers to take him to a homosexual club. The hustler who had tried to pick him up previously is there. He offers Dave money to fuck him in front of three lesbians looking for kicks. Dave accepts. Dave fucks the young man. When he looks up, he is surrounded by "women and grils *[sic]* with their clothes hiked up and panties down around their nylon clad knees, with fingers all busily fingerfucking away at another female's cunt." The hustler is instructed by the lesbians to let the sperm from his ass trickle into a glass dish so they can inspect it. The lesbians "were tearing off each others *[sic]* panties to turn and clasp heads diving in between parted thighs for a female '69'!" Dave gets paid the promised amount plus a bonus. Finis.

In the second vignette, Paul is over forty and wealthy. He uses his money to pursue his favorite pleasure, assfucking young men. He dislikes women and avoids male hustlers. He uses his wealth to encourage younger boys to take up his own preferences. Paul waits for Bob, a new boy. Bob arrives. Bob tells Paul how he and a younger boy, Robin, had found photographs of "girls in nothing buth *[sic]* their undies and stockings" and had hidden to "oggle *[sic]*" the photographs and, as a result, had jerked each other off. Paul shows Bob both heterosexual and homosexual pornography. Paul sucks off Bob. Bob sucks off Paul. Bob looks at more pornography, especially of a male assfucking a woman and of a man assfucking a man. Bob says: "Ooooh! I never realized what thrills there were, Paul! Can we try that too!" Paul invites Bob to spend school vacation on his boat. Bob suggests inviting Robin too. Bob asks to try it now "like they were in those pictures." Bob's response to being fucked is: "Ahh! It huts *[sic]* a bit! But it's lovely! Go on! Ram it up me! Split me! Fuck me!" Bob is referred to as Paul's victim, and the act is described as "just as he had seen it in the picture—with the girl and the boy!" After Bob leaves, Paul contemplates the pleasure in having two sex slaves. He decides to photograph it. Bob and Robin arrive at Paul's house. Paul enters the room as Bob and Robin are making love. Paul takes a photograph. They go to the boat. Bob shows Robin the pornographic photographs. When Robin sees the assfucking, he sucks Bob's cock. Paul, from a skylight above, takes photographs. Paul calls to Bob, instructs him to do sixty-nine. Paul masturbates as he watches Bob and Robin and also steers the boat. All come. Bob steers the boat. Paul, Robin, and Bob have tea. They arrive at an island. The boys cook dinner. They are naked with hard-ons. Paul takes photographs. All eat nude. Paul fucks Bob and sucks Robin's cock, puts his finger up Robin's ass. Robin looks at the photographs again. Bob looks at the photographs again. Paul takes a photograph. They go to sleep. Paul makes breakfast. Bob does the dishes. Paul pretends that he is going to spank Robin, but instead greases his ass. Paul fucks Robin as Bob watches. Paul continues fucking Robin as Bob fucks Paul. Robin and Bob mutually jerk off. Paul takes a photograph. They visit the island. The two boys seduce Paul. Paul falls asleep. As a prank, the boys take his clothes. He swims back to the boat. How will he wreak vengeance? He orders the boys to undress, whips them, forces them to swim so that salt gets into the whip cuts. Bob fucks Robin. Paul takes a photograph. Robin sucks off Paul. The next day, two girls arrive in a boat. The males move away. The girls lie naked on the beach. Paul concludes that they think the island is deserted. From their posture, it is obvious that they have been "indulging in some form of fucking." Paul develops his photographs. He joins the boys on the deck. The three watch the women in "a Lesbian '69.'" As they watch the women, Paul jerks off both boys. They agree when Paul says: "I still think that having cocks to play with, we have the advantage when it comes to fucking!" Paul fucks Bob and Robin. Robin is fucked "as a girl might be." Paul goes for a walk. He threatens to whip the boys if there is a drop of sperm on them when he returns. He watches the lesbians. Their asses getting tan from the sun reminds him that he wants to tan the asses of "these females that had invaded his masculine kingdom!" He asks them what they are doing, takes off his leather belt and beats them. He returns to the boat. Bob is sucking Robin. Paul takes a photograph. The males leave the island. They spot the boat of the lesbians. Paul is gratified that both are standing, too sore he assumes to sit, which leads the males to speculate on "female assholes to be fucked" during the rest of their holiday. Finis.

In the third vignette, it is Saturday and Jules Auger is at the helm of his boat. Narrator and Jules return to their bedroom, where Narrator fucks Jules. They sleep. Narrator showers. Storm joins him in the shower and sucks his cock. Narrator sucks Storm's cock. Narrator goes to Gordon for the night, then crawls into bed with Jules. On Sunday, everything is the same, except that Patrick joins Narrator in the shower. On Monday, they dock and go to the studio. Narrator wonders whether he will ever be able to leave the homosexual life, "be normal with a woman and marry and have children." Narrator resolves to stay homosexual only long enough to become a successful actor. Narrator thinks about Mary. He can't believe that she is a lesbian. She is "too normal for that." He wants to fuck her. He has to escape from Jules Auger to make love to Mary Moray. Jules calls Narrator into the projection room. Narrator's name is Rod. Gordon, Patrick, and Storm are there. Jules fondles Rod's genitals. Rod is very good in the rushes, very manly. He only has to pretend to be homosexual a few more years to get to the top. Rod thinks of Mary as he agrees to have a sex binge with the boys. In a cafeteria Rod glimpses Mary and gets hot. The men go to Jules's home in Palm Springs. They all disrobe on the way to the pool, this time including "the young colored chauffer *[sic]*" who is "hotter than any woman you ever had and he's got twice as much as most men." The chauffeur, George, makes love to Rod. Rod makes love to George. Rod is on fire. They do sixty-nine. George declares his love. Rod says that George is more thrilling than the "shapely, desirable young cunts [that] had thrilled my prick in the past." Gordon sucks Storm. Jules and Patrick rest. George leaves. Gordon fucks Storm. Rod sleeps. Jules wakes Rod to take him to bed. Rod fucks Jules. Rod showers. Rod is nauseated by homosexual love. Rod moves to a penthouse paid for by Jules. He wants Mary Moray's twat. Gordon warns Rod not to eye Mary. If Jules finds out that any of his lovers fuck a woman, they are blackballed as actors. Rod agrees to do what Jules wants. Then he accidentally runs into Mary. She suggests they spend the weekend together. They go to his place. She says: "Sometimes I think all man *[sic]* are a little bit queer." She says: "I want you to be my fucker. And I don't let many men have me that way." He carries her to the bedroom just as Jules enters the apartment. Jules says he has bought and paid for Rod. Mary cries. Jules fires Mary. Mary stumbles out the door in tears. Rod undresses. He wants to subject Jules to pain like he's never known. Rod beats Jules with a leather belt. Rod sucks his cock. Rod fucks him as painfully as he can: "Jules was just like any other bitch I'd fucked in the ass in my time. . . . I was the male stud and Jules was my woman." Rod thinks of Mary. Rod thinks he has killed Jules. Jules comes to, babbling that he is in heaven. Jules is in love with Rod. Rod says: "You're my femme aren't you baby? You'll trot over and flopp *[sic]* for me anytime I whistle, won't you?" Rod tells Jules he is going to fuck Mary. Jules says he will have her killed. Mary disappears. Rod has to find her to overcome "the stigma of being an active homosexual." Rod is invited to a party on Jules's boat. The men explain that Jules has a new boy, Darien. Rod announces that he will not go to the party. Jules telephones, they argue, Jules claims that the new boy means nothing, says he loves Rod. Rod says that he wants to fuck a woman in Jules's presence. Jules says that he will have any woman killed whom Rod fucks. Rod finds out where Mary is through her heterosexual friend, Larry. Larry stays in Rod's apartment. Rod goes to find Mary. Some men, hired by Jules to kidnap Rod and take him to Jules's party, kidnap Larry instead. Rod thinks this is funny as he sees the men coming and learns their purpose. Rod finds Mary. They go to a motel. Mary confesses to lesbian experiences. He sucks her. She sucks him. They go to fuck, but he is soft, limp. Mary does everything she can to arouse him, but nothing works. Then he thinks of Jules and goes mad with desire. He imagines that she is Jules as she sucks his cock. He forces her to swallow the sperm. She gags and curses. They drive home in silence. She apologizes to him. He wants to see her again. She is grateful. They agree to meet in one week. Rod returns to his penthouse, but hears Jules and friends inside so goes elsewhere. He goes to Andy and George the chauffeur. They undress. Andy fucks Rod. Rod sucks George. Andy sucks Rod. For Rod, they are better than any woman. Jules thinks Rod was with a woman. Rod is ostracized at work. He lets it be known that he was with two men to appease Jules. Rod goes home. Larry is there with an erection. Larry, the heterosexual, says that Jules and his cohorts gang-raped him. After two days he started to like it. He discovered that he had always been queer. He beats up Rod for setting him up. He keeps hitting him. He beats him with a belt. Rod knows Larry wants him. He wants Larry. Rod sucks Larry's cock. Rod loves Larry. They sleep. Rod wakes to find Larry assfucking him. They shower. They blackmail Jules with threats of kidnapping charges and announce that they are a team. On the way out of Jules's office, Rod pinches the nipples of the secretary. She screams. Rod and Larry howl with laughter. Larry was "the aggressor, the male member of our union." Rod was "proud to be his femme." At a cast party, Mary enters. Rod and Mary take a walk to his trailer. Mary undresses. He wants her. She wants him. But again, he is soft, limp. He falls asleep. Suddenly Larry and Mary are making love. Larry says he likes women after all. Mary says that she made Larry a man again and is sorry she had not been able to help Rod. Larry and Mary announce they will marry. Rod feels nothing for either of them. He is already thinking of "a young Negro lad . . . He wanted to fuck me. That was all that mattered." Rod admits "the truth." He is homosexual. He "could only be happy loving men and being loved by them. Who could ask for more?" Finis.

Throughout *I Love a Laddie*, the literal expression of male power is in the intense, repeated use of the penis, which here resembles the mythical Hydra. The penis is central, whatever the act or environment. Degree of hardness and frequency of use signify penile virility, nearly unlimited in the sexual scenarios described. The men in themselves or relative to each other are vehicles for the penis. The penis is the central character in each story. The emphasis is not so much on who does what to whom as it is on the perpetual motion of the penis, its efficacy in producing pleasure for its proud carrier and receiver. In the second vignette, Paul, the wealthy middle-aged man with the two boys, whose penile virility is established beyond doubt, also uses a camera as if it were a penis. The camera becomes part of the sexual action. The camera is not a substitute for the penis; rather, it is as if he had two. He chooses which penis to use. Taking a photograph becomes a form of sexual action in itself, equal in significance to fucking or cocksucking, more mature in that in producing a collection of photographs, it produces wealth.

The penis causes pain, but the pain enhances the pleasure. It is as if the ability of the penis to cause pain were an intrinsic quality of the penis, not a use to which the penis is put. The pain also authenticates the power of the penis—its size, the force behind it. As a result, fucking is inherently sadistic because it is necessarily both pain and pleasure; and when penile pain is supplemented by purposeful cruelty, it occasions the highest sexual ecstasy, emotional love, or both. The pain is experienced as a commitment on the part of the one fucking to the one being fucked. The degree of pain is equivalent to the degree of love coming from the lover to the beloved of the moment. But in no sense is the beloved annihilated. His virility continues to animate his own behavior, either in relation to others or in the sphere of social power. Even Rod's commitment to be Larry's "femme" is articulated as an act of will on his part. This will is distinctly masculine. Rod, who is, after all, named Rod, continues to embody on the screen manly virility, and his social power in his career increases. His recognition of his homosexuality—characterized by his thoughts about the future lover who wants to fuck him—does not place homosexuality per se in the area of the feminine, despite his endless ruminations on becoming a real man by fucking Mary and his repeated failures to do so (she is, after all, named Mary). His aggressive pursuit of sex retains its masculine character, and his virility—the energy of his penis—is never questionable. What he accomplishes in his recognition of himself as homosexual is to discard the female altogether, to change his frame of reference so that females no longer figure in at all. Mary's claim to have made Larry a man again is transparently ridiculous, since the heterosexual Larry (before he was gang-raped) was markedly (even in this context) dull and stupid. His virility was expressed vividly only in his sexual relationship to Rod. In fact, within the context of the vignette, Larry's alliance with Mary unmans him, since sex with a woman is shown to be rather pale and silly: less cock is involved in it. Mary's lesbianism contributes to the impression that Larry has been caught by someone who will make him less masculine, take him away from the penis, which is manhood. Moray, her last name, also names numerous kinds of savage, voracious eels: the vagina dentata castrates, as does the lesbian.

Lesbians are in each vignette. In the first, Dave fucks the hustler for pay to amuse a group of grotesque lesbians. In the second, Paul beats the two lesbians who invade his masculine territory; and it is on sighting their boat at the end that he and the boys begin to contemplate fucking "female assholes." In the third, Mary is first called a lesbian by Larry, in his first heterosexual incarnation, because she would not allow him to fuck her in a past encounter. She admits her lesbian experiences to Rod and also tells him that she does not often allow a man to fuck her. Throughout, claims are made, explicitly and by inference, for the superiority of male-male sex, and it is no exaggeration to say that a particular hatred of lesbians is very notable in all three vignettes. Lesbians are characterized as manipulators and controllers of men, invaders of male domain, or dangerous adversaries who can take a man from a man if so disposed.

Women in general are sources of sexual arousal within the vignettes and, apparently, for the reader as well. Within the vignettes, the heterosexual use of women is invoked to seduce boys; the heterosexual presence of women (women turned out to please men) is titillating; the epithets used to name women are sexual in nature, insulting, degrading, violent, utterly contemptuous. Garry, the manager of the hotel, wears a negligee, but this does not make him feminine—his penile strength is endlessly celebrated; rather, the negligee evokes the feminine in the mind of the reader. This evocation of the feminine is constantly exploited to emphasize by contrast the extreme masculinity of the men who worship cock. None of the men is really portrayed as feminine, despite occasional disdainful references to mannerisms or descriptions of a male being fucked "like a girl." Without the presence of the female, masculinity cannot be realized, even among men who exclusively want each other; so the female is conjured up, not just to haunt or threaten, but to confirm the real superiority of the male in the mind of the reader. In an interview in the *Gay Community News*, gay activist and writer Allen Young described and interpreted a photograph that has, as part of its composition, this same sort of heterosexual reference:

> For example, [in gay male pornography] I've seen pictures of a guy jacking off to an issue of *Playboy;* in other words, a guy is looking at a naked woman and jacking off and I as a gay man am supposed to look at the picture and feel more excited looking at that boy because he's straight. The message is that a straight man is more desirable than a faggot. Obviously this is a put down to the gay man.[6]

The excitement is supposed to come, in fact, from the visual reminder of male superiority to women in which homosexual men participate. Without that wider frame of reference, masculinity is essentially meaningless. The feminine or references to women in male homosexual pornography clarify for the male that the significance of the penis cannot be compromised, no matter what words are used to describe his (temporary) position or state of mind. The evocation of femininity or the presence of women is in itself a part of the sexual excitement because superiority means power and in male terms power is sexually exciting. In pornography, the homosexual male, like the heterosexual male, is encouraged to experience and enjoy his sexual superiority over women.

In *I Love a Laddie,* the seduction of boys, the enlarged genitalia of a black male who is in a servile social position, and wealth as a sign of mature masculinity complete a portrait of male power that is imperializing in its motivation, attuned to the nuances of dominance in its implicit values, rooted in the hierarchical absolutes of male-over-male power within the larger culture.

The photograph shows two women in an elegant living room. Both women have cream-colored skin, taut and flawless. The room is cream colored: carpeting, sofa, table, walls. The furniture is taut in design: very modern and simple. One woman, blond-haired, lies on the sofa, her ass raised on the arm of the sofa, her legs bent back toward her stomach, the spread of her legs shown by the distance between her feet poised in the air. She is wearing a garter belt, nylon stockings that stop a few inches above her knees, and spiked heels the same color as her hair. Her eyes are closed, her eye shadow is dark gray. Her mouth is slightly open, her lips are distinctly pinkish. One of her hands disappears between her legs; the other, emerging from a hidden arm, seems to be fondling her own breast, which is not visible because one sees the profile of the breast closest to the camera. The most prominent part of her body is her buttock, raised, highlighted by the intensity of the light on it. The rest of her ass, even in profile, is obscured by the head of the second woman. The second woman is on her knees beside the sofa arm, her features indistinguishable, her mouth apparently kissing the first woman's exposed buttock, but in fact her face is merely profiled against the woman's raised buttock. The second woman is perpendicular to the reclining woman, so that her ass, fully exposed, directly faces the camera. She is wearing a cream-colored robe which is draped across her back and falls to one side to highlight her naked ass. Her legs are spread. Pubic hair shows underneath. She is wearing spiked heels the same color as her hair, dark brown. The light is concentrated on the ass of the woman on her knees.

In the photograph, all visual significance is given to the ass of the woman on her knees, which is in the foreground, exaggerated by the light markedly on it, and to its echo, the raised buttock of the woman reclining. The camera is the penile presence, the viewer is the male who participates in the sexual action, which is not within the photograph but in the perception of it. The photograph does not document lesbian lovemaking; in fact, it barely resembles it. The symbolic reality of the photograph—which is vivid—is not in the relationship between the two women, which not only does not provoke but actually prohibits any recognition of lesbian eroticism as authentic or even existent. The symbolic reality instead is expressed in the posture of women exposed purposefully to excite a male viewer. The ass is exposed and vulnerable; the camera has taken it; the viewer can claim it. The spiked heels suggest cruelty, associated with the lesbian, the quintessential castrator. At the same time, the spiked heels suggest a slavish conformity to male-dictated fashion, a crippling of the female, binding of the feet, which is underlined in the long and languid accompanying text by the declaration that neither woman has ever before made love with a woman (so this is just for you, dear boy) and the assurance that men are magnificent. The exposed ass is an emblem for the values in the photograph as a whole. The contact between the women does not exclude the male; it explicitly invites him. The woman on her knees, legs spread open, conjures up the propitiating, submissive gesture of the animal who takes the same stance (ethologists take note: without the spiked heels) allegedly to appease an aggressive male. The photograph is the ultimate tribute to male power: the male is not in the room, yet the women are there for his pleasure. His wealth produces the photograph; his wealth consumes the photograph; he produces and consumes the women. The male defines and controls the idea of the lesbian in the composition of the photograph. In viewing it, he possesses her. The lesbian is colonialized, reduced to a variant of woman-as-sex-object, used to demonstrate and prove that male power pervades and invades even the private sanctuary of women with each other. The power of the male is affirmed as omnipresent and controlling even when the male himself is absent and invisible. This is divine power, the power of divine right to divine pleasure, that pleasure accurately described as the sexual debasing of others inferior by birth. In private, the women are posed for display. In private, the women still sexually service the male, for whose pleasure they are called into existence. The pleasure of the male requires the annihilation of women's sexual integrity. There is no privacy, no closed door, no self-determined meaning, for women with each other in the world of pornography.

2

Men and Boys

Just so does Miller return us to the first question of humanism. What, finally, is a Man?

Norman Mailer, *Genius and Lust: A Journey Through the Major Writings of Henry Miller*

With a disgust common to all feminists who have tried to be participants in the so-called humanism of men, only to discover through bitter experience that the culture of males does not allow honest female participation, Virginia Woolf wrote: "I detest the masculine point of view. I am bored by his heroism, virtue, and honour. I think the best these men can do is not to talk about themselves anymore."[1] Men have claimed the human point of view; they author it; they own it. Men are humanists, humans, humanism. Men are rapists, batterers, plunderers, killers; these same men are religious prophets, poets, heroes, figures of romance, adventure, accomplishment, figures ennobled by tragedy and defeat. Men have claimed the earth, called it Her. Men ruin Her. Men have airplanes, guns, bombs, poisonous gases, weapons so perverse and deadly that they defy any authentically human imagination. Men battle each other and Her; women battle to be let into the category "human" in imagination and reality. Men battle to keep the category "human" narrow, circumscribed by their own values and activities; women battle to change the meaning that men have given the word, to transform its meaning by suffusing it with female experience.

Boys are birthed and raised by women. At some point, boys become men, dim their vision to exclude women.

All children view things as animate. As Jean Piaget's work in developmental psychology has shown, children hear the wind whisper and the trees cry. As Bruno Bettelheim expresses it: "To the child, there is no clear line separating objects from living things; and whatever has life has life very much like our own."[2] But adult men treat women, and often girls, and sometimes other males, as objects. Adult men are convinced and sincere in their perception of adult women in particular as objects. This perception of women transcends categories of sexual orientation, political philosophy, nationality, class, race, and so forth. How does it happen that the male child whose sense of life is so vivid that he imparts humanity to sun and stone changes into the adult male who cannot grant or even imagine the common humanity of women?

In *The Dialectic of Sex*, Shulamith Firestone shows that the boy has a choice: remain loyal to the mother who is in reality degraded, without authority against the father, unable to protect the child from the father's violence or the violence of other adult men, or become a man, one who has the power and the right to hurt, to use force, to use his will and physical strength over and against women and children. Be the mother—do the housework—or be the father—carry a big stick. Be the mother—be fucked—or be the father—do the fucking. The boy has a choice. The boy chooses to become a man because it is better to be a man than a woman.

Becoming a man requires that the boy learn to be indifferent to the fate of women. Indifference requires that the boy learn to experience women as objects. The poet, the mystic, the prophet, the so-called sensitive man of any stripe, will still hear the wind whisper and the trees cry. But to him, women will be mute. He will have learned to be deaf to the sounds, sighs, whispers, screams of women in order to ally himself with other men in the hope that they will not treat him as a child, that is, as one who belongs with the women.

A boy, or his mother, is threatened, hit, or molested. A boy experiences male force as its victim or as a witness. This nearly universal event is described by John Stoltenberg is an essay, "Eroticism and Violence in the Father-Son Relationship":

> The boy will be a witness as the father abuses his wife—once or a hundred times, it only needs to happen once, and the boy will be filled with fear and helpless to intercede. Then the father will visit his anger upon the boy himself, uncontrollable rage, wrath that seems to come from nowhere, punishment out of proportion to any infraction of rules the boy knew existed—once or a hundred times, it only needs to happen once, and the boy will wonder in agony why the mother did not prevent it. From that point onward, the boy's trust in the mother decays, and the son will belong to the father for the rest of his natural life.[3]

The boy seeks to emulate the father because it is safer to be like the father than like the mother. He learns to threaten or hit because men can and men must. He dissociates himself from the powerlessness he did experience, the powerlessness to which females as a class are consigned. The boy becomes a man by taking on the behaviors of men—to the best of his ability.

The boy escapes, into manhood, into power. It is his option, based on the social valuation of his anatomy. This route of escape is the only one now charted.

But the boy remembers, he always remembers, that once he was a child, close to women in powerlessness, in potential or actual humiliation, in danger from male aggression. The boy must build up a male identity, a fortressed castle with an impenetrable moat, so that he is inaccessible, so that he is invulnerable to the memory of his origins, to the sorrowful or enraged calls of the women he left behind. The boy, whatever his chosen style, turns martial in his masculinity, fierce, stubborn, rigid, humorless. His fear of men turns into aggression against women. He keeps the distance between himself and women unbridgeable, transforms women into the dreaded She, or, as Simone de Beauvoir expresses it, "the Other." He learns to be a man—poet man, gangster man, professional religious man, rapist man, any kind of man—and the first rule of masculinity is that whatever he is, women are not. He calls his cowardice heroism, and he keeps women *out*—out of humanity (fabled Mankind), out of his sphere of activity whatever it is, out of all that is valued, rewarded, credible, out of the diminishing realm of his own capacity to care. Women must be kept out because wherever there are women, there is one haunting, vivid memory with numberless smothering tentacles: he is that child, powerless against the adult male, afraid of him, humiliated by him.

Boys become men to escape being victims by definition. Girls would become men if girls could, because it would mean *freedom from:* freedom from rape most of the time; freedom from continuous petty insult and violent devaluation of self; freedom from debilitating economic and emotional dependence on someone else; freedom from the male aggression channeled against women in intimacy and throughout the culture.

But male aggression is rapacious. It spills over, not accidentally, but purposefully. There is war. Older men create wars. Older men kill boys by generating and financing wars. Boys fight wars. Boys die in wars. Older men hate boys because boys still have the smell of women on them. War purifies, washes off the female stink. The blood of death, so hallowed, so celebrated, overcomes the blood of life, so abhorred, so defamed. The ones who survive the bloodbath will never again risk the empathy with women they experienced as children for fear of being found out and punished for good: killed this time by the male gangs, found in all spheres of life, that enforce the male code. The child is dead. The boy has become a man.

MEN DEVELOP a strong loyalty to violence. Men must come to terms with violence because it is the prime component of male identity. Institutionalized in sports, the military, acculturated sexuality, the history and mythology of heroism, it is taught to boys until they become its advocates—men, not women. Men become advocates of that which they most fear. In advocacy they experience mastery of fear. In mastery of fear they experience freedom. Men transform their fear of male violence into a metaphysical commitment to male violence. Violence itself becomes the central definition of any experience that is profound and significant. So, in *Love's*

Body, philosopher Norman O. Brown, a sexual radical in the male system, posits that "[l]ove is violence. The kingdom of heaven suffereth violence, from hot love and living hope."[4] In the same text, Brown defines freedom in the same way: "Freedom is poetry, taking liberties with words, breaking the rules of normal speech, violating common sense. Freedom is violence."[5] Swim in male culture; drown in the male romanticization of violence. On the Left, on the Right, in the Middle; authors, statesmen, thieves; so-called humanists and self-declared fascists; the adventurous and the contemplative; in every realm of male expression and action, violence is experienced and articulated as love and freedom. Pacifist males are only apparent exceptions: repelled by some forms of violence as nearly all men are, they remain impervious to sexual violence as nearly all men do.

Men choose their spheres of advocacy according to what they can bear and/or what they can do well. Men will advocate some forms of violence and not others. Some men will renounce violence in theory, and practice it in secrecy against women and children. Some men will become icons in male culture, able to discipline and focus their commitment to violence by learning a violent skill: boxing, shooting, hunting, hockey, football, soldiering, policing. Some men will use language as violence, or money as violence, or religion as violence, or science as violence, or influence over others as violence. Some men will commit violence against the minds of others and some against the bodies of others. Most men, in their life histories, have done both. In the area of sexuality, this fact was acknowledged with no recognition of its significance by the scholars of the Institute for Sex Research (the Kinsey Institute) who studied sex offenders:

> If we labeled all punishable sexual behavior as a sex offense, we would find ourselves in the ridiculous situation of having all of our male histories consist almost wholly of sex offenders, the remaining few being not only nonoffenders but nonconformists. The man who kisses a girl *[sic]* in defiance of her expressed wishes is committing a forced sexual relationship and is liable to

> an assault charge, but to solemnly label him a sex offender would be to reduce our study to a ludicrous level.[6]

Rather than "reduce [their] study to a ludicrous level," which would be unthinkable, the honorable scientists chose to sanction as normative the male commitment to the use of force documented by their study.

Men are distinguished from women by their commitment to do violence rather than to be victimized by it. Men are rewarded for learning the practice of violence in virtually any sphere of activity by money, admiration, recognition, respect, and the genuflection of others honoring their sacred and proven masculinity. In male culture, police are heroic and so are outlaws; males who enforce standards are heroic and so are those who violate them. The conflicts between these groups embody the male commitment to violence: conflict is action; action is masculine. It is a mistake to view the warring factions of male culture as genuinely distinct from one another: in fact, these warring factions operate in near-perfect harmony to keep women at their mercy, one way or another. Because male supremacy means precisely that men have learned to use violence against others, particularly against females, in a random or disciplined way, loyalty to some form of male violence, its advocacy in language or action, is a prime criterion of effective masculine identity. In adoring violence—from the crucifixion of Christ to the cinematic portrayal of General Patton—men seek to adore themselves, or those distorted fragments of self left over when the capacity to perceive the value of life has been paralyzed and maimed by the very adherence to violence that men articulate as life's central and energizing meaning.

MEN RENOUNCE whatever they have in common with women so as to experience no commonality with women; and what is left, according to men, is one piece of flesh a few inches long, the penis. The penis is sensate; the penis is the man; the man is human; the penis signifies humanity. Though this *reductio ad absurdum* is the central male reality in psyche and in culture, male reductionism is more absurdly expressed when men go one step further and reduce the penis itself to sperm en masse, or to the one divinely inspired sperm that manages to fertilize an egg. Always in the vanguard, R. D. Laing, in his 1976 book *The Facts of Life*, expressed this same male reductionism in an even more bizarre way: "One could remain in love with one's placenta the rest of one's life."[7] Laing expresses both grief and rage over the loss of his *(sic)* placenta,* but this anguish has not yet managed to surpass in cultural significance the sorrow of those who, from the castigators of Onan on, mourn lost sperm. In *Eumenides*, Aeschylus insisted that all life originates in sperm, that the male is the sole source of life and that therefore the sole power over life resides properly with him. The linguistic antecedents of the word *penis* include, in Old English and Old High German, the meanings "offspring" and "fetus." In the last several centuries nothing has modified the male compulsion to keep reducing life to fragments of male physiology; then to make the fragments magical, sources of both power and menace. The dimension of menace is especially important in enabling men to value bits and pieces of themselves. Sperm, for instance, is seen as an agent of death, the woman's death, even when it is viewed as the originator of life, male life. Childbearing is glorified in part because women die from it. As Martin Luther put it: "If a woman grows weary and at last dies from childbearing, it matters not. Let her only die from bearing; she is there to do it."[8] Our own beloved Norman Mailer, in *The Prisoner of Sex*, contemplated that "women had begun to withdraw respect from men about the time pregnancy lost its danger . . . If [death] had once been a possibility real enough for them to look at their mate with eyes of love or eyes of hate but know their man might yet be the agent of their death, conceive then

*Antiabortion activists are energetically attempting to forge a medical definition of the placenta as belonging to the fetus, not the mother; and a whole host of male-created therapies that explore trauma before birth give the fetus a male social identity with its implicit male social suffering, male social alienation, and male social privilege.

of the lost gravity of the act . . ."[9] Mailer here is not lamenting the advent of female-controlled contraception, though he does lament it; he is mourning Semmelweis's discovery of the cause of the epidemics of puerperal fever that killed masses of childbearing women, including Mary Wollstonecraft.

The obsessive belief that the penis/sperm, once lodged in the woman, is a male fetus, together with the erotic dimension of the penis/sperm as agent of female death, accounts in large part for the continuing male commitment to forced female pregnancy. The vagina/womb, as Erik Erikson articulated, is perceived by the male as empty space that must be filled by a penis or a child (male until proven otherwise, in which case devalued), which is the penis realized— or the woman herself is empty, that is, a nonentity, worthless.

Force—the violence of the male confirming his masculinity—is seen as the essential purpose of the penis, its animating principle as it were, just as sperm ideally impregnates the woman either without reference to or against her will. The penis must embody the violence of the male in order for him to be male. Violence is male; the male is the penis; violence is the penis or the sperm ejaculated from it. What the penis can do it must do forcibly for a man to be a man. The reduction of human erotic potential to "sex," defined as the force of the penis visited on an unwilling woman, is the governing sexual scenario in male-supremacist society. Havelock Ellis, considered a feminist by scholars in the male tradition, sees the penis as properly and intrinsically suggesting a whip and the whip as a logical and inevitable expression of the penis:

> We must regard the whip as a natural symbol for the penis. One of the most frequent ways in which the idea of coitus first faintly glimmers before an infantile mind—and it is a glimmer which, from an evolutionary standpoint, is biologically correct—is as a display of force, of aggression, of something resembling cruelty. Whipping is the most obvious form in which to the young mind this idea might be embodied. The penis is the only organ of the body which in any degree resembles a whip.[10]

Throughout male culture, the penis is seen as a weapon, especially a sword. The word *vagina* literally means "sheath." In male-supremacist society, reproduction takes on this same character: force leading, at some point inevitably, to death; the penis/sperm valued as potential agent of female death. For centuries, female reluctance to "have sex," female dislike of "sex," female frigidity, female avoidance of "sex," have been legendary. This has been the silent rebellion of women against the force of the penis, generations of women as one with their bodies, chanting in a secret language, unintelligible even to themselves, a contemporary song of freedom: I will not be moved. The aversion of women to the penis and to sex as men define it, overcome only when survival and/or ideology demand it, must be seen not as puritanism (which is a male strategy to keep the penis hidden, taboo, and sacred), but as women's refusal to pay homage to the primary purveyor of male aggression, one on one, against women. In this way, women have defied men and subverted male power. It has been an ineffectual rebellion, but it has been rebellion nonetheless.

BOYS AND MEN do experience sexual abuse at the hands of men. The homophobe's distorting concentration on this fact, which cannot and must not be denied, neatly eliminates from view the primary victims of male sexual abuse: women and girls. This is congruent with the fact that crimes against females are ultimately viewed as expressions of male normalcy, while crimes against men and boys are viewed as perversions of that same normalcy. Society's general willingness to do anything necessary to protect boys and men from male sexual aggression is testimony to the value of a male life. Society's general refusal to do anything meaningful to protect women and girls from male sexual aggression is testimony to the worthlessness of a female life. A male life must be protected for its own sake. A female life warrants protection only when the female belongs to a male, as wife, daughter, mistress, whore; it is the owner who has a right to have his rights over his females protected from other men. A female's bodily integrity or well-being is not protected because of the value of the woman as a human being in her own right.

The relatively low incidence of male sexual assault against males, as contrasted with the pervasive assaults against females, cannot be attributed to de jure proscriptions. Rape of women, battery of wives, forcible incest with daughters, are also proscribed by male law but are widely practiced with virtual impunity by men. The key is not in what is forbidden but in what is sanctioned, really and truly sanctioned. Sexual violence against women and girls is sanctioned and encouraged for a purpose: the active and persistent channeling of male sexual aggression against females protects men and boys rather effectively from male sexual abuse. The system is not perfect, but it is formidable.

The homophobe's citing of actual or potential or projected or feared sexual abuse of boys in particular also functions to sustain male supremacy by obscuring this crucial fact: male sexual aggression is the unifying thematic and behavioral reality of male sexuality; it does not distinguish homosexual men from heterosexual men or heterosexual men from homosexual men. An absence or repudiation of this aggression, which is exceptional and which does exist in an eccentric and minuscule minority composed of both homosexual and heterosexual men, distinguishes some men from most men, or, to be more precise, the needle from the haystack.

Prostitution, especially boy prostitution, and prisons are the primary social institutions through which men express explicit sexual aggression against other males. Sexual abuse of males by men does take place in other areas, though its frequency, if not its effect, is unknown.

While females as a class are always targeted for sexual abuse, boys and men are targeted according to their devalued position in an exclusively male hierarchy. Youth, poverty, and race are the special characteristics that target males as possible victims of other men. Youth functions to target a male because a youth is not yet fully dissociated from women and children. The experiencing of sexual aggression is initiatory; the boy can cross over, soak up the aggression of the aggressor and use it against others. Boys who have had this experience still grow into men who defend the sexual privileges of adult men, no matter what abuses those privileges entail. These males protect themselves against being victimized, and even the memory of victimization, by turning into victimizers. Men who have been molested as children, and who as adults have a clearly defined homosexual orientation, sometimes express confusion as to whether they did or did not like the experience. Part of the reason for this confusion is that they longed for sexual contact with boys or men but were afraid of discovery or harm. Generally, boys and girls who have active sexual longings do not imagine the hit-and-run sexuality of the adult male. They are still tied, to differing extents, to the nonphallic, more diffuse eroticism they experienced with their mothers. They have longings and desires that are not reducible to genital sexual contact. Women who were molested as children also experience confusion as to what they really wanted when the adult male exercised his sexual will on them, but must, as a condition of forced femininity, accept the male as constant aggressor and forced sex as normative. In women, this often results in a passivity bordering on narcolepsy, morbid self-blame, and punishing self-hatred. Men molested as children resolve their confusion through action: in crossing over to the adult side, they remove themselves from the pool of victims. Since as adults they can experience the commission of forcible sex with others as freedom, they can say, as poet Allen Ginsberg did on a Boston television show, that they were molested as children and liked it. This is the public stance of the boy who has become the man, no matter what his private or secret ambivalences might be. Unlike women, men as adults are not likely to be molested again.

Significantly, forcible father-son incest, or sexual abuse of boys by stepfathers or near relatives, seems to be rare within families, while the sexual abuse of girls by fathers, stepfathers, and near relatives is pervasive. It is possible that evidence of extensive sexual abuse of boys within families has simply not yet been uncovered, since child abuse in all of its forms is one of this country's best-kept secrets. But it is more likely that the sexual abuse of boys by close relatives is actually rare because such abuse is potentially dangerous to the adult male and would deeply endanger the power of men as a class. The boy will, at some point, be stronger, more virile, than the father. He will also be less socialized, that is, not yet fully reconciled to the abandonment of all commitment to the humanity of women. A sexually abused boy can become sexual aggressor in turn, attack the father and, on the physical level, win. Adult men tend not to rape their own sons or close male relatives so as not to risk rape from them. While the interests of men sometimes conflict, this is one rift that the male-supremacist system could not survive. One-to-one sexual combat between fathers and sons would rend the fabric of patriarchy. The father's self-interest demands that the boy's burgeoning sexual aggression, developed to begin with in response to the father as a personal or social reality, be channeled against others, not against the patriarch himself. The father creates the monster to control him, not to suffer sexual retribution at his hands.

Poverty is also the mark of a potential male victim. Prison populations are poor and so are prostitute populations. Money is one instrument of male force. Poverty is a humiliating, and therefore a feminizing, experience; the poor male is less powerful than the wealthier male. The one with the money in general controls the sexual experience whatever its nature. In a money society, money is power, and the buying of another male, especially a boy, is forcible sex. Consent, properly understood in a society where men have turned both desire and freedom into dirty jokes, is a reality only between or among peers, and the poor and the rich are never peers. And boys, in particular poor boys, are not and cannot be the peers of adult men.

Racism also targets males as likely victims of sexual abuse. Prison populations in the United States are disproportionately made up of black males. The indifference of society at large to the sexual abuse of men in prisons is directly attributable to the fact that prisons are populated by the poor and by blacks. When society is confronted with the enormity of the rape problem in male prisons, suddenly the outrage occasioned by male sexual abuse in any other sphere does not exist; rape of the sacred male when he is in prison is easy to ignore or to forget. Those who do care about forcible violation of males in prison tend to offer the logical solution: since forcible violation of females is normal, introduce females into the prison population; then the prisoners can have socially sanctioned sex.

No one really knows the extent of male sexual abuse of other males. Largely in response to the prejudice against male homosexuals that is endemic in the United States and the discriminatory attribution of sexual crimes to homosexual men, the reality of such abuse is often denied even by those who have experienced it. But sexual abuse of boys does exist—contained, controlled, discouraged by enforced heterosexuality which has as one of its main purposes the protection of males as a whole from the rampant sexual aggression characteristic of men as a class: the abuse of boys is considered an atrocious crime primarily because the lives of boys are valued far above the lives of girls; males are more vulnerable to sexual abuse the lower they are in the male hierarchy; the labeling of male homosexuals as child molesters particularly functions to hide the fact that women and girls are the population most often and most consistently victimized and violated by men. As long as male sexuality is expressed as force or violence, men as a class will continue to enforce the taboo against male homosexuality to protect themselves from having that force or violence directed against them. Women will be their surrogates, and every institution in the society will continue to demand that men do to women what men would find insufferable if done to themselves. T. E. Lawrence, the fabled Lawrence of Arabia, beaten and raped as an adult, expressed in a letter to Charlotte Shaw the desperation that such violation by rape is to one not raised to endure it, that is, to a man:

> You instance my night at Deraa. Well, I'm always afraid of being hurt; and to me, while I live, the force of that night will lie in the agony which broke me, and made me surrender. . . .
>
> About that night. I shouldn't tell you, because decent men don't talk about such things. I wanted to put it plain in the book *[Seven Pillars of Wisdom]*, wrestled for days with my self-respect . . . which wouldn't, hasn't let me. For fear of being hurt, or

> rather to earn five minutes respite from a pain which drove me mad, I gave away the only possession we are born into the world with—our bodily integrity. It's an unforgiveable matter, an irrecoverable position: and it's that which has made me foreswear decent living, and the exercise of my not-contemptible wits and talents.[11]

T. E. Lawrence attempted to exorcise this experience by repeating it: by having himself flagellated by a younger man whom he paid, he himself controlling his own humiliation and physical torment. This only emphasizes the riveting trauma of losing "the only possession we are born into the world with—our bodily integrity"; and the male option of finding the means to control sexual reality, however devastating that reality has been.

It must also be noted that glorious ancient Greece, so often cited as the ideal male homosexual society, that is, a society in which sex among men and boys was entirely acceptable, operated in accordance with these same principles: male sexual aggression against boys and among men was highly regulated by custom and in practice; sexual relations between men and boys expressed a rigid hierarchy of male power; the youth used was feminized vis-à-vis older men; sex was not consensual, that is, among peers (in fact, on Crete and in other parts of Greece, boys were kidnapped into sexual apprenticeship); the boy became the man, changed status, his reward at the end of an apprenticeship; populations of women and slaves, neither of which had any rights of citizenship, absorbed the brunt of male sexual aggression. Male homosexuality in male-supremacist societies has always been contained and controlled by men as a class, though the strategies of containment have differed, to protect men from rape by other men, to order male sexuality so that it is, with reference to males, predictable and safe. Females and devalued males who participate in the low status of women are logically the preferred victims, since male sexuality as it exists in male-supremacist contexts requires victims, not fully present equals, in order to realize itself. The devalued males can often change status, escape; women and girls cannot. And the devalued male who cannot change his devalued status can always find solace in his own rights of tyranny and privilege, however circumscribed, over women and girls in his own family, class, race, or group.

It is unlikely that male-male sexuality will be or can be tolerated by men as a class until the very nature of masculinity is changed, that is, until rape is no longer the defining paradigm of sexuality. Those gay men of our own time who offer ancient Greece as a utopian model are only confirming that, for them, the continued scapegoating of women and the sexual exploitation of less powerful males would be an insignificant price to pay for a comfortable solution to their own social and sexual dilemma. As adult men, they would have freedom as they understand it, the freedom of the sexual predator; women, girls, and devalued males would continue to be the prey. This moral bankruptcy is not in any sense unique to homosexual men; rather, it is part of what they have in common with all men.

I saw, as so many times before, that *sublata nullum discrimen inter feminas* ("when the lamp is taken away, all women are alike").

Giacomo Casanova, *History of My Life*[12]

I was born at 1715 hours on October 7th, 1927, into a family that consisted of my mother and father, living in a small three-room flat on the south side of Glasgow. My father could not admit to anyone for several days that I was born.

My mother went into "a decline." A woman was brought in to nurse me who after six weeks turned out to be a drunken slut and another woman was brought in. She was a drunken slut as well.

R. D. Laing, *The Facts of Life*[13]

And it is this that makes the cocksureness of women so dangerous, so devastating. It is really out of scheme, it is not in relation to the rest of things. So we have the tragedy of cocksure women. They find, so often, that instead of having laid an egg, they have laid a vote, or an empty-ink-bottle, or some other absolutely unhatchable object, which means nothing to them.

D. H. Lawrence, "Cocksure Women and Hensure Men," *Sex, Literature and Censorship*[14]

The interest of the employed woman tends to become one with that of her employer; between them they combine to crush the interests of the child who represents the race, and to defeat the laws made in the interests of the race which are those of the community as a whole. The employed woman wishes to earn as much wages as she can and with as little interruption as she can . . .

This impulse on the employed woman's part is by no means always and entirely the result of poverty, and would not, therefore, be removed by raising her wages. . . . her home means nothing to her; she only returns there to sleep, leaving it next morning at daybreak or earlier; she is ignorant even of the simplest domestic arts; she moves about in her own home like a stranger and awkward child.

Havelock Ellis, *Studies in the Psychology of Sex*[15]

The queen is the most dangerous of creatures. He is always on the verge of threatening a man's virility. This is not solely because the queen represents a man's antithesis, the extreme evil to be avoided at all costs (American education as a whole being devoted to making boys different from girls), but because the queen is so nearly a woman that even a hidebound heterosexual may make a mistake.

Georges-Michel Sarotte, *Like a Brother, Like a Lover*[16]

"You were saying that a lot of your magazine offends you. Then why do you keep on publishing?"

"Because men all over the country need *Hustler.* They feel inferior, and they are. Women are naturally superior; they're our only hope. I mean, my mother lives with me. I've always been close to her. She's a saint. And I'm in favor of the women's movement. It's just that they take no responsibility for scaring men. Why do you think there's so much bisexuality on campuses? Why do you think men molest children? Because they're afraid of relating to liberated women."

Larry Flynt, interviewed by Jeffrey Klein[17]

. . . Why does Samuel Butler say, "Wise men never say what they think of women"? Wise men never say anything else apparently.

Virginia Woolf, *A Room of One's Own*[18]

Male perceptions of women are askew, wild, inept. Male renderings of women in art, literature, psychology, religious discourses, philosophy, and in the common wisdom of the day, whatever the day, are bizarre, distorted, fragmented at best, demented in the main. Everything is done to keep women out of the perceptual field altogether, but, like insects, women creep in; find the slightest chink in the male armor and watch her, odious thing, crawl in. Even this presence, on hands and knees as it were, is so disorienting, so fiercely threatening, that attributions of malice must be made—immediate, intense, slanderous, couched in language that conveys the man's absolute authority to speak. In male reality, women cannot enter male consciousness without violating it. The male is contaminated and distressed by any contact with woman-not-as-object. He loses ground. His own masculinity cannot withstand what he regards as an assault unless he steps on the uppity thing, crushes it by hook or by crook, by insult, open hand flat against the face or clenched fist crushed into it. The dark comforts him because it dims personality; he has sex in the dark to convince himself that all women are the same, without individual substance or importance, a la Casanova. Dependence on women is abhorrent to him, so even at birth he was surrounded by drunken sluts, a la Laing. Women who want to work or vote are vicious, having abandoned every shred of female decency, which is qualitatively different and entirely distinct from male decency, a la D. H. Lawrence and Havelock Ellis. Male decency miraculously survives the commission of murder and rape; female decency is abnegated when the woman steps out of the house to work or vote. A male masquerading as a female is dangerous because men cannot distinguish him from the real thing (*thing* here used literally, not idiomatically) a la Sarotte. The male will even, a la Larry Flynt, attribute some specious kind of superiority to the female to justify his cruel abuses of women in reality and in this context, remembered for a split second, mother was a saint. In the main, the abominable She is held responsible for everything bad, fearful, or alienating that ever happened to the fully-human-He. Any assertion of female self leads to the inevitable decline of society; and when the abominable She calls attention to herself as human, not object, she violates the male's most essential sense of masculine self. Every attempt she makes to reclaim the humanity he has stolen from her makes her subject to insult, ridicule, and abuse. In his view, she is not a woman unless she acts like a woman as he has defined woman. His definition need not be coherent. It is never scrutinized for logic or consistency or even threadbare common sense. He can theorize, fantasize, call it science or art; whatever he says about women is true because he says it. He is the authority on what she is because he has made her, cut away at her as if she were a piece of stone until the prized inanimate object is extracted. As filmmaker Agnes Varda, crediting Simone de Beauvoir as the source, expressed it in her film *One Sings, the Other Doesn't:* Women are made, not born.

Men want women to be objects, controllable as objects are controllable. Women who deviate from the male definition are monstrous, sluts, depraved. Since all women do deviate to some degree, all women are viewed to some degree as monstrous, sluts, depraved, with appetites that, if unleashed, would swallow up the male, destroy him. Men know that the object does breathe, but rather than face up to the meaning of this knowledge, they prefer to believe that under the object lurks a hungry, angry viper; that the object is a rock that must never be moved or picked up or the viper will strike. Suddenly, one is confronted with the fragile, vulnerable male, threatened by reptilian female genitalia (for instance, the vagina dentata), or the devouring mother, or the insatiable lust of the nymphomaniac. The fear that what men have suppressed in women will emerge to destroy them makes the control of women an urgent and absolute necessity. Men dare to claim not only that they are fragile but that the power of women over them is immense and real.

In *The Mermaid and the Minotaur*, Dorothy Dinnerstein proposes that this delusion originates in the infantile experience of the all-powerful mother; all infantile ambivalences and rage are taken out on women for the duration of a male life. (According to Dinnerstein, women are self-punishing because of this same infantile rage.)

The solution, as Dinnerstein sees it, is child care by men as well as women, so that the vengeance can be more fairly doled out.

But it is the male who is powerful, and even the child, early on, knows it, perceives it, acts to mitigate the danger, to protect himself from it. This means making an alliance with the one who has the power, the father; and this is what all boys try to do. To understand, or to know even without understanding, that survival demands this alliance means that the boy has passed beyond any infantile experience of the mother's power over his immediate well-being. He has experienced her powerlessness, and it is this more mature experience of female powerlessness, of the female's inability to protect the boy from the power of the adult male, that is the basis of his adult behavior.

Adult men have made their seedy pact with and for male power. They have entered the kingdom and once there, they will not return voluntarily to the degraded world of the female. Because as men they can define reality without reference to truth, they turn their own experience on its ass to justify their capitulation to the power of the father, their cowardly abandonment of the mother. Their guilt must be very great. In all their communication, shouted and whispered, no matter what men have done to them, they name women the threat, and the truth is that any loyalty to women does threaten a man's place in the community of men. Anything, including memory or conscience, that pulls a man toward women as humans, not as objects and not as monsters, does endanger him. But the danger is always from other men. And no matter how afraid he is of those other men, he has taken a vow—one for all and all for one—and he will not tell. Women are scapegoated here too, called powerful by men who know only too well how powerless women are—know it so well that they will tell any lie and commit any crime so as not to be touched by the stigma of that powerlessness.

EVERYTHING IN LIFE is part of it. Nothing is off in its own corner, isolated from the rest. While on the surface this may seem self-evident, the favorite conceit of male culture is that experience can be fractured, literally its bones split, and that one can examine the splinters as if they were not part of the bone, or the bone as if it were not part of the body. This conceit replicates in its values and methodology the sexual reductionism of the male and is derived from it. Everything is split apart: intellect from feeling and/or imagination; act from consequence; symbol from reality; mind from body. Some part substitutes for the whole and the whole is sacrificed to the part. So the scientist can work on bomb or virus, the artist on poem, the photographer on picture, with no appreciation of its meaning outside itself; and even reduce each of these things to an abstract element that is part of its composition and focus on that abstract element and nothing else—literally attribute meaning to or discover meaning in nothing else. In the mid-twentieth century, the post-Holocaust world, it is common for men to find meaning in nothing: nothing has meaning; Nothing is meaning. In prerevolutionary Russia, men strained to be nihilists; it took enormous effort. In this world, here and now, after Auschwitz, after Hiroshima, after Vietnam, after Jonestown, men need not strain. Nihilism, like gravity, is a law of nature, male nature. The men, of course, are tired. It has been an exhausting period of extermination and devastation, on a scale genuinely new, with new methods, new possibilities. Even when faced with the probable extinction of themselves at their own hand, men refuse to look at the whole, take all the causes and all the effects into account, perceive the intricate connections between the world they make and themselves. They are alienated, they say, from this world of pain and torment; they make romance out of this alienation so as to avoid taking responsibility for what they do and what they are. Male dissociation from life is not new or particularly modern, but the scale and intensity of this disaffection are new. And in the midst of this Brave New World, how comforting and familiar it is to exercise passionate cruelty on women. The old-fashioned values still obtain. The world may end tomorrow, but tonight there is rape—a kiss, a fuck, a pat on the ass, a fist in the face. In the intimate world of men and women, there is no mid-twentieth century distinct from any other century. There are only the old values, women there for the taking, the means of taking determined by the male. It is ancient and it is modern; it is feudal, capitalist, socialist; it is caveman and astronaut, agricultural and industrial, urban and rural. For men, the right to abuse women is elemental, the first principle, with no beginning unless one is willing to trace origins back to God and with no end plausibly in sight. For men, their right to control and abuse the bodies of women is the one comforting constant in a world rigged to blow up but they do not know when.

In pornography, men express the tenets of their unchanging faith, what they must believe is true of women and of themselves to sustain themselves as they are, to ward off recognition that a commitment to masculinity is a double-edged commitment to both suicide and genocide. In life, the objects are fighting back, rebelling, demanding that every breath be reckoned with as the breath of a living person, not a viper trapped under a rock, but an authentic, willful, living being. In pornography, the object is slut, sticking daggers up her vagina and smiling. A bible piling up its code for centuries, a secret corpus gone public, a private corpus gone political, pornography is the male's sacred stronghold, a monastic retreat for manhood on the verge of its own destruction. As one goes through the pictures of the tortured and maimed, reads the stories of gang rape and bondage, what emerges most clearly is a portrait of men who need to believe in their own absolute, unchangeable, omnipresent, eternal, limitless power over others. Every image reveals not the so-called object in it but the man who needs it: to keep his prick big when every bomb dwarfs it; to keep his sense of masculine self intact when the world of his own creation has made that masculine self a useless and rather silly anachronism; to keep women the enemy even though men will destroy him and he by being faithful to them will be responsible for that destruction; to sustain his belief in the righteousness of his real abuses of women when, in fact, they would be insupportable and unbearable if he dared to experience them as what they are—the bullying brutalities of a coward too afraid of other men to betray or abandon them. Pornography is the holy corpus of men who would rather die than change. Dachau brought into the bedroom and celebrated, every vile prison or dungeon brought into the bedroom and celebrated, police torture and thug mentality brought into the bedroom and celebrated—men reveal themselves and all that matters to them in these depictions of real history, plasticized and rarefied, represented as the common erotic stuff of male desire. And the pictures and stories lead right back to history—to peoples enslaved, maimed, murdered—because they show that, for men, the history of atrocity they pretend to mourn is coherent and utterly intentional if one views it as rooted in male sexual obsession. Pornography reveals that slavery, bondage, murder, and maiming have been acts suffused with pleasure for those who committed them or who vicariously experienced the power expressed in them. Pornography reveals that male pleasure is inextricably tied to victimizing, hurting, exploiting; that sexual fun and sexual passion in the privacy of the male imagination are inseparable from the brutality of male history. The private world of sexual dominance that men demand as their right and their freedom is the mirror image of the public world of sadism and atrocity that men consistently and self-righteously deplore. It is in the male experience of pleasure that one finds the meaning of male history.

3

The Marquis de Sade (1740–1814)

> As flies to wanton boys are we to the gods;
> They kill us for their sport.
>
> Shakespeare, *King Lear*

Donatien-Alphonse-François de Sade—known as the Marquis de Sade, known to his ardent admirers who are legion as The Divine Marquis—is the world's foremost pornographer. As such he both embodies and defines male sexual values. In him, one finds rapist and writer twisted into one scurvy knot. His life and writing were of a piece, a whole cloth soaked in the blood of women imagined and real. In his life he tortured and raped women. He was batterer, rapist, kidnapper, and child abuser. In his work he relentlessly celebrated brutality as the essence of eroticism; fucking, torture, and killing were fused; violence and sex, synonymous. His work and legend have survived nearly two centuries because literary, artistic, and intellectual men adore him and political thinkers on the Left claim him as an avatar of freedom. Sainte-Beuve named Sade and Byron as the two most significant sources of inspiration for the original and great male writers who followed them. Baudelaire, Flaubert, Swinburne, Lautréamont, Dostoevski, Cocteau, and Apollinaire among others found in Sade what Paul Tillich, another devotee of pornography, might have called "the courage to be." Simone de Beauvoir published a long apologia for Sade. Camus, who unlike Sade had an aversion to murder, romanticized Sade as one who had mounted "the great offensive against a hostile heaven"[1] and was possibly "the first theoretician of absolute rebellion."[2] Roland Barthes wallowed in the tiniest details of Sade's crimes, those committed in life as well as on paper. Sade is precursor to Artaud's theater of cruelty, Nietzsche's will to power, and the rapist frenzy of William Burroughs. In England in 1966, a twelve-year-old boy and a ten-year-old girl were tortured and murdered by a self-proclaimed disciple of Sade. The crimes were photographed and tape-recorded by the murderer, who played them back for pleasure. In 1975 in the United States, organized crime reportedly sold "snuff" films to private collectors of pornography. In these films, women actually were maimed, sliced into pieces, fucked, and killed—the perfect Sadean synthesis. Magazines and films depicting the mutilation of women for the sake of sexual pleasure now abound. A major translator into English of Sade's thousands of pages of butchery and the one primarily responsible for the publication of Sade's work in accessible mass-market editions in the United States is Richard Seaver, a respected figure in establishment publishing. Seaver, instrumental in the propagation of Sade's work and legend, has reportedly written a film of Sade's life that will be made by Alain Resnais. Sade's cultural influence on all levels is pervasive. His ethic—the absolute right of men to rape and brutalize any "object of desire" at will—resonates in every sphere.

Sade was born into a noble French family closely related to the reigning monarch. Sade was raised with the prince, four years his senior, during his earliest years. When Sade was four, his mother left the Court and he was sent to live with his grandmother. At the age of five, he was sent to live with his uncle, the Abbé de Sade, a clergyman known for his sensual indulgences. Sade's father, a diplomat and soldier, was absent during Sade's formative years. Inevitably, biographers trace Sade's character to his mother's personality, behavior, and alleged sexual repression, despite the fact that very little is known about her. What is known, but not sufficiently noted, is that Sade was raised among the male mighty. He wrote in later years of having been humiliated and controlled by them.

At the age of fifteen, Sade entered the military as an officer. At this age, he apparently began gambling and frequenting brothels. Purchasing women was one of the great passions of his life, and most of the women and girls he abused during his lifetime were whores or servants. Sade advanced in the military and was promoted several times, each promotion bringing with it more money.

Those leftists who champion Sade might do well to remember that prerevolutionary France was filled with starving people. The feudal system was both cruel and crude. The rights of the aristocracy to the labor and bodies of the poor were unchallenged and not challengeable. The tyranny of class was absolute. The poor sold what they could, including themselves, to survive. Sade learned and upheld the ethic of his class.

Nearly twenty-three, Sade fell in love with a woman of his own class, Laure de Lauris. Sade's urgent desire to marry her was frustrated when she begged her father not to permit the marriage under any circumstances. Sade was enraged by her "betrayal" of him, possibly occasioned by the venereal disease both had contracted. Sade blamed her for infecting him, and his biographers, always credulous, take him at his word despite his already long and sordid sexual history. There is no cited evidence that Laure de Lauris had any other sexual partner.

That same year, Sade entered into an arranged marriage with Renée-Pélagie de Montreuil, elder daughter of a wealthy family. Within six weeks after his marriage, Sade had rented an isolated house in which he acted out his sexual desires on women whom he bought.

Five months after his marriage, Sade terrified and assaulted a twenty-year-old working-class woman, Jeanne Testard. Testard, a fan maker, had agreed to service a young nobleman. She was taken to Sade's private house and locked in a room. Sade made clear to her that she was a captive. She was subjected to verbal abuse and humiliation. In particular, Sade raged against her conventional Christian religious beliefs. He told her that he had masturbated into a chalice in a chapel and that he had taken two hosts, placed them inside a woman, and fucked her. Testard told Sade that she was pregnant and could not tolerate maltreatment. Sade took Testard into a room filled with whips, religious symbols, and pornographic pictures. He wanted Testard to whip him, and then he wanted to beat her. She refused. He took two crucifixes, crushed one, and masturbated on the other. He demanded that she destroy the one on which he had masturbated. She refused. He threatened her life with two pistols that were in the room and a sword that he was wearing. She crushed the crucifix. He wanted to give her an enema and have her shit on the crucifix. She refused. He wanted to sodomize her. She refused. Sade threatened, harangued, and lectured her through a very long night during which she did not eat or sleep. Before releasing her, he made her sign a blank piece of paper and promise to tell no one about what had transpired. He wanted her to agree to meet him the following Sunday so that he could fuck her with a host inside of her.

On being freed, Testard went to the police. Sade was arrested, apparently because police interviews with prostitutes revealed that Sade had abused scores of them. Sade was punished because he had become careless in his excesses. He was imprisoned for two months at Vincennes in squalor most distressing to a gentleman. He wrote letters to the authorities in which he begged them to keep the nature of his crime secret from his family.

After his release, Sade began a series of affairs with actresses and dancers, who in the eighteenth century were almost always also courtesans. He kept several of these women and continued purchasing less distinguished women as well.

Sade's abuse of prostitutes became so alarming that, within a year after his brutal treatment of Testard, the police warned procuresses not to provide Sade with women. Sade's valet scavenged the streets for victims, some of whom, according to Sade's neighbors, were male.

During this same period, he also managed to impregnate his wife, who gave birth to a son.

In 1768, Easter Sunday early in the morning, Rose Keller, in her mid-thirties, a German immigrant, a widow, a cotton spinner who had been unemployed for approximately a month, approached Sade to beg for alms. He offered her work housecleaning. She accepted. He told her that she would be well fed and treated kindly.

Sade took Keller to his private house. He took her to a dark room in which the windows were boarded and said he was going to get her food. He locked her in the room. Keller had waited for about an hour when Sade came to take her into another room. He told her to undress. She refused. He tore her clothes off, threw her face down onto a couch, tied her arms and legs with ropes. He whipped her brutally. He took a knife and told her that he would kill her. According to Keller, Sade kept cutting her with a knife and rubbing wax into the wounds. Keller believed she would die and begged Sade not to kill her until she could make her Easter confession. When Sade was finished with her, he took her back to the first room and ordered her to wash and rub brandy into her wounds. This she did. He also rubbed into the wounds an ointment that he had invented. He was proud of his invention, which he claimed healed wounds quickly. Later, Sade alleged that he had paid Keller to be whipped so that he could test his ointment. Sade brought Keller food. He took her back to the room where he had beaten her and locked her in. Keller bolted the door from the inside. She unblocked some of the locked shutters with a knife, injuring herself in the process, made a rope of bedding, and climbed out of the window and down the wall. Sade's valet pursued her and offered her money to return. She pushed him off and ran.

Keller was badly hurt and her clothes were ripped. She ran until she encountered a village woman, to whom she poured out her story. Other women joined. They examined her and then took her to an inappropriate official, since the local magistrate was away. A police official called in from elsewhere took her statement. Keller was examined by a surgeon and was given refuge.

Sade's mother-in-law, Madame de Montreuil, settled a large sum of money on Rose Keller to persuade her to withdraw criminal charges. Despite the settlement, Sade was imprisoned for nearly eight months, during which time he impregnated his wife again. When he returned to Lacoste, his home with his wife, she left for Paris, where, seven months later, Sade's second son was born. Sade's pursuit of other women began on his release. Sade weaved in and out of Renée-Pélagie's life. In April 1771 a daughter was born.

In September 1771 Sade began an affair with his wife's younger sister, Anne-Prospère.

In June 1772, Sade traveled to Marseilles with his valet, known as Latour. During the course of Sade's brief stay there, Latour procured five prostitutes for Sade. Sade (in varying combinations) beat, fucked, and forcibly sodomized the women, with his usual threats of worse violence and death. He also had his valet sodomize at least one of the women and himself. In Marseilles, Sade added another dimension to his sexual repertoire: he encouraged the women to eat candies that had been laced with drugs. The women did not know what they were eating. Sade's defenders claim that the candies were treated with a harmless aphrodisiac and something to encourage flatulence, which Sade found particularly charming. Two of the women became violently ill from the candies, had intense abdominal pain, vomited blood and black mucus. The women believed that they had been poisoned, and there is little doubt that had they consumed the quantities of the candy that Sade had wanted them to eat, they would have become deadly ill. One of the women went to the police. An investigation of Sade's brutality with the five prostitutes—the forced flagellation, the forced sodomy, the attempted poisoning—led to an order to arrest both Sade and Latour. Sade, with Anne-Prospère as his lover and Latour as his valet, fled to Italy to escape arrest.

Sade and Latour were found guilty of poisoning and sodomy (a capital crime irrespective of force) in absentia. They were sentenced to death. In lieu of the death sentence that could not be carried out, the two men were burned in effigy.

Sade's mother-in-law, Madame de Montreuil, faced with Sade's incorrigibility, perhaps in an effort to separate Anne-Prospère from Sade, used her formidable political influence to have Sade imprisoned in Italy. For the next four months, Sade wrote letters to high officials in Italy and France in which he bemoaned the injustice of his imprisonment and pleaded to be freed. At the end of the fourth month, he escaped. Shortly after his escape, Sade wrote his mother-in-law several times to ask for money. When it was not forthcoming, Sade returned to Lacoste. On his return to France, another order was issued for his arrest. He again escaped. After a few weeks, he again returned to Lacoste. Renée-Pélagie filed a complaint against her mother, probably in the hope that this pressure would encourage Madame de Montreuil to use her influence to have the charges against Sade dropped. Despite the complaint against Madame de Montreuil, a new warrant was issued for Sade's arrest. He went into hiding, then returned again to Lacoste. Renée-Pélagie continued to try to have her mother arrested. Her efforts were rewarded with a promise from high government officials that an appeal would be presented in the parliament to cancel Sade's sentence. This would then lead to invalidation of the *lettre de cachet* (an order from the king that a given person be imprisoned without trial and with no predetermined sentence) that had also been issued against Sade.

Sade, with an end to his legal troubles in sight, intensified his pursuit of pleasure. He had a procuress known as Nanon find him five fifteen-year-old girls who were taken to Lacoste and forced to submit to Sade's brutality. Sade's wife was a participant in these new sexual extravaganzas. She became the prime apologist for Sade's violence against the girls, even though, as one of them testified, Renée-Pélagie was herself "the first victim of a fury which can be described only as madness."[3] Parents of three of the girls pressed charges against Sade, who refused to release his captives. One of the girls was horribly injured. She was sent to Sade's uncle, the Abbé, to keep her from testifying against Sade. Renée-Pélagie did everything possible to keep a doctor from treating the girl, since evidence of bodily injury could be used against Sade and herself as well. Madame de Montreuil, perhaps to protect her daughter, joined with Renée-Pélagie and Sade to try to coerce the parents into dropping their complaints. Meanwhile, Sade forcibly kept the girls at Lacoste. They would be returned to their parents only if no charges of kidnapping were made.

Sade brought more women and girls to Lacoste. Human bones were found in Sade's garden; he claimed one of his mistresses had planted them as a joke. Nanon, the procuress, became pregnant by Sade. Madame de Montreuil had a *lettre de cachet* issued for her arrest. Nanon was imprisoned; her infant daughter died at Lacoste shortly after she was born because the wet nurse's milk went dry.

Sade was again threatened with arrest. He escaped again to Italy. The fifteen-year-old girl who had been most severely injured and had been sent to Sade's uncle had not, in nine months, recovered from her injuries. She was finally taken to a hospital where the Sade family conspired to keep her from talking with anyone to whom she might reveal what had happened to her. By this time, the Abbé believed that Sade should be imprisoned.

For a year, Sade traveled in Italy. He complained of being lonely. One of the kidnapped girls, still kept at Lacoste, died. Another escaped and went to the police. Against the advice of Renée-Pélagie, Sade returned to Lacoste. More women were procured for him. Sade kept spending money on women while Renée-Pélagie lived in near penury. He hired servants, locked them up, forced them to submit to him. A father of a servant hired by Sade tried to shoot him. The daughter signed a statement defending Sade. The authorities ordered the woman returned to her father. She was not.

Another attempt was made to arrest Sade. He hid. On being informed by Madame de Montreuil that his mother was dying in Paris, he went there. She died before he arrived, but in Paris Sade was arrested under a *lettre de cachet*. Madame de Montreuil had told the police Sade's whereabouts. He was sent to Vincennes, where he was imprisoned for nearly six years. In 1784, he was transferred to the Bastille. In 1789, the people of France were near revolution. Sade rigged up an improvised loudspeaker from his cell and exhorted the people to lay siege to the Bastille. He was moved to Charenton, a lunatic asylum. On July 14, 1789, the Bastille was stormed and its warden killed. In 1790, Sade was released from Charenton along with all prisoners who had been imprisoned under *lettres de cachet* by the old regime.

During the years of his imprisonment in Vincennes and the Bastille, Sade wrote the body of literature for which he is best known (though his literary career did not begin in prison; he had done some writing and even produced and directed theatrical events sporadically). On Sade's release, Renée-Pélagie, whom Sade had subjected to extraordinary scorn and abuse during his imprisonment, left him and obtained a legal separation. Sade's bitterness toward her was unrelenting. Apparently he felt that he had given her the best years of his life, which were less than perfect only because he had been maliciously persecuted. He especially blamed Renée-Pélagie for the loss of manuscripts that had been taken or destroyed during the siege of the Bastille. She had failed to rescue them, as he had demanded, and may have burned some herself. In the ensuing years, he set about re-creating the lost work. After his release, Sade also met his daughter as an adult for the first time. He hated her on sight. Early in 1791, Sade began living with Marie-Constance Renelle, to whom *Justine* is dedicated and with whom he had what his biographers consider a sincere, loving, devoted relationship. Sade was no longer a young rake. In prison he had become very fat, and the French Revolution had deprived him of his power as an aristocrat. Necessity, that fabled parent of invention, gave birth in a few short months to Citizen Sade.

For nearly four years, Sade walked a political tightrope. He played the role of one who had been abused by the old regime, who had no loyalties to the old nobility and was entirely committed to the new society. He made politically correct speeches, renamed streets to reflect the ideology of the revolution, and worked to keep his own property from the legitimate claims of the revolution and of Renée-Pélagie. According to his biographers, Sade's essential humanism was demonstrated during the Terror when he was on a committee that passed judgment on the Montreuils: he could have denounced them and had them killed, but he did not. It is more likely that Sade, a consummate survivor, had understood that, during the Terror, guilt by past association could endanger his own life. Condemnation of the Montreuils could eventually have led to his own death for his having consorted with them.

Revolutionary leader Jean-Paul Marat discovered the nature of the crimes for which Sade had been imprisoned under the old regime. He denounced Sade but by mistake someone with a similar name was executed. Marat, although he became aware of his mistake, did not live to rectify it: he was assassinated by Charlotte Corday.

Toward the end of 1793, Sade was imprisoned. The charge was that in 1791 he had volunteered to serve the king. Sade insisted that he had thought the regiment in which he had volunteered to serve was loyal to the revolution. He remained in prison and in July 1794 was sentenced to death. The administration of the prisons was so inefficient that Sade could not be found. He was not executed. Later that same month, Robespierre was executed, and the Terror ended. Two months later, Sade was released.

In 1800, Napoleon came to power. In March 1801, Sade was again arrested, this time for authoring obscene literature (*Justine*, published in part in 1791 and in a new version in 1797; and *Juliette*, published in 1797). Except for his imprisonment for antirevolutionary activity in 1793, all Sade's imprisonment in France up to this point (he was sixty) had been for committing brutal crimes against persons. Sade was imprisoned by administrative order. He denied that he had authored either *Justine* or *Juliette* and particularly denounced *Justine* as filth. He was imprisoned at Sainte-Pélagie for two years, during which time he sexually assaulted other prisoners. As a result of his assaultive behavior in Sainte-Pélagie and because of a change in policy that separated the treatment of criminals from the treatment of the insane, Sade was transferred to Bicête, an asylum. He had been there for forty-four days when, on the basis of an appeal by his sons, he was transferred to Charenton, where living conditions were considerably better—his especially, since his family paid the institution handsomely for his room and board. Marie-Constance Renelle was allowed to live at Charenton with him. Sade was also permitted to produce expensive theatrical events, which were open to the public.

Several attempts were made to have Sade transferred back to prison, since medical opinion was that he was a criminal, not a madman. But Sade was useful to the head of Charenton, especially as director of drama. Sade stayed at Charenton until he died in 1814 at the age of seventy-four. In the last year or two of his life, still cohabiting with Renelle, he had an affair with Madeleine Leclerc, perhaps fourteen years old, essentially sold to him by her mother. As he noted in his diary, from her he wanted and obtained absolute submission as he had, all his life, understood and appreciated it.

> Fiddling with the hairs on an elephant's nose is indecent when the elephant happens to be standing on the baby.
>
> John Gardner, *On Moral Fiction*

In a woman-hating culture, it is particularly difficult to make credible the claim that a crime committed against a woman must matter. The belief that women exist to be used by men is so old, so deep set, so widely accepted, so commonplace in its everyday application, that it is rarely challenged, even by those who pride themselves on and are recognized for their intellectual acumen and ethical grace. Keening, wild, and wailing or sober, severe, and rigorous, feminists keep pointing to a woman who is real and does exist and who must matter. Others look and see only insignificant shadows moving under the feet of those real people to whom real things happen—men—so that in a room of a hundred "people," half men, half women, a male-defined observer will see fifty men and fifty shadows. Rape a shadow and watch it disappear. Rape a shadow, and does it matter? Sometimes, it appears that shadows pursue. They cannot be lost. They follow, nipping at the heels. Attributions of malice are made. Shadows become ominous, haunting. In histories and biographies, in philosophical and literary essays, male-supremacist culture perpetuates the power of men over women by turning women into shadows. The shameful inequities of life are maintained by the distortions and manipulations pervasive in so-called nonfiction. What happens to men is portrayed as authentic, significant, and what happens to women is left out or shown not to matter. Women are portrayed as the shadows that tamely follow or maliciously haunt men, never as the significant beings who matter.

So sexual philosopher Georges Bataille, in *Death and Sensuality*, can write without embarrassment (or, until the women's movement, without fear of contradiction): "In his life de Sade took other people into account, but his conception of fulfilment worked over and over in his lonely cell led him to deny outright [in writing] the claims of other people."[4] Sade, of course, had denied outright the claims of other people since his youth, but the "other people" were primarily women, real women, and so are of no significance to Bataille.

In the same way, Donald Thomas, one of Sade's recent biographers, can claim: "The cruelties of his fiction are quite at variance with almost all Sade's conduct . . ."[5] Thomas also insists that Sade's sexual desires were "indulged largely in his fiction."[6] The abused bodies of women, piled up in heaps through a cruel and conscienceless life, are dismissed by facile distortion or complete denial. Not above writing false history to trivialize Sade's brutalities against women, Thomas, with this intellectual sleight of hand, makes the victim disappear into thin air:

> The Marquis de Sade's true difficulty was not that he had an inclination for beating some of the girls *[sic]* whom he hired or that he submitted them to unorthodox sexual acts, but that he did this in the middle of the eighteenth century when they were more likely to complain and be heard.[7]

It is fair to point out that the feudal system rather effectively discouraged whores from going to the police with complaints against noblemen.

Simone de Beauvoir, in an essay entitled "Must We Burn Sade?" first published in the early fifties, also manages to make the crime and the victims nearly invisible: "Actually, whipping a few girls *[sic]* (for a consideration agreed upon in advance) is rather a petty feat; that Sade set so much store on it is enough to cast suspicion on him."[8]

The rights of women as persons are entirely, if disingenuously, denied by Richard Seaver and Austryn Wainhouse, Sade's translators into English, in their foreword to a collection of Sade's work:

> With his usual perception about himself, Sade once noted in a letter to his wife that, had the authorities any insight, they would not have locked him up to plot and daydream and make philosophical disquisitions as wild and vengeful and absolute as any ever formulated; they would have set him free and surrounded him with a harem on whom to feast. But societies do not cater to strange tastes; they condemn them. Thus Sade became a writer.[9]

Again, brutalities against women are somehow transposed, this time into something less dangerous and less significant than writing. The victims of Sade's sexual terrorism are less important than "philosophical disquisitions." This valuation is not the final result of any moral anguish; it is entirely unselfconscious.

In tome after tome, Sade's biographers write the women Sade assaulted in either invisible ink or spleen. Norman Gear, in *The Divine Demon*, is both fanciful and cute:

> Had he not been more than punished for his sins? And what, after all, had they amounted to? He had given a few girls and women a little pain, but not so much really, and none of them had been seriously harmed. He had seduced some girls, but he had never raped one. Most of the women he had used in his orgies had come to him willingly enough, for payment, or, oddly enough, because they liked him. . . . Even poor Rose Keller had soon recovered from her thrashing, and had been very well rewarded for a week with a sore behind. As for the whores in Marseilles—they had been paid for their services and had not endured worse than it was their common lot to endure.[10]

Jean Paulhan, a Sadean missionary, is outraged that Sade, a significant being, should have been imprisoned for violating shadows:

> It seems established that Sade gave a spanking to a whore in Paris: does that fit with a year in jail? Some aphrodisiac sweets to some girls *[sic]* in Marseilles: does that justify ten years in the Bastille? He seduces his sister-in-law: does that justify a month in the Conciergerie? He causes no end of bother to his

> powerful, his redoubtable in-laws . . . does that justify two years in a fortress? He enables several moderates to escape (we are in the midst of the Terror): does that justify a year in Madelonnettes? It is acknowledged that he published some obscene books, that he attacked Bonaparte's entourage; and it is not impossible that he feigned madness. Does that justify fourteen years in Charenton, three in Bicête, and one in Sainte-Pélagie? Would it not strongly appear as if, for a whole string of French governments, any and every excuse sufficed for clapping him behind bars?[11]

Paulhan cites neither Sade's actual crimes nor his actual terms of imprisonment; his version of the correspondences between the two is entirely whimsical. But the consequences of his inexactitude are not: Sade the Victim is writ large; Sade's victims are written out.

Sade's biographers attempt to justify, trivialize, or deny (even though records confirming the facts exist) every assault Sade ever committed against women and girls. Especially, tireless efforts are made to discount the kidnapping and torture of Rose Keller, Sade's first nonprostitute victim of record.

Violence against prostitutes, regardless of its ferocity, is nothing less than an acceptable fact of life. Who, the biographers ask with mock wonderment, can deny that these "girls" are there to be used? The man's right to sexual pleasure on his own terms is the given, the natural right. Sexual pleasure includes by definition or intrinsically justifies the use of force, trickery, or violence. The cost to the prostitute's health or well-being means nothing. Her own will has no value and no claim to value. The use of force against prostitutes means less than nothing. Freedom, that hallowed word, is valued only when used in reference to male desire. For women, freedom means only that men are free to use them.

In describing what is usually referred to as the Rose Keller incident—a sublime euphemism—even Sade's biographers seem to recognize that their hero did do something very mean indeed—unless Rose Keller was a whore or a liar, in which case Sade's use of her was of no consequence. So they set out to prove that she was both, a task made easy not by the truth (she was neither) but by the power of the biographers to define their own terms within the accepted bounds of a woman-hating society. Rose Keller was a whore because all women, especially working-class women, are whores; Rose Keller was a whore because any woman who is hungry or unemployed will whore; Rose Keller was a whore because there is no absolute proof for every day of her life that she was not a whore; Rose Keller was a whore because Sade said she was a whore; Rose Keller was a whore because, after being tortured and escaping, she accepted money from Sade's mother-in-law. Rose Keller was a liar because all women are liars, especially when they accuse men of forcing them to any sexual activity; Rose Keller was a liar because Sade said she was a liar; Rose Keller was a liar because she accepted money, which proved that she had made up the story to obtain money; Rose Keller was a liar because who was she anyway compared to the heroic Sade?

Hobart Ryland, the translator of Sade's *Adelaide of Brunswick* into English, claimed that Keller "made up a fantastic story."[12] Geoffrey Gorer shed doubt on Keller's credibility by meticulous analysis of detail: "A woman so badly wounded would surely have had some difficulty in climbing walls."[13] Thomas acknowledged that "[g]rievous bodily harm had been done to the young woman," and he sternly admonished that "there was no question of excusing it even if she was a whore."[14] Excusing it nonetheless, Thomas characterized Sade's torture of Keller as "a rather disagreeable hour or two, and a few minutes of actual discomfort not far removed in degree from a visit to an eighteenth-century dentist."[15] The money made it all worthwhile and "sensible men saw it in perspective and knew that it was just an incident."[16] Ronald Hayman, author of a so-called critical biography, strikes the same wretched note: "Scores of men were taking their pleasure in very much the same way; scores of girls *[sic]*, no doubt, were exploiting the situation for what it was worth. Money was an effective pain-killer."[17] Angela Carter, in a recent pseudofeminist literary essay, claims that Keller "turn[ed] her hand to blackmail and who can blame her?"[18] Entering the realm of literary affectation heretofore reserved for the boys,

Carter writes: "The affair enchants me. It has the completeness and lucidity of a script by Brecht. A woman of the third estate, a beggar, the poorest of the poor, turns the very vices of the rich into weapons to wound them with."[19] Her flight of fancy nearly matches that of Hayman, who warns:

> Again we should not take it for granted that Sade was enjoying himself. Was he even doing what he felt he wanted to do? As Gide said: "One can never know to what extent one feels and to what extent one plays at feeling. This ambivalence constitutes the feeling."[20]

But it is Roland Barthes who most callously robs Rose Keller of her real life in order to sustain Sade's legend in pretty, if meaningless, prose:

> In the total disengagement from value produced by the pleasure of the Text, what I get from Sade's life is not the spectacle, albeit grandiose, of a man oppressed by an entire society because of his passion, it is not the solemn contemplation of a fate, it is, *inter alia*, that Provençal way in which Sade says "milli" (mademoiselle) Rousset, or milli Henriette, or milli Lépinai, it is his white muff when he accosts Rose Keller . . .[21]

Sade's white muff matters.

All of the girls and women hurt by Sade are treated by biographers and intellectuals with this same endemic contempt. An exchange of money, male to female, especially wipes away crime, negates harm—whether the commentator is a pedestrian biographer or a grand literary critic. The use of money to buy women is apparently mesmerizing. It magically licenses any crime against women. Once a woman has been paid, crime is expiated. That no real harm was done, no matter what actually was done, is a particularly important theme. This point is echoed in the Kinsey Institute's study of sex offenders (see pages 188–198) and in a vast body of contemporary social analyses that, explicitly or implicitly, define sexual freedom as men doing what they want without foolish resistance from "puritanical" or "repressed" women who are incapable of knowing or telling sexual truth. According to Gear, the poisoned prostitutes in Marseilles had "upset stomachs and were none the worse for their adventures."[22] According to Thomas, the Marseilles prostitutes, whom he acknowledges were poisoned, went to the police because they "were only too anxious now to find a villain on whom all their ills and all official disapproval could be placed."[23] According to Hayman, "it was obvious that the poisoning was accidental . . . [Sade] had no conceivable motive for wanting to murder them."[24] To give credit where it is due: Edmund Wilson, in 1952, reacting to the mindless defenses of Sade's crimes among the literati, asserted that "there is not a shred of evidence for assuming that [the candies] were not intended, if not to kill the girls *[sic]*, at least to have painful results, and the behavior of Sade himself, as reported by one of the girls *[sic]*, seems decidedly to show that they were."[25] Once one has entered the realm of existing discourse on Sade, Wilson's willingness to believe the testimony of "one of the girls" is almost shocking.

The avenging wrath of Sadean sycophants is reserved, however, for Madame de Montreuil, Sade's mother-in-law, the one woman who during his lifetime tried to stop him. The critics' strategy with the unpropertied victims is to erase them. Madame de Montreuil cannot be erased. She was responsible for Sade's imprisonment in Italy, for the issuance of several *lettres de cachet* against him. She also, at various stages of Sade's life, tried to buy him out of trouble, to reconcile Sade to his marriage and to his wife. As an active woman, a mother, one who took action to restrict the cruel indulgences of a male, Madame de Montreuil's life monumentally insults Sade's biographers. According to Gorer, "her one aim was de Sade's destruction."[26] He also speculates that she was jealous of Sade's relationship with her younger daughter; this jealousy "drove her to attack and ruin him to the best of her ability during the next thirty years."[27] According to the various biographers: Madame de Montreuil lusted for Sade but he refused her; had nothing to do with her time and therefore turned to intrigues against her son-in-law; was a vengeful and sadistic woman who chose Sade as her victim; had a thin skin and resented the endless gossip about Sade's various atrocities, and therefore tried to have the state murder him; lusted after her younger daughter, whom Sade took from her; had to marry off her younger daughter, with which Sade interfered; was ruthless and evil because women who meddle in the affairs of men are. Edmund Wilson demonstrates some charity in stating: "No: one cannot blame Sade's family for locking him up."[28] But Madame de Montreuil, mother of two daughters who were both ruined by Sade, caretaker of his children in the years when Renée-Pélagie lived with Sade as a participant in his crimes, is not redeemed by any critic's vague sympathy. In the literature on Sade, she is the villain, the one who was cruel, the one who abused power, the one who was sadistic, the one who was dangerous, the one who should have been stopped.

Throughout the writings on Sade, his own mother and Renée-Pélagie are insulted in a lethargic and haphazard way. Other women were more important to Sade; his literary friends are happy to have the same set of priorities. Those incapable of imagining the suffering of one who has been kidnapped and tortured, poisoned and raped, cannot be expected to grasp the long-term, complex suffering of women in legal captivity. Sade's mother is especially blamed for withdrawing into religion. She is also blamed for dying, since Sade was arrested when he attempted to visit her on her deathbed. Renée-Pélagie is especially blamed for leaving Sade and for burning some of his manuscripts, which she may or may not have done. She is also blamed for aging, becoming fat, going blind. She is also blamed for being sexually repressed, that is, not particularly eager to satisfy Sade's appetites. She is not blamed for her years of loyalty to Sade, her efforts to keep him out of prison, her attempts to have her mother arrested, or her participation with Sade in the sexual and physical torture of five fifteen-year-old girls. Sade's violence against Renée-Pélagie, as opposed to his violence against other women, was fully sanctioned by the law. As her husband, he had the authority to do what he wanted to her. He also had the authority to spend her money, which he did. The savagery of his life created the strange desperation of hers. The nightmare of her life has been lost in the celebration of his.

Repeat the syllables
until the lesson is pumped through the heart:
Nicriven, accused of lasciviousness, burned 1569.
Barbara Gobel, described by her jailors
as "the fairest maid in Wurzburg,"
burned 1629, age nineteen.
Frau Peller, raped by Inquisition torturers
because her sister refused
the witch-judge Franz Buirman, 1631.
Maria Walburga Rung, tried at a secular court
in Manheim as a witch,
released as "merely a prostitute,"
accused again by the episcopal court
at Eichstadt, tortured into confession,
and then burned alive, 1723, age twenty-two.

What have they done to me?

Robin Morgan,
"The Network of the Imaginary Mother"

Camus captured the essence of Sade's legend when he wrote: "His desperate demand for freedom led Sade into the kingdom of servitude . . ."[29] Throughout the literature on him, with some small qualifying asides, Sade is viewed as one whose voracious appetite was for *freedom;* this appetite was cruelly punished by an unjust and repressive society. The notion is that Sade, called by Apollinaire "that freest of spirits to have lived so far,"[30] was a monster as the word used to be defined: something unnaturally marvelous. Sade's violation of sexual and social boundaries, in his writings and in his life, is seen as inherently revolutionary. The antisocial character of his sexuality is seen as a radical challenge to a society deadly in its repressive sexual conventions. Sade is seen as an outlaw in the mythic sense, a grand figure of rebellion in action and in literature whose sexual hunger, like a terrorist's bomb, threatened to blow apart the established order. The imprisonment of Sade is seen to demonstrate the despotism of a system that must contain, control, and manipulate sexuality, not allow it to run free toward anarchic self-fulfillment. Sade is seen as the victim of that cruel system, as one who was punished because of the bravery of his antagonism to it. The legend of Sade is particularly vitalized by the false claim, widely believed, that he rotted in prison for most of his life as punishment for obscene writings. Sade's story is generally thought to be this: he was a genius whose mind was too big for the petty puritans around him; he was locked up for his sexual abandonment, especially in writing; he was kept in jail because nothing less could defuse the danger he presented to the established order; he was victimized, unjustly imprisoned, persecuted, for daring to express radical sexual values in his life and in his writing; as "that freest of spirits to have lived so far," his very being was an insult to a system that demanded conformity. It was left to Erica Jong to insist in an article in *Playboy* ("You Have to Be Liberated to Laugh") that Sade was jailed for his sense of humor.

Writers on Sade are fascinated by both his life and his work, and it is impossible to know whether Sade's legend could have been sustained if one had existed without the other. Edmund Wilson, repelled by Sade's work, is fascinated by his life. Simone de Beauvoir, repelled by Sade's life, is fascinated by his work. Most of the writers on Sade advocate rather than analyze him, are infatuated with him as a subject precisely because his sexual obsessions are both forbidden and common. The books and essays on Sade are crusading, romanticizing, mystifying in the literal sense (that is, intentionally perplexing to the mind). Infused with a missionary passion, they boil down to this: Sade died for you—for all the sexual crimes you have committed, for all the sexual crimes you want to commit, for every sexual crime you can imagine committing. Sade suffered because he did what you want to do; he was imprisoned as you might be imprisoned. The "you" is masculine. The freedom Sade is credited with demanding is freedom as men conceive it. Sade's suffering or victimization, whatever its cause or degree, is authentic because a man experienced it (Sade in being imprisoned, the writers in morbid contemplation of a man brought down). No woman's life has ever been so adored; no woman's suffering has ever been so mourned; no woman's ethic, action, or obsession has been so hallowed in the male search for the meaning of freedom.*

The essential content of Sade's legend was created by Sade himself, especially in his prison letters and in the rambling philosophical discourses that permeate his fiction. Maurice Heine, a Left libertarian, and his disciple Gilbert Lély, the first so-called Sade scholars, rewrote Sade's elaborate self-justifications, in the process transmuting them into accepted fact. Sade wrote his own legend; Heine and Lély resurrected it; subsequent writers paraphrased, defended, and embellished it.

In the letters, Sade is militant, with the pride of one martyred in righteousness: "Misfortune will never debase me . . . ," he wrote to Renée-Pélagie from Vincennes in 1781. "Nor will *I* ever take a slave's heart. Were these wretched chains to lead me to the grave, you will always see me the same. I have the misfortune to have received from Heaven a resolute soul which has never been able to yield and will never do so. I have absolutely no fear of offending anyone."[31]

It was Sade who painted the picture of Madame de Montreuil that his biographers now turn out, without the master's touch, by the dozens. As Sade wrote: "This terrible torture is not enough according to this horrible creature: it has to be increased further by everything her imagination can devise to redouble its horror. You will admit there is only one monster capable of taking vengeance to such a point."[32]

Sade's defense of everything he ever did is very simple: he never did anything wrong. This defense has two distinct parts. First, he did not do anything he was accused of doing that might warrant

*"[And] no woman's *crime*," wrote Robin Morgan to me in a letter, July 20, 1979, "for that matter, has (sure as hell) ever been so justified, excused, romanticized, glamorized."

imprisonment, because no one could prove that he did, including eyewitnesses whose word could never match his own: "A child's testimony? But this was a servant; thus, in his capactiy as a child and as a servant he cannot be believed."[33] Second, everything he had done was common practice. These two contradictory strains of self-defense often fuse to reveal the Sade obscured by his mesmerized apologists. Here he defends himself, again to his wife, vis-à-vis his abuse of the five fifteen-year-old girls originally procured by Nanon, who later bore his child:

> I go off with them; I use them. Six months later, some parents come along to demand their return. I give them back [he did not], and suddenly a charge of abduction and rape is brought against me. It is a monstrous injustice. The law on this point is . . . as follows: it is expressly forbidden in France for any procuress to supply virgin maidens, and if the girl supplied is a virgin and lodges a complaint, it is not the man who is charged but the procuress who is punished severely on the spot. But even if the male offender has requested a virgin he is not liable to punishment: he is merely doing what all men do. It is, I repeat, the procuress who provided him with the girl and who is perfectly aware that she is expressly forbidden to do so, who is guilty. Therefore this first charge against me in Lyon of abduction and rape was entirely illegal: I have committed no offence. It is the procuress to whom I have applied who is liable to punishment—not I.[34]

The use of women, as far as Sade was concerned, was an absolute right, one that could not fairly be limited or abrogated under any circumstances. His outrage at being punished for his assaults on females never abated. His claim to innocence rested finally on a simple assertion: "I am guilty of nothing more than simple libertinage such as it is practised by all men more or less according to their natural temperaments or tendencies."[35] Sade's fraternal ties were apparent only when he used the crimes of other men to justify his own.

Sade designated "libertinage" as the main theme of his work. Richard Seaver and Austryn Wainhouse, in a foreword to a collection of Sade's work, point out with grave emphasis that "libertine" comes from the Latin *liber*, which means "free." In fact, originally a libertine was a manumitted slave. Sade's use of the word contradicts its early meaning, despite the claim of his sycophantic translators. For Sade, libertinage was the cruel use of others for one's own sexual pleasure. Sade's libertinage demanded slavery; sexual despotism misnamed "freedom" is Sade's most enduring legacy.

Sade's work is nearly indescribable. In sheer quantity of horror, it is unparalleled in the history of writing. In its fanatical and fully realized commitment to depicting and reveling in torture and murder to gratify lust, it raises the question so central to pornography as a genre: why? why did someone do (make) this? In Sade's case, the motive most often named is revenge against a society that persecuted him. This explanation does not take into account the fact that Sade was a sexual predator and that the pornography he created was part of that predation.

It is not adequate to describe Sade's ethic as rapist. For Sade, rape was a modest, not fully gratifying mode of violation. In Sade's work, rape is foreplay, preparation for the main event, which is maiming unto death. Rape is an essential dimension because force is fundamental to Sade's conception of sexual action. But over time, with repetition, it pales, becomes boring, a stupendous waste of energy unless accompanied by the torture, and often the murder, of the victim. Sade is the consummate literary snuff artist: orgasm eventually requires murder. Victims are sliced up, impaled on stakes, burned alive, roasted slowly on spits, eaten, decapitated, flayed until they die. Women's vaginas and rectums are sewn up to be torn through. Women are used as tables on which burning food is served, on which candles are burned. One would require the thousands of pages Sade himself used to list the atrocities he described. Nevertheless, some themes emerge.

In Sade's fiction, men, women, boys and girls are used, violated, destroyed. At the top, in control, are the libertines, mostly old men, aristocrats, powerful by virtue of gender, wealth, position, and cruelty. Sade describes the sexuality of these men essentially as addiction: each sex act contributes to the development of a tolerance; that is, arousal requires more cruelty each time, orgasm requires more cruelty each time; victims must increase in abjectness and numbers both. Everyone inferior to the aristocrats on top in wealth, in social status, or in her or his capacity for cruelty becomes sexual fodder. Wives, daughters, and mothers are particularly singled out for ridicule, humiliation, and contempt. Servants of both sexes and female prostitutes are the main population of the abused, dismembered, executed. Lesbian acts decorate the slaughter; they are imagined by a man for men; they are so male-imagined that the divine fuck imbued with murder is their only possible resolution.

In the bulk of Sade's work, female victims greatly outnumber male victims, but his cruelty is all-inclusive. He manifests a pansexual dominance—the male who knows no boundaries but still hates women more.

While the aristocrats on top are never maimed, they are, at their own command, whipped and sodomized. They remain entirely in control even when whipped or sodomized. Everything done to them or by them is for the purpose of bringing them to orgasm on their own terms. Sade established impotence as a characteristic of the aging libertine: viler and viler crimes are necessary to achieve erection and ejaculation. George Steiner, perhaps to his credit, fails to appreciate the significance of the progression of lust in Sade's work, especially in *The 120 Days of Sodom:* "In short: given the physiological and nervous complexion of the human body, the numbers of ways in which orgasm can be achieved or arrested, the total modes of intercourse are fundamentally finite. The mathematics of sex stop somewhere in the region of *soixante-neuf;* there are no transcendental series."[36] Displaying his own brand of misogyny, Steiner goes on to say that "things have remained fairly generally the same since man first met goat and woman."[37] But Sade is saying precisely that men become sated too soon with what they have had, whatever it is, especially woman, also goat.

In Sade's fiction, the men on top exchange and share victims in an attempt to forge a community based on a common, if carnivorous, sexuality. The shared victim results in the shared orgasm, a bond among the male characters and between the author and his male readers.

The men on top also share the shit of the victims. They control elimination and physical cleanliness, a stratagem that suggests the Nazi death camps. They eat turds and control the diets of their victims to control the quality of the turds. While Freudian values apply here—the anal being indicative of greed, of obsession with material wealth—excrement, like blood, like flesh itself, is ingested because these men have gone beyond vampirism toward a sexuality that is entirely cannibalistic.

Much is made of the fact that two of Sade's main characters, Justine and Juliette, are women. Juliette especially is cited as an emancipated woman because she takes to maiming and murder with all the spectacular ease of Sade's male characters; she is the one who knows how to take pleasure, how to transform pain into pleasure, slavery into freedom. It is, Sade's literary friends claim, a matter of *attitude:* here we have Justine, raped, tortured, violated, and she hates it, so she is a victim; here we have Juliette, raped, tortured, violated, and she loves it, so she is free. As expressed by Roland Barthes:

> The scream is the victim's mark; she makes herself a victim because she chooses to scream; if, under the same vexation she were to ejaculate *[sic]*, she would cease to be a victim, would be transformed into a libertine: *to scream/to discharge*, this paradigm is the beginning of choice, i.e. Sadian meaning.[38]

"Sadian meaning," then, reduces to the more familiar preachment: if you can't do anything about it (and I will see to it that you cannot), lie back and enjoy it. In the critical writings on Sade's pornography, rape in the criminal sense exists mainly as a subjective value judgment of the one who was used, to whom hysteria is always attributed. Women, according to Sade, Barthes, and their ilk, can and should choose to experience the rape of women as men experience it: as pleasure.

Sade's view of women was hailed by Apollinaire as prophetic: "Justine is woman as she has been hitherto, enslaved, miserable and less than human; her opposite, Juliette, represents the woman whose advent he anticipated, a figure of whom minds have as yet no conception, who is arising out of mankind, who shall have wings, and who shall renew the world."[39]

Justine and Juliette are the two prototypical female figures in male pornography of all types. Both are wax dolls into which things are stuck. One suffers and is provocative in her suffering. The more she suffers, the more she provokes men to make her suffer. Her suffering is arousing; the more she suffers, the more aroused her torturers become. She, then, becomes responsible for her suffering, since she invites it by suffering. The other revels in all that men do to her; she is the woman who likes it, no matter what the "it." In Sade, the "attitude" (to use Barthes's word) on which one's status as victim or master depends is an attitude toward male power. The victim actually refuses to ally herself with male power, to take on its values as her own. She screams, she refuses. Men conceptualize this resistance as conformity to ridiculous feminine notions about purity and goodness; whereas in fact the victim refuses to ally herself with those who demand her complicity in her own degradation. Degradation is implicit in inhabiting a predetermined universe in which one cannot choose what one does, only one's attitude (to scream, to discharge) toward what is done to one. Unable to manifest her resistance as power, the woman who suffers manifests it as passivity, except for the scream.

The so-called libertine re-creates herself in the image of the cruelest (most powerful) man she can find and in her alliance with him takes on some of his power over others. The female libertines in Sade's work are always subordinate to their male counterparts, always dependent on them for wealth and continued good health. They have female anatomies by fiat; that is, Sade says so. In every other respect—values, behaviors, tastes, even in such a symptomatic detail as ejaculating sperm, which they all do—Sade's libertine women are men. They are, in fact, literary transvestites.

Sade himself, in a footnote to *Juliette*, claimed an authenticity for Juliette based on his conviction that women are more malevolent than men: ". . . the more sensitive an individual, the more sharply this atrocious Nature will bend him into conformance with evil's irresistible laws; whence it is that women surrender to it more heatedly and perform it with greater artistry than men."[40] The message that women are evil and must be punished permeates Sade's work, whether the female figures in question are supposed to represent good or evil. The vileness of women and an intense hatred of female genitalia are major themes in every Sadean opus. Both male and female characters evince a deep aversion to and loathing of the vagina. Anal penetration is not only preferred; often the vagina must be hidden for the male to be aroused at all. Sade's female libertines are eloquent on the inferiority of the vagina to the rectum. While boys and men are used in Sade's lust murders, women are excoriated for all the characteristics that distinguish them from men. In Sade's scheme of things, women are aggressively slaughtered because women are repulsive as both biological and emotional beings. The arrogance of women in claiming any rights over their own bodies is particularly offensive to Sade. Any uppity pretense to bodily integrity on a woman's part must be fiercely and horribly punished. Even where Sade, in one or two places, insists on women's right to abort pregnancies at will, his sustained celebration of abortion as erotically charged murder places abortion squarely within the context of his own utterly and unredeemably male value system: in this system, women have no bodily rights.

A religious scholar, John T. Noonan, Jr., names Sade as "the first in Western Europe to praise abortion . . ."[41] Citing Noonan, Linda Bird Francke, in *The Ambivalence of Abortion*, claims that Sade's advocacy of abortion was instrumental in the papal decision that abortion must be prohibited from gestation on. Characterizing Sade's work as part of the proabortion movement, she asserts that Sade "actually extolled the values of abortion."[42] Sade extolled the sexual value of murder and he saw abortion as a form of murder. For Sade, abortion was a sexual act, an act of lust. In his system, pregnancy always demanded murder, usually the murder of the pregnant woman, rendered more exciting if she was in an advanced stage of pregnancy. Nothing could be calculated to please Sade more than the horrible deaths of women butchered in illegal abortions. This is Sade's sexuality realized.

In Sade's work, both male and female children are maimed, raped, tortured, killed. Men especially go after their daughters, sometimes raising them specifically to become paramours, most often abusing them and then passing them on to close male friends to be used and killed. Sade's obsession with sexual violence against children of both sexes is transformed by his literary lackeys, true to form, into another demonstration of Sade's progressive sexual radicalism. As Geoffrey Gorer wrote: "According to de Sade, very young children are shameless, sexually inquisitive and endowed with strong sexual feelings. Children are naturally polymorphous perverts."[43] Actually, according to Sade, adult men find it particularly gratifying to kidnap, rape, torture, and kill children.

Sade is concerned too with the violation of the mother—not only as wife to her husband but also as victim of her children. A constant conceit throughout Sade's fiction is that fathers are wondrous sexual beings, mothers stupid and repressed prudes who would be better off as whores (or as the whores they really are). As a philosopher, Sade maintains consistently that one owes nothing to one's mother, for the father is the source of human life:

> . . . Be unafraid, Eugénie [the heroine], and adopt these same sentiments; they are natural: uniquely formed of our sires' blood, we owe absolutely nothing to our mothers. What, furthermore, did they do but co-operate in the act which our fathers, on the contrary, solicited? Thus, it was the father who desired our birth, whereas the mother merely consented thereto.[44]

Contempt for the mother is an integral part of Sade's discourse:

> It is madness to suppose one owes something to one's mother. And upon what, then, would gratitude be based? Is one to be thankful that she discharged *[sic]* when someone once fucked her?[45]

A daughter's turning on her mother, forcing her mother to submit to rape and torture, defaming and debasing her mother, and finally luxuriating in the killing of her mother is a crucial Sadean scenario.

Sade's ideas on women and sexual freedom are explicated throughout his work. He has few ideas about women and sexual freedom and no fear of repetition. Women are meant to be prostitutes: ". . . your sex never serves Nature better than when it prostitutes itself to ours; that 'tis, in a word, to be fucked that you were born . . ."[46] In rape a man exercises his natural rights over women:

> If then it becomes incontestable that we have received from Nature the right indiscriminately to express our wishes to all women, it likewise becomes incontestable that we have the right to compel their submission, not exclusively, for I should then be contradicting myself, but temporarily [the doctrine of "nonpossessiveness"]. It cannot be denied that we have the right to decree laws that compel woman to yield to the flames of him who would have her; violence itself being one of that right's effects, we can employ it lawfully.[47]

Sade pioneered what became the ethos of the male-dominated sexual revolution: collective ownership of women by men, no woman ever justified in refusal. Sade took these ideas to their logical conclusion: state brothels in which all females would be forced to serve from childhood on. The idea of unrestricted access to an absolutely available female population, there to be raped, to which one could do anything, has gripped the male imagination, especially on the Left, and has been translated into the euphemistic demand for "free sex, free women." The belief that this urge toward unrestrained use of women is revolutionary brings into bitter focus the meaning of "sexual freedom" in leftist sexual theory and practice. Sade says: use women because women exist to be used by men; do what you want to them for your own pleasure, no matter what the cost to them. Following leftist tradition, Peter Weiss, in the play known as *Marat/Sade*, paraphrased Sade in this happily disingenuous way: "And what's the point of a revolution/without general copulation."[48]

In a variation of leftist theme, Christopher Lasch, in *The Culture of Narcissism*, sees Sade not as the originator of a new ethic of sexual collectivity, but as one who foresaw the fall of the bourgeois family with its "sentimental cult of womanhood"[49] and the fall of capitalism itself. According to Lasch, Sade anticipated a "defense of woman's *[sic]* sexual rights—their rights to dispose of their own bodies, as feminists would put it today . . . He perceived, more clearly than the feminists, that all freedoms under capitalism come in the end to the same thing, the same universal obligation to enjoy and be enjoyed."[50] Lasch's particular, and peculiar, interpretation of Sade appears to derive from his stubborn misunderstanding of sexual integrity as feminists envision it. In Sade's universe, the obligation to enjoy is extended to women as the obligation to enjoy being enjoyed—failing which, sex remains what it was, as it was: a forced passage to death. The notion that Sade presages feminist demands for women's sexual rights is rivaled in self-serving absurdity only by the opinion of Gerald and Caroline Greene, in *S-M: The Last Taboo*, that "[i]f there was one thing de Sade was not, it was a sexist."[51]

De Beauvoir had understood that "[t]he fact is that the original intuition which lies at the basis of Sade's entire sexuality, and hence his ethic, is the fundamental identity of coition and cruelty."[52] Camus had understood that "[t]wo centuries ahead of time and on a reduced scale [compared to Stalinists and Nazis], Sade extolled totalitarian societies in the name of unbridled freedom . . ."[53] Neither they nor Sade's less conscientious critics perceived that Sade's valuation of women has been the one constant in history—imagined and enacted—having as its consequence the destruction of real lives; that Sade's advocacy and celebration of rape and battery have been history's sustaining themes. Sade's spectacular endurance as a cultural force has been because of, not despite, the virulence of the sexual violence toward women in both his work and his life. Sade's work embodies the common values and desires of men. Described in terms of its "excesses," as it often is, the power of

Sade's work in exciting the imaginations of men is lost. Nothing in Sade's work takes place outside the realm of common male belief. In story and discourse, Sade's conception of romance is this: "I've already told you: the only way to a woman's heart is along the path of torment. I know none other as sure."[54] Sade's conception of sexuality is this:

> . . . there is no more selfish passion than lust; none that is severer in its demands; smitten stiff by desire, 'tis with yourself you must be solely concerned, and as for the object that serves you, it must always be considered as some sort of victim, destined to that passion's fury. Do not all passions require victims?[55]

These convictions are ordinary, expressed often in less grand language, upheld in their rightness by the application of male-supremacist law especially in the areas of rape, battery, and reproduction; they are fully consonant with the practices (if not the preachments) of ordinary men with ordinary women. Had Sade's work—boring, repetitive, ugly as it is—not embodied these common values, it would long ago have been forgotten. Had Sade himself—a sexual terrorist, a sexual tyrant—not embodied in his life these same values, he would not have excited the twisted, self-righteous admiration of those who have portrayed him as revolutionary, hero, martyr (or, in the banal prose of Richard Gilman, "the first compelling enunciator in modern times of the desire to be other than what society determined, to act otherwise than existing moral structures coerced one into doing"[56]).

Sade's importance, finally, is not as dissident or deviant: it is as Everyman, a designation the power-crazed aristocrat would have found repugnant but one that women, on examination, will find true. In Sade, the authentic equation is revealed: the power of the pornographer is the power of the rapist/batterer is the power of the man.

4

Objects

The creation of a rich and dependable object world; the building-in of secure sequences of behavioral time; the comfortable mastery of space; firm links between the acting organism and the external world; all of these add up to solid answers to our four common human problems. "What shall I do? What may I hope? What can I know? What *is* man?"

Ernest Becker, *The Revolution in Psychiatry*

I was so drunk all the time that I took bottles for girls and girls for bottles.

Anton Chekhov, in a letter, April 25, 1887

A sex toy is anything that isn't you when you're having whatever it is you define as sex.

Ian Young, quoted in "Devices and Desires," by Gerald Hannon, *The Body Politic*

There is something every woman wears around her neck on a thin chain of fear—an amulet of madness. For each of us, there exists somewhere a moment of insult so intense that she will reach up and rip the amulet off, even if the chain tears at the flesh of her neck.

Robin Morgan, "Goodbye to All That," *Going Too Far*

Through most of patriarchal history, which is estimated variously to have lasted (thus far) five thousand to twelve thousand years, women have been chattel property. Chattel property, in the main, is movable property—cattle, wives, concubines, offspring, slaves, beasts of burden, domesticated animals. Chattel property is reckoned as part of a man's estate. It is wealth and accumulations of it both are wealth and demonstrate wealth. Chattel property for the most part is animate and sensate, but it is perceived and valued as commodity. To be chattel, even when human, is to be valued and used as property, as thing.

It is fashionable to think that women, who have come a long way, baby, are entirely removed from chattel status. It is fashionable to think that the chattel status of women is ancient, buried with the old cities of defunct civilizations. But in the United States and England, married women were economic chattel through most of the nineteenth century. Married women were allowed to own property—which meant that they themselves were considered persons, not property—toward the end of the nineteenth century, but that right was made effectual only in the first decades of the twentieth century. In some states in the United States, married women still cannot engage in some economic transactions without the consent or participation of their husbands.

In the areas of sex and reproduction, the chattel status of women is preserved in law and in practice. A married woman is obligated to engage in coitus with her husband. He, not she, controls access to her body. With few exceptions, a married woman cannot be raped by her husband as rape is legally defined, because marriage means that the husband has a legal right to coital access. When women were clearly and unambiguously sexual chattel, the wife could be "chastised" by her husband at will—whipped, flogged, caned, hit, tied up, locked up—to punish her for real or imagined bad behavior or to improve her character. The bad behavior, then as now, was often an attempt to refuse the husband sexual access. The English suffragists thought a new era had arrived when, in 1891, a court set limits to the force a husband could use against his wife. As Sylvia Pankhurst recorded:

> The Jackson case of 1891, described by the *Law Times* as "the Married Woman's Charter of personal liberty," wherein it was

> decided that a husband might not imprison his wife to enforce his conjugal rights, was eagerly hailed, and was an evidence of the change which was coming over opinion in general.[1]

But the general opinion did not change, not in England, not in the United States. Today there are laws against battery, which so often includes both captivity and rape: unenforced laws. In practice, assault and battery of a wife by a husband is both commonplace and protected by a male-supremacist system that, in its heart of hearts, still views the wife's body as her husband's sexual property; and, needless to say, the rape part of any battery is almost never against the law at all. Using FBI statistics, feminists calculate that in the United States one woman is raped every three minutes, one wife battered every eighteen seconds. There are currently an estimated twenty-eight million battered wives in the United States. In thirteen states, the right of marital rape has been extended by statute to cohabitation. In five of those states, a man who rapes a so-called *voluntary social companion* is partially protected by statute. In one of those states, West Virginia, he is fully protected. In only three states is the right of a husband to rape fully abrogated. The right to obtain an abortion at will, defined as a right of privacy by the United States Supreme Court in 1973, has been limited in some states by a requirement of male consent, despite a subsequent 1976 Supreme Court decision holding that no one has a right to exercise veto power over a woman's decision to abort. The chattel status of women, especially married women, is not yet dead. It is not even vestigial, some useless and unusable remain which long ago lost its function or importance. It is still central in fixing male sexual and reproductive control of women.

With this formidable history and ongoing reality of women as sexual property, it is not surprising that men conspicuously view themselves as authentic persons and the others clustered around them, especially their sexual intimates, especially women and children, as objects.

The tradition of regarding sensate beings as objects is now particularly honored, even enforced, in psychiatry and psychology.

The whole world outside man himself is viewed as the object world, a series of things to which man/men must learn to relate. This project of learning to relate to objects outside himself is, needless to say, awesomely difficult but nevertheless necessary because, as Ernest Becker, a so-called humanist in the realm of psychology, puts it: ". . . we know that man needs objects in order to come into being as an organism, and subsequently in order to provide for continuing action and experience. The organism needs objects in order to feel its own powers and presence."[2] Man, the organism in question, uses objects—women, children, animals (cattle are still important—the myth of the cowboy), sensate beings called objects as a matter of course—to feel *his* own power and presence. The use of the word *object* to characterize persons who are not adult men is considered normative and appropriate. Psychologists do not make a distinction between men who relate to persons as such and men who relate to persons as objects. Instead, they consider it appropriate to relate to some persons as objects, inappropriate to relate to other persons as objects, and inappropriate to relate to some objects as sexual objects. One of the reasons that male homosexuality is so disreputable in the realm of psychology is that it is deemed inappropriate for a man to relate to another man as an object, the only sexual response possible in the male sexual system as it now stands. A man must function as the human center of a chattel-oriented sensibility, surrounded by objects to be used so that he can experience his own power and presence. He must not reduce himself to the level of women, for instance, by becoming an object for another man. This degrades the whole male sex, which is inappropriate.

The notion that appropriate responses to appropriate objects signify the mentally healthy male enables Becker to write:

> . . . the schizophrenic, who relates to people only on the basis of their sex, is not showing a hypersexuality so much as a poverty in the behavioral range: he reduces the object to that aspect with which he can cope.[3]

Though Becker suggests that viewing women merely as vaginas is not wonderful, the nearly universal reduction of women to sex ("that aspect with which he can cope") in psychology or in high culture or among his peers does not, apparently, indicate a poverty of behavior. Becker himself, of course, does not show a poverty of behavior in reducing persons to objects because that is normal, neutral, and not reductive. "One's whole life," Becker claims, "is an education in broadening his range of behavior to objects."[4] So, too, Christopher Lasch characterizes the contemporary run of patients seen by psychologists as shallow because of their inadequate response to objects:

> These patients, though often ingratiating, tend to cultivate a protective shallowness in emotional relations. They lack the capacity to mourn, because the intensity of their rage against lost love objects, in particular against their parents, prevents their reliving happy experiences or treasuring them in memory.[5]

Lasch himself, of course, is not shallow in regarding loved persons, in particular one's parents, as "love objects." The mourning of a lost object does not seem to Lasch either shallow or futile.

The first object in a male's personal history and in cultural importance is the mother. It is in properly internalizing her as an object that the male learns everything from heterosexuality to heterosexuality (homosexuality being generally regarded as a failure to learn), including: how to be a separate human being, that is, how to separate from the first object; how to possess suitable objects that are appropriate substitutes for the first object; and what to expect from an object by way of care and devotion, including being kept clean, fed, groomed, smiled at, and humored. According to Mahler, Pine, and Bergman, who use the standard vocabulary: "The establishment of affective (emotional) object constancy depends upon the gradual internalization of a constant, positively cathected, inner image of the mother."[6] The inability "to use the mother as a real external object as a basis for developing a stable sense of separateness from, and relatedness to, the world of reality"[7] may well be responsible for psychosis (autism and schizophrenia) in children. Even when the first object does her duty and by divine grace manages to get the infant positively cathected to an inner image of her while being an external reality from which he can separate and through which he can relate to the whole world of reality, still, according to Becker, the infant/he will not be happy: "The infant's long period of helpless dependence fills him with one great anxiety: the anxiety of object-loss, the fear of losing the succoring maternal object."[8] This clarifies, at least, the sense in which the object is alive: she is an object that/who succors, which, in its Latin past, meant "runs to help." He is afraid that he will lose the object that runs to help: and here one finds the chattel sense of motherhood as it resonates in the modern realm of male-supremacist psychology—she is the first object that belongs to the male in his life, movable property that runs to help.

Like any human chattel without a revolution in which to fight, her rebellions will be personal, small, sometimes mean, and relatively ineffectual. Since the infant/he is dependent on her—as masters are on servants and slaves—she will subvert her male child's rights over her, his very masculinity, to make him less her master and more her equal. The indignity implicit in the futile effort of this actual adult to establish an equal authenticity with the infant dependent on her should be obvious. She will have the bizarre idea that she is an adult person, an idea that prohibits the demands of service required of her as a mother in a male-supremacist context. She will perhaps think that the child, as he grows, will come to know and love her for herself, for her own qualities as a person. But the father and/or the society built on his real power will step in and destroy the subversion inherent in this idea by requiring her son to define himself in opposition to her, as her opposite. He cannot have her qualities; she cannot have his. If he is to be a person, she must be regarded as an object. She will be damned and cursed for any attempt, small or large, to step outside the bounds of this valuation of her; and the boy will be encouraged to carry out the male revenge on her. As Bettelheim counsels:

> There is no need for the child to repress [revenge] fantasies; on the contrary, he can enjoy them to the fullest, if he is subtly guided to direct them to a target which is close enough to the

> true parent but clearly not his parent. What more suitable object of vengeful thoughts than the person who has usurped the parent's place: the fairy-story step-parent? If one vents vicious fantasies of revenge against such an evil usurper, there is no reason to feel guilty or need to fear retaliation, because that figure clearly deserves it. . . . Thus, the fairy story permits the child to have the best of both worlds; he can fully engage in and enjoy revenge fantasies about the step-parent of the story, without any guilt or fear in respect to the true parent.[9]

Notice the incredible obfuscation of gender: which fairy tales involve a wicked stepfather? The male child is encouraged to learn that the mothering female is wicked and is a "suitable object of vengeful thoughts"; he is encouraged to enjoy fantasies of revenge against this figure who is more like his mother than she is like anyone else; ideally, he will not feel guilt or fear. The strategy endorsed by Bettelheim with reference to fairy tales is basic to children's stories of all sorts: the male child is taught to experience his mother not as she is but as an object with symbolic meaning. The adult male never seems to move beyond the boy enjoying his fantasies of revenge on a female object, except in one respect: he acts, using real women. Still calling revenge fantasy, he acts.

The way in which the adult male acts was described with sublime understatement and delicacy by pseudofeminist Havelock Ellis: "She is, on the physical side, inevitably the instrument in love; it must be his hand and his bow which evoke the music."[10] Rabid antifeminists Ferdinand Lundberg and Marynia F. Farnham make the same point with less elegance:

> Here, we should again like to point out to female egalitarians, is a good place to ponder this fact: for the male, sex involves an objective act of his doing but for the female it does not. As an act in which he is playing the leading role (leading, that is, within the confines of the copulatory process) it is both superficially and deeply important to the male that it be carried out without faltering. Any failure to carry through the act is *his* failure, not the woman's. Her role is passive. It is not as easy as

> falling off a log for her. It is easier. It is as easy as being the log itself.[11]

Does one (female) prefer to be perhaps a violin or definitely a log? This is the range of choice. It is also the range of political difference in the sexual philosophies of "profeminist" and antifeminist psychologists: one side insists that in the physical act of love a woman is an unspecified stringed instrument; the other side insists that in the copulatory process a woman is a log. Male-defined discourse is full of such knotty and poignant disputes.

Note too that the male commits an objective act. Men are able to be objective, an exalted capacity, precisely because they are not objects. To be objective means that one knows the world, sees it as it is, acts on the objects in it appropriately. Objectivity by definition requires a capacity to know, an ability to see. Women, the logs at issue, cannot be objective or act objectively because objects do not see or know. A log does not cognize. A log is what it is—a log. A log that resists being rolled is a log that does not know its nature or its place. A log that resists being rolled by definition is not a log. A woman who resists being a log is by definition not a woman.

Is it any wonder, then, that a hypothetical freshman conjured up by Becker in *The Revolution in Psychiatry* is somewhat confused. He is courting "the attractive blonde in his English class"; he is having trouble responding to her "as a total organismic behavioral object"; it is likely "that *Playboy* magazine had provided him with a sufficient vocabulary and imagery of what girls 'are like' (if his red-blooded American interests were along these lines)"; even though *Playboy* has given him an accurate idea "of what *a girl* is like," only his "own dependable response pattern . . . can convey the real meaning of 'girl.'"[12] And if *Playboy* has given him a sufficient and accurate vocabulary and imagery of what a girl *(sic)* is like, when he conquers his trouble in responding to her as a total organismic behavioral object, what will he do and what will she be? Hannah Tillich gave the emblematic answer:

> In Paris, Paulus took me to a street that had what looked at first like the window displays in one of the big Fifth Avenue

> department stores. But the dummies in different outfits were human beings. I was intrigued. This was the dream street of male desire and female submission. Here was the simply dressed girl looking like a neighbor or the sleeping beauty in pink veils; here was the girl with high boots and a whip or the lady in violet velvet; here was the girl begging for punishment. It was a window into hidden truth.[13]

The advantage of the living dummy over the inert kind was expressed by the French eroticist Théophile Gautier in his naughty novel, *Mademoiselle de Maupin*, first published in 1835. The poet-protagonist D'Albert says: "A woman possesses this unquestionable advantage over a statue, that she turns of herself in the direction you wish, whereas you are obliged to walk round the statue and place yourself at the point of sight—which is fatiguing."[14] A woman, D'Albert claims, is "a toy which is more intelligent than if it were ivory or gold," this superior intelligence demonstrated in the fact that it "gets up of itself if we let it fall."[15]

The inevitable and intrinsic cruelty involved in turning a person into an object should be apparent, but since this constricting, this undermining, this devaluing, is normative, no particular cruelty is recognized in it. Instead, there is only normal and natural cruelty—the normal and natural sadism of the male, happily complemented by the normal and natural masochism of the female. Each psychologist puts this view forth in his own quiet, unassuming way. Anthony Storr, considered an expert on violence, suggests that "[i]t is probably true that men are generally more 'sadistic' and women more 'masochistic.' . . . there are many women who nag unmercifully in the hope that their man will finally treat them with the force that they find exciting."[16] The object is allowed to desire if she desires to be an object: to be formed; especially to be used. The log can desire to be cut down to size, chopped, rolled, burned: formed and used in ways appropriate to its nature. As Anthony M. Ludovici wrote in response to the first wave of feminism:

> . . . I cannot uphold the view that Woman has any destiny to work out for herself. She has no "true Womanhood" that has yet to be sought and found while we leave her alone. We cannot

> leave her alone. The moment we leave her alone she ceases to be true Woman: where, then, could she go alone to seek and find her "true Womanhood"?[17]

This same view was expressed with rawer passion by Otto Weininger in *Sex and Character** (1903), an influential book in pre-Hitler Europe that equated women and Jews as worthless, lying, cheating, deceiving. While he has since been surpassed as an anti-Semite by the men whom he influenced, he still holds his own as a misogynist:

> When man became sexual he formed woman. That woman is at all has happened simply because man has accepted his sexuality. Woman is merely the result of this affirmation; she is sexuality itself. Woman's existence is dependent on man; when man, as man, in contradistinction to woman, is sexual, he is giving woman form, calling her into existence.[18]

The unembodied woman apparently described by Weininger—she does not exist until man calls her into existence—is not really unembodied, just truncated: "To put it bluntly, man possesses sexual organs; her sexual organs possess woman."[19] To put it more bluntly: she is cunt, formed by men, used by men, her sexual organs constituting her whole being and her whole value.

And what is the value of this sexual object to men, since it is they who form her, use her, and give her what value she has? The pioneering male masochist Leopold von Sacher-Masoch, who spent most of his life bullying bewildered women into wearing furs and halfheartedly whipping him, candidly wrote in his diary that "my cruel ideal woman is for me simply the instrument by which I terrorise myself."[20] The nature of the act does not change the nature of the act: the female is the instrument; the male is the center of

---

*Freud considered the book "remarkable" and its author "highly gifted but sexually deranged." Cf. *Two Case Histories*, vol. 10, *The Standard Edition of the Complete Psychological Works of Sigmund Freud*, eds. and trans. James Strachey and Anna Freud (London: Hogarth Press and Institute of Psycho-Analysis, 1962), p. 36n.

sensibility and power. Roland Barthes, with himself as the lover, essentially endorses the same view of the object's value and purpose:

> Enough that, in a flash, I should see the other in the guise of an inert object, like a kind of stuffed doll, for me to shift my desire from this annulled object to my desire itself; it is my desire I desire, and the loved being is no more than its tool.[21]

The object's purpose is to be the means by which the lover, the male, experiences himself: his desire. Girls, who also play with dolls, only learn to change diapers or arrange hair.

The object, the woman, goes out into the world formed as men have formed her to be used as men wish to use her. She is then a provocation. The object provokes its use. It provokes its use because of its form, determined by the one who is provoked. The carpenter makes a chair, sits on it, then blames the chair because he is not standing. When the object complains about the use to which she is put, she is told, simply and firmly, not to provoke. Antifeminist H. L. Mencken, in a response to the first wave of feminism, offered this generous solution:

> The way to put an end to the gaudy crimes that the suffragist alarmists talk about is to shave the heads of all the pretty girls in the world, and pluck out their eyebrows, and pull their teeth, and put them in khaki, and forbid them to wriggle on dance-floors, or to wear scents, or to use lip-sticks, or to roll their eyes.[22]

James Brain, an anthropologist who supports the second wave of feminism, asserts that women's bodies in themselves

> can seem to be signaling their readiness for sex at any time—a problem to which no one has any totally adequate answer, unless one considers the orthodox Muslim solution of completely covering a woman from head to foot in enveloping black garments to be one.[23]

Brain is absolutely clear that "[r]ape can never be condoned, excused, or justified. On the other hand, woman *[sic]* should realize the powerful effect that their clothes have in stimulating male sexual interests."[24] The wide wide world of male ideas again astonishes.

But it is left to Norman Mailer to proclaim the true nature and power of women who are made, not born: in particular, to focus on, explicate, and enthuse about the extraordinary tribute inherent in being used as a cunt (if and only if one is a woman) by a man. Mailer finds this tribute most exhilarating and indelible in the world of Henry Miller:

> In all of [Miller's] faceless, characterless, pullulating broads, in all those cunts which undulate with the movements of eels, in all those clearly described broths of soup and grease and marrow and wine which are all he will give us of them—their cunts are always closer to us than their faces—in all the indignities of position, the humiliation of situation, and the endless presentation of women as pure artifacts of farce, their asses all up in the air, still he screams his barbaric yawp of utter adoration for the power and the glory and the grandeur of the female in the universe, and it is his genius to show us that this power is ready to survive any context or abuse.[25]

The power Mailer refers to is the power to excite lust, to provoke the fuck, especially the power to cause erection: the appropriate sphere of power for a cunt, whether in the air or on the ground. For the fuck to exist, the cunt must exist: and abuse and humiliation only serve to enhance the cuntiness of a cunt, which is her power, glory, and so forth, no matter how horribly she is used or degraded. The appropriate use of an object—called cunt, instrument, tool, or woman—can never cease to be appropriate if the user correctly uses the object's nature and function. Objects exist or are made in order to be used: in this case, used so that the male can experience his desire, or his desire to desire, or his alienation from his desire, or his desire to enact desire, or his desire to play a stringed instrument or to roll a log, or his desire to make dependable response patterns to organismic behavioral objects. Women are used in the making and made in the using.

The love of or desire for or obsession with a sexual object is, in male culture, seen as a response to the qualities of the object itself. Since the first preoccupation is with the form of the object, men make great claims for the particular forms that provoke lust or the ability to fuck in them. What Becker refers to as a dependable response pattern, in the field of sexual psychology, is most often called objectification. Objectification is the accomplished fact: an internalized, nearly invariable response by the male to a form that is, in his estimation and experience, sufficiently whatever he needs to provoke arousal. The proper bounds of objectification as an appropriate response to an appropriate object are set by psychologists, the high priests of secular culture: the form of a woman, a composite of women's attributes, a part of a woman's body. Anything or anyone else is seen as some kind of substitute for a woman or the male-defined sexual parts of her body. It is inappropriate to substitute. Male supremacy depends on the ability of men to view women as sexual objects, and deviations from this exercise in male power and female oblivion are discouraged. Nevertheless, objectification occurs on a massive scale with regard to inappropriate objects: males, leather, rubber, underwear, and so on. Objectification—that fixed response to the form of another that has as its inevitable consequence erection—is really a value system that has ejaculation as its inexorable, if momentary, denouement. Objectification, carried by the male not only as if it were his personal nature but as if it were nature itself, denotes who or what the male loves to hate; who or what he wants to possess, act on, conquer, define himself in opposition to; where he wants to spill his seed. The primary target of objectification is the woman. In male culture, men do argue about the proper bounds of objectification, especially about the viability of objectifying other males; but men do not argue about the moral meaning of objectification as such. It is taken for granted that a sexual response is an objectified response: that is, a response aroused by an object with specific attributes that in themselves provoke sexual desire. Objectification is a rather sterile word for the phenomenon that Thomas Hardy explored in *The Well-Beloved:*

> To his Well-Beloved he had always been faithful, but she had had many embodiments. Each individuality known as Lucy, Jane, Flora, Evangeline, or whatnot, had been merely a transient condition of her. He did not recognize this as an excuse or as a defence, but as a fact simply. Essentially she was perhaps of no tangible substance; a spirit, a dream, a frenzy, a conception, an aroma, an epitomized sex, a light of the eye, a parting of the lips.[26]

Sometimes objectification operates on what appears to be a silly and commonplace level, as when Ernest Hemingway had his fourth wife, Mary Welsh, dye her reddish hair blond. As she recorded: "Deeply rooted in his field of esthetics was some mystical devotion to blondness, the blonder the lovelier, I never learned why. He would have been ecstatic in a world of women dandelions."[27] Sometimes objectification is clearly sinister, for instance when it signifies, as it often does, racial hatred. As Robert Stoller points out, not necessarily with aversion, ". . . some people need the excremental: . . . to choose people they consider fecal (e.g., black, Jewish, poor, uneducated, prostituted)."[28] Stoller's formulation refers to those instances where objectification of the despised category facilitates intercourse. Jean-Paul Sartre describes the same sort of objectification with reverse consequences: "Some men are suddenly struck with impotence if they learn from the woman with whom they are making love that she is a Jewess. There is a disgust for the Jew, just as there is a disgust for the Chinese or the Negro among certain people."[29] The relationship between the supposedly silly and commonplace objectification of blonds as beautiful and the sinister objectification of those considered in some way filth is, of course, a direct one: the same value system is embodied in this range of sexual obsession, sexual response. With this value system in mind, it becomes clear that the love of blonds is in fact as socially significant as, and inseparable from, the hatred of those who are seen to embody opposite qualities or characteristics. Objectification, in fact and in consequence, is never trivial.

Men, perpetually searching to justify their perpetual search for objects that move them to experience their own desire transmuted to power, claim especially to love beauty as such; and under the formidable guise of aesthetic devotion, objectification is defended or presented as the recognition of the beautiful. Women ideally embody beauty: so the theory goes, even though men in practice seem to hate the female body per se. The notion that female beauty inspires male love is pervasive. One can hardly argue (so it seems) with the aesthetic values of the sublime artists of male culture who freeze the female form in time and render it exquisite, as in, for instance, the Venus de Milo, ancient Aphrodite, the women of Rubens, and so forth. It is nearly unconscionable to challenge, for instance, the aesthetic sensibility in Keats's exquisite "Ode on a Grecian Urn," where the object is first the urn itself, then the figures on it:

> Bold Lover, never, never canst thou kiss;
> Though winning near the goal—yet, do not grieve;
> She cannot fade, though thou hast not thy bliss,
> For ever wilt thou love, and she be fair![30]

The meaning of the male idealization of beauty is hidden by the very beauty of the art that proclaims woman, at her highest, a beautiful object. Keats has found the ideal crystallization of objectifying love: the bold lover perpetually desires the unchanging beauty of the unchanging female frozen in time; he will always love and she will always be fair; he will always love because she will always be fair. This same model of love is found in every soap and cosmetic commercial. In Keats, objectification is raised to its highest aesthetic level. With pinups too the bold lover will forever love and she be fair.

The love that the male feels for the ideal beauty is evoked (or provoked) by beauty itself. Scarcely any woman dares to ignore male ideas of ideal female beauty altogether because these ideas will significantly determine the quality and limits of any woman's life. But these ideas—which change from society to society or from time to time, or which exist in contrasting or opposing formulations at the same time within the same society—have a common premise: the object must be that which it is supposed to be; its behavior must be appropriate to its function. Inappropriate behavior ruins female beauty. Since women are capable of everything but permitted almost nothing (without the consequences of male revenge or grudge), acts that enhance the sensual or aesthetic dimension of a man become virtual physical stains on a woman. The one static standard of female beauty is that the woman must conform to the male's definition of her as an object with respect to function as well as form. George Sand, for instance, attributed her own lack of beauty in male eyes (and therefore her own) to her intellectual and physical activity. In so doing, she gives a still-accurate picture of what the female beauty in Western culture may be and of what she must not do:

> I had a sound constitution, and as a child seemed likely to become beautiful, a promise I did not keep. This was perhaps my fault, since at the age when beauty blossoms I was already spending my nights reading and writing. . . .
>
> Not to work so that my eyes would sparkle; not to run and play in the sun when God's sun attracts me so; not to walk in sturdy wooden shoes for fear of deforming my ankles; to wear gloves, that is, to renounce the quickness and strength of my hands; to doom myself to be clumsy and feeble; never to tire myself, when everything urges me to use up my energy; to live, in short, under a bell jar; to be neither burned, nor chapped, nor faded before my time—such things were always impossible for me.[31]

Reading and writing, especially writing, have been seen as the antithesis of beauty in the female, as deadly as cyanide. Physical activity, even when prohibited, has been better tolerated.

Women are reared, and often forced, to conform to the specific requirements of ideal beauty, whatever they are at any given time. From foot-binding to waist binding to breast binding, ideal beauty often requires deforming of the natural body. From clitoridectomy to breast enlargement or reduction to surgically altered noses, ideal beauty often requires mutilation of the natural body. From hair dyeing to face painting to necessary ornamentation (for instance, high-heeled shoes), ideal beauty often requires distortion or denial of the natural body. Ranging from idiocy to atrocity, any and all strategies are employed so that the natural female body will fit the male idea of ideal female beauty.

The mystification of female beauty in male culture knows no limit but one: somehow the beauty herself ends up dead or mutilated. Even an unregenerate materialist like Herbert Marcuse cannot stay earthbound when expostulating on beauty personified in the female—in this case Medusa, cut into pieces by Perseus:

> As desired object, the beautiful pertains to the domain of the primary instincts, Eros and Thanatos. The mythos links the adversaries: pleasure and terror. Beauty has the power to check aggression: it forbids and immobilizes the aggressor. The beautiful Medusa petrifies him who confronts her. "Poseidon, the god with azure locks, slept with her in a soft meadow on a bed with springtime flowers" [Hesiod, *Theogony*, trans. Norman O. Brown]. She is slain by Perseus, and from her truncated body springs the winged horse Pegasus, symbol of poetic imagination.[32]

Poetry, the genre of purest beauty, was born of a truncated woman: her head severed from her body with a sword, a symbolic penis, so that poetry is born not only of a dead woman but of one sadistically mutilated. Poe, whose debt to Perseus cannot be overestimated, wrote that "[t]he death of a beautiful woman is, unquestionably, the most poetical topic in the world."[33] The function of beauty in the realm of the so-called erotic was further elucidated by Bataille when he wrote: "Beauty is desired in order that it may be befouled; not for its own sake, but for the joy brought by the certainty of profaning it."[34] Beauty, then, consistently has meaning in the sphere of female death or violation. An object is always destroyed in the end by its use when it is used to the fullest and enough; and in the realm of female beauty, the final value of the object is precisely to be found in its cruel or deadly destruction.

Female knowledge of objectification usually stops at a necessary but superficial understanding: beauty is rewarded and lack of beauty is punished. The punishments are understood as personal misfortune; they are not seen as systematic, institutional, or historical. Women do not understand that they are also punished through sexual use for being beautiful; and women do not understand the lengths to which men go to protect themselves and their society from contamination by ugly women who do not induce a lustful desire to punish, violate, or destroy, though men manage to punish, violate, or destroy these women anyway. The Goncourt brothers, honored as authorities both on women and on eighteenth-century France, praised the eighteenth-century convent as "a refuge rather than a prison," benign because it kept women scarred by smallpox out of the sight of men:

> [The convent] is above all the haven of broken lives, the almost obligatory asylum of women suffering from small-pox, a malady all but forgotten to-day, but one which disfigured a good quarter of the women of that time. Society, with every argument at its command, and the family, with every conceivable exhortation, urged the victim of this scourge toward the obscurity of the cloister. Even her mother consented, out of love, to surrender her luckless child, whose unsightliness excluded her from society and who ended by submitting to the pitiless precept of the time—"An ill-favored woman is a being without state in Nature or place in the world."[35]

According to the Goncourts, two hundred thousand women or more, called *laiderons* ("foul faces"), were locked up in eighteenth-century French convents. The ostracism and exclusion of women who are not perceived as beautiful enough to be desirable from work and social participation is the modern equivalent of segregating the *laiderons;* instead of being locked in, the modern *laideron* is locked out.

Since the value of the object is finally in its violation or destruction, it is no surprise to find that there are men who have sexually objectified the woman who is that violated object: especially the prostitute ravaged by the life or the racially degraded woman, both of whom are seen as pure and dangerous sexuality, used, reeking with violation. This woman is the sexual object for those men who want to violate, as Baudelaire expressed it, the abominable:

> Woman is hungry and wishes to eat. Thirsty
> and wishes to drink.
> She is in heat and wishes to be fucked.
> Is that not splendid?
> Woman is natural, that is to say abominable.[36]

The prostitute is the emblematic used woman, natural in that she most purely fulfills her sexual function; the despised—by virtue of race, class, or ethnicity—compose the bulk of the prostituted; prostitution signifies in and of itself male power in every sphere and constitutes in and of itself a bedrock of sexual excitement. As Flaubert wrote: "It is perhaps a perverted taste, but I love prostitution for itself and independently of what it means underneath. I've never been able to see one of these women, in low-cut dresses, pass, beneath the light of the gas lamps, without my heart beating fast."[37] But it is precisely what prostitution means "underneath" that makes for the excitement. At the end of *Sentimental Education*, Flaubert's novel about the passage of male youths into cynical maturity, Frédéric and Deslauriers, two great friends, remember the first time they visited a brothel: ". . . the very pleasure of seeing at a single glance so many women at his disposal affected [Frédéric] so powerfully that he turned deathly pale, and stood still, without saying a word."[38] The whores laugh, he runs, and since he has the money, his friend is compelled to follow him. The novel ends as the two men agree that "[t]hat was the happiest time we ever had."[39] Looking back, they realize that they had never again experienced such a formidable sense of power, such an absolute recognition of the meaning of their masculinity, and that this feeling constituted happiness.

The prostitute is seen as the antithesis of the man. In Baudelaire's language, the man is civilized, the dandy; the woman is natural, the abominable. The language changes from writer to writer, but what remains constant is that this intense sense of estrangement from the female provides the necessary basis for sexual excitement. The woman whom the male knows as a person, not as object, can never, as Havelock Ellis puts it, be "a real girl":

> But only the girl with whom one has not grown up from childhood, and become accustomed to, can ever be to us in the truly sexual sense, a real girl. That is to say, she alone can possess these powerful stimuli to the sense of sexual desirability, never developed in the people one has grown unconsciously used to, which are essential to the making of a real girl.[40]

Ellis goes on to claim that this inability to be aroused by a girl *(sic)* with whom one has grown up has biological origins in both man and lower animals. The baboon-next-door, apparently, is not "a real girl" either.

For Becker "the making of a real girl" distinguishes man from other animals; "the making of a real girl" takes on sublime significance as man searches for meaning and especially for a meaningful sense of his own importance. Becker is simply more abstract than Ellis:

> No ontology of human striving can be complete without discussing what is most peculiar to man—the urge to love. When we understand that man is the only animal who must *create* meaning, who must open a wedge into neutral nature, we already understand the essence of love. Love is the problem of an animal who must *find* life, *create* a dialogue with nature in order to experience his own being. It is another dimension of the need to be brought into the world, by being brought into contact with life at its quickest and most striking. As Spinoza saw, love is the increase of self by means of the object. Love is the sentiment of a peculiarly alienated animal, one who is separate from the natural, instinctive process, and must be urged back into the world.[41]

The intense and obsessive use of person as object is seen as the solution to man's alienation—not as the source of it nor as one of its most numbing manifestations.

Not only does "love . . . increase [the] self by means of the object"; but the fact of objectification—this diminished capacity to perceive and respond to life—is viewed as a key and dynamic element of individuality. Since men characteristically respond only to sexual fragments, bits and pieces, slivers of flesh costumed this way or that, this very incapacity is consistently transformed into one of love's defining virtues. Krafft-Ebing, a pioneering sexologist currently out of fashion (unlike Kinsey and Ellis) because his goal was to move sexual deviation out of the realm of the criminal into the realm of the medical (not into the realm of the normal), enunciated a still-current appraisal of the value of objectification:

> In the considerations concerning the psychology of the normal sexual life in the first chapter of this work it was shown that, within psychological limits, the pronounced preference for a certain portion of the body of persons of the opposite sex, particularly for a certain form of this part, may attain great psychosexual importance. Indeed, the especial power of attraction possessed by certain forms and peculiarities for many men—in fact, the majority—may be regarded as the real principle of individualism in love.[42]

The automatic, predetermined, fixed, intransigent response to a particular form or part of the body is supposed to be a manifestation of individuality rather than a paralyzation of individuality. The male's individuality, in effect, can be reckoned by how little he responds to, how little he perceives, how little he values. Sexual myopia, then, becomes the paradigm for individuality.

Sexologist C. A. Tripp very much in fashion, considers male sexual objectification an evolutionary high point: ". . . the selection of a particular partner whose smallest details may be so invested with meaning as to bring a person's *[sic]* sexual response to fever pitch—represents more than a culmination of individual development. It can also be seen as the culmination of a trend in evolution."[43] In Tripp's rather surreal portrait of progress, the person in question is male, since Tripp, a disciple of Kinsey, insists that women have virtually no sex drive at all; and psychologists of all persuasions concur that real objectification is a male event, since objectification is necessary for arousal and arousal always means erection. Objectification signifies the male's capacity for individualism and also his extreme selectivity and discernment, most clear, according to Tripp, in the situation of the homosexual male, where both partners by definition objectify:

> Homosexual promiscuity, in particular, frequently entails a remarkable amount of discrimination. Even a person who never wants a second contact with any of his partners may spend much time selecting from dozens or even hundreds of possibilities. In fact, some of the most promiscuous individuals sustain considerable frustration not from any lack of opportunity but from being exceedingly selective.[44]

Tripp believes that this evolutionary summit has a biological source: "The cortical organization of human *[sic]* sexuality is such that it eventually becomes keyed to specific cues, or to whole contexts of association."[45] The cortical organization of the male—responsible in Tripp's view for the fact of sexual objectification and all its attendant virtues (individuality, selectivity, discrimination, and promiscuity itself)—is superior to that of the female, who lumbers along with her mere capacity for unlimited orgasm and her dull taste for personality. Tripp's phrase "whole contexts of association," which sounds expansive rather than constricting, in reality means a program, a scenario, a response to preordained events that must proceed according to script for the male to maintain arousal. "On close examination," Tripp explains, fully articulating the wisdom of our time, "nearly every adult's *[sic]* highest level of response is limited to relatively few situations that fulfill specific personal demands—demands that are decidedly fetishlike in character."[46]

And, in that case, what is it in this loved body which has the vocation of a fetish for me?
Roland Barthes, *A Lover's Discourse*

The word *fetish* comes from the Portuguese *feitiço*, which means "charm" or "made thing." A fetish is a magical, symbolic object. Its first meaning is religious: the magical object is regarded with irrational, extreme, extravagant trust or reverence (to paraphrase Merriam-Webster). In its sexual meaning, the magic of the fetish is in its power to cause and sustain penile erection. In *The Outer Fringe of Sex*, Maurice North offers a neutral definition of fetishism:

> a preference for a particular part of the body not directly entering into coitus, an article of clothing or some other extrasexual object or combination of any of the aforementioned that is carried to the point where this *fetish-object* becomes dominant in the individual's sex life, or without which sexual satisfaction is incomplete or impossible.[47]

Krafft-Ebing, in his definition, reveals a preoccupation with perpetuating heterosexual intercourse as the norm of sexual behavior:

> The concentration of the sexual interest on a certain portion of the body that has no direct relation to sex (as have breasts and external genitals)—a peculiarity to be emphasized—often leads body-fetishists to such a condition that they do not regard coitus as the real means of sexual gratification, but rather some form of manipulation of that portion of the body that is effectual as a fetish.[48]

Fetishism is seen as an inappropriate narrowing of sexual responsiveness; objectification is seen as an appropriate narrowing of sexual responsiveness. The two are not really distinct at all; they reveal a continuum of incapacity. Fetishism too, as part of the male condition, is dignified as a sign of the human condition: "Fetishism, in other words," writes Becker, "represents a relatively desperate attempt by a limited organism to come to grips in some satisfying way with a portion of reality. And, of course, the more limited the reality is, the more striking and overpowering—as when a cat singles out a robin on a lawn."[49]

The image of the cat hunting the robin is not, of course, either accidental or irrelevant. The fetish is the magical object that causes erection. The irrational, extreme, extravagant trust or reverence felt by the male is not for the fetish object but for the erection. The fetish is valued because it consistently enables penile erection. Sex itself—behavior toward the fetish—remains predatory, hostile; it is the use of things to experience self. This usage and hostility when directed at real objects are considered, in the main, abnormal; when directed at whole women or their breasts or genitals it is considered normal and appropriate.

Freud claimed that "the fetish is a substitute for the woman's (the mother's) penis that the little boy once believed in and—for reasons familiar to us [fear of castration]—does not want to give up."[50] Storr suggests that the fetish stands in for female genitals, "since the fetishist feels towards the fetish the same excitement and fascination which is aroused by the genital organs in the normal male."[51] Since in Storr's view fetishes substitute for female genitals, the fetishes themselves are likely to be feminine symbols, especially articles of clothing particularly associated with women. "Women," Storr claims, using the common, solipsistic argument of psychologists, "have no need of fetishes because they do not have to achieve or sustain an erection."[52] Storr maintains, however, that women do use fetishes—to attract men: "[a] fetish may, as it were, be a flag hung out by the woman to proclaim her sexual availability . . ."[53] Since there is virtually no bodily part or piece of apparel or substance that is not fetishized by some men somewhere, it would be hard indeed for a woman not to hang out a flag without going naked, which would be construed as definitely hanging out a flag. From underwear to rubber boots and raincoats to leather belts to long hair to all varieties of shoes to feet in and of themselves: all these and more are fodder for male fetishists. The fact is that men can and do fetishize everything; and no woman can possibly know how to match up any given man with any given fetish, nor how to anticipate, nor how to avoid, "provoking" sexual arousal due to a fetishized response. What women can know, but do not sufficiently appreciate, is that common male fetishes determine female fashion: attracting a male through acceptable style or dress means that one has conformed to the requirements of one or more common male fetishes. Combat boots and dung-colored rags do the same.

Kinsey, in his volume on the human female, categorizes fetishism as "an almost exclusively male phenomenon"; then he softens the meaning by a gender-neutral description of what fetishism entails:

> Persons who respond only or primarily to objects which are remote from the sexual partner, or remote from the overt sexual activities with a partner, are not rare in the population. This is particularly true of individuals who are erotically aroused by high heels, by boots, by corsets, by tight clothing, by long gloves, by whips, or by other objects which suggest sado-masochistic relationships . . .[54]

All of the fetishes listed by Kinsey, in the male frame of reference, suggest bondage. As with Becker's image of the cat ready to pounce on the robin, the sexual meaning attributed to the fetish cannot exist outside a context of power and predation.

The shoe is a commonly fetishized article of dress, though how the shoe comes to substitute for the female is a male mystery. Charles Winick suggests that

> [t]he shoe is the one item of costume which reflects gender most sensitively, perhaps because the foot's position in the shoe is so analogous to the position of the sexual organs during intercourse.[55]

Explanations like Winick's are commonplace in the literature on foot and shoe fetishism: note the logic or absence thereof. Also note the elevation of male obsession into the sphere of the meaningful.

All kinds of shoes are fetishized, but in the West the high-heeled shoe and the boot have the widest, most enduring significance. Lars

Ullerstam, in *The Erotic Minorities*, writes that "[w]hen women's fashion decrees high-heeled boots, many men walk the streets with a permanent erection."[56] "Women's fashion" is a euphemism for fashion created by men for women; the failure to follow the dicta of this fashion has severe economic repercussions for any woman. The clear, unavoidable male concern with female footwear demonstrates the scale of male fascination with female feet. Hannah Tillich, with her characteristic good humor, noted the extraordinary effect her bare feet had on Paul Tillich:

> When I took off my shoes, Paulus became ecstatic about my feet. In later years, I often said that if I hadn't walked barefoot with him that day, we would never have married. That was after I had learned that his preoccupation with feet had always been extraordinary.[57]

The Chinese were preoccupied with feet for a thousand years, during which they bound and crippled the feet of young girls and the deformed foot was the main focus of sexual interest. The bound foot was the fetish; the binding and the sexual use of the crippled female were saturated with the values of bondage and conquest. The preoccupation in the West with high-heeled shoes is no less ominous.

The sexual fetish often has a function that obscures its significance as a magical cause of erection. The shoe, for instance, is seen by women in many ways, but almost never as a magical cause of erection in the male. Some women even wear shoes because the streets are dirty or cold or dangerous to the bare foot. The cultural level on which the fetish manifests varies greatly. Paul Tillich, for instance, was a great Christian thinker. Underneath the high-minded, humanistic philosophizing was a grimmer reality, as Hannah Tillich revealed in her memoir:

> The old man [Paul Tillich] had pushed the buttons on his custom-made screen. There was the familiar cross shooting up the wall. "So fitting for a Christian and a theologian," she [Hannah Tillich] sneered. A naked girl hung on it, hands tied

> in front of her private parts. Another naked figure lashed the crucified one with a whip that reached further to another cross, on which a girl was exposed from behind. More and more crosses appeared, all with women tied and exposed in various positions. Some were exposed from the front, some from the side, some from behind, some crouched in fetal position, some head down, or legs apart, or legs crossed—and always whips, crosses, whips.[58]

Which comes first, the fetish or the philosophy, is an unsolvable riddle: but every fetish, expressed on whatever level, manifests the power of the erect penis, especially its power in determining the sensibility of the male himself, his ethical as well as his sexual nature. Since men never judge ethical capacity on the basis of justice toward women, the sexual meaning of the fetish remains subterranean, while on the cultural level the fetish is expanded into myth, religion, idea, aesthetics, all necessarily and intrinsically male-supremacist. The uniting theme is the hatred expressed toward women.

MALE CULTURE THRIVES on argument and prides itself on distinctions. Objectification is natural, normal, to be encouraged; fetishism is unnatural, abnormal, to be discouraged. But surely fetishism proceeds logically from objectification: and if the perception of persons as objects is not a crime against the person so perceived, then there is no crime, because every violation of the female proceeds from this so-called normal phenomenon. And, in the final analysis, it must be recognized that the woman is the fetish, not just object, but magical charm, charged with symbolic meaning: the made thing that most consistently provokes erection. In Marcuse's words (arguing *against* the mysticism of Norman O. Brown's *Love's Body*): "This is it. The woman, the land is here on earth, to be found here on earth, living and dying, female for male, distinguished, particular, tension to be renewed, Romeo's and Don Juan's, self and another, yours or mine, fulfillment in alienation."[59]

Mother, whore, beauty, abomination, nature or ornament, she is the thing in contradistinction to which the male is human. Without her as fetish—the charmed object—the male, including the male homosexual, would be unable to experience his own selfhood, his own power, his own penile presence and sexual superiority. Male homosexual culture consistently uses the symbolic female—the male in drag, effeminacy as a style, the various accoutrements that denote female subjection—as part of its indigenous environment, as a touchstone against which masculinity can be experienced as meaningful and sublime. Male homosexuals, especially in the arts and in fashion, conspire with male heterosexuals to enforce the male-supremacist rule that the female must be that made thing against which the male acts to experience himself as male. Woman is not born; she is made. In the making, her humanity is destroyed. She becomes symbol of this, symbol of that: mother of the earth, slut of the universe; but she never becomes herself because it is forbidden for her to do so. No act of hers can overturn the way in which she is consistently perceived: as some sort of thing. No sense of her own purpose can supercede, finally, the male's sense of her purpose: to be that thing that enables him to experience raw phallic power. In pornography, his sense of purpose is fully realized. She is the pinup, the centerfold, the poster, the postcard, the dirty picture, naked, half-dressed, laid out, legs spread, breasts or ass protruding. She is the thing she is supposed to be: the thing that makes him erect. In literary and cinematic pornography, she is taught to be that thing: raped, beaten, bound, used, until she recognizes her true nature and purpose and complies—happily, greedily, begging for more. She is used until she knows only that she is a thing to be used. This knowledge is her authentic erotic sensibility: her erotic destiny. The more she is a thing, the more she provokes erection; the more she is a thing, the more she fulfills her purpose; her purpose is to be the thing that provokes erection. She starts out searching for love or in love with love. She finds love as men understand it in being the thing men use. As Mario, the master eroticist in the film *Emmanuelle*, says to the heroine after he has had her repeatedly raped and used: "Real love is the erection, not the orgasm." As Adrienne Rich wrote: "No one has imagined us."[60]

5

Force

Indeed the Pentateuch is a long painful record of war, corruption, rapine, and lust. Why Christians who wished to convert the heathen to our religion should send them these books, passes all understanding. It is most demoralizing reading for children and the unthinking masses, giving all alike the lowest possible idea of womanhood, having no hope nor ambition beyond conjugal unions with men they scarcely knew, for whom they could not have had the slightest sentiment of friendship, to say nothing of affection.

Elizabeth Cady Stanton, *The Woman's Bible*

And it should be realised, too, that captives, animals or men *[sic]*, are not constantly absorbed by the notion of escape, for all their restless pacing behind the bars . . . The long glance, the unquiet step are only reflexes, brought about by habit or the size of their prison. Open the door that the bird, the squirrel, the wild beast have been eyeing, besieging, imploring, and instead of the leap, the sudden flurry of wings you expected, the disconcerted creature will stiffen and draw back into the depths of its cage. I had plenty of time to think, and I was constantly hearing the same grand, contemptuous, sarcastic words, shining links of a fine-wrought chain: "After all, you are perfectly free. . . ."

Colette, *My Apprenticeships*

There are two photographs, part of a four-page layout with text. In the first photograph, there are two women. The woman on the left is older. Her head is swathed in a black turban. Her skin is a tawny brown. Her race is ambiguous. From her ear hangs a shiny silver half-moon earring. From her neck, on a barely visible cord, is a small ivory tooth. Her body is draped in a bright red robe that has Oriental characters on it. The neck of the robe is opened into a deep V but her breasts do not show. On her left wrist is a silver bracelet. On her left hand are two large silver rings. In her left hand is a pair of silver scissors. One finger of her left hand appears to touch the pubic area of the second woman. The scissors, held between the thumb and first finger, are slightly raised above the pubic area. Her right hand, with one large silver ring, holds up a black garter, unfastened to provide access to the pubic area of the second woman. The first woman's eyes are downcast so that only her heavily made-up eyelids show. Her eyes appear to be focused on the pubic area of the second woman. The first woman wears bright red lipstick the color of her robe and has nails painted the same color. The color is usually called blood red. The second woman has curly, light brown hair. She is clearly white-skinned. The text, titled "Barbered Pole," identifies her as Polish and turns her into an ethnic joke. She wears a red-and-black lace corset with black garters, one garter attached to the black nylon stocking on her right leg. Her left leg extends under the arm and behind the first woman, so that her legs are spread wide open. The garter belt on the left is unfastened and lifted up by the first woman and draped over her hand. The second woman wears a pinker shade of lipstick, her cheeks are very pink, her nails are painted blood red. Her exposed pubic area is just below the visual center of the photograph. The scissors poised above her pubic area are dead center. The second photograph is a close-up of the pubic area, which fills the whole frame: flesh, spread thighs, the vulva. The vulva is pink and highlighted. The scissors rest right next to the vulva, pointed toward it. A comb with hair in its teeth is just above the vaginal opening. It is held by a hand with bloodred fingernails, one of which is pointed toward the vulva. Most of the hair has been cut or shaved away (in accompanying photographs), except for a discernible V pattern right above the vulva. Red specks that could be blood or bruises or cuts are on the skin of the inner thighs. The text in part reads: "When Katherina was asked why she was having her pubic hair styled, she told us that it was purely for her own self."

The first woman is defined through age, color, and activity. She is old in the male value system, beyond sexual desirability. She is used, hardened, potentially dangerous yet performing a menial service. Her proper sexual role is to prepare, to groom, a younger woman for sexual service. She is a woman of color, though it is not clear which color. Turban, ivory tooth, heavy silver jewelry with the half-moon earring, Oriental characters on her robe, a gypsylike appearance as if a fortune-teller, suggest that she is an old witch woman filled with racial mysteries, malice, and magic—a prototypical female figure in the racist imagination. Both her servility and hostility to the white woman are articulated in the activity she performs, menial in relation to the white woman yet also potentially dangerous to her. This is the classic situation of the racially degraded servant: her literal ability to hurt the one she serves is, in a moment, absolute, but she cannot survive beyond the literal act because her group is powerless, she will be destroyed, and so she serves.

The white woman—Polish, in ethnic humor characterized as extremely stupid—stares into the camera with an unflinching gaze, with no hint of embarrassment, modesty, or shame. She is unafraid. She wants what she is getting. She is, in a literal sense, imperiled, at the mercy of the woman of color, but she does not even acknowledge her. The Polish joke in the layout may be that the Polish woman thinks that all of this is "purely for her own self."

The white woman is the whore, the sexual object of the moment. The woman of color is the sexual veteran. The woman of color is the menial. The white woman is the boss. The older woman is the preparer. The younger woman is the thing prepared. In the realm of age, the relationship parodies the mother-daughter arrangement in the male-supremacist system: the mother teaches her daughter how to groom herself or grooms her; the mother is the carrier and enforcer of male aesthetic values vis-à-vis the female body; the mother's success is measured by the daughter's success in becoming what the mother has tried to make her. The older woman has the weapon in her hand. Still, the older woman serves. The one she actually serves is not pictured.

These are two women together, within the male framework a lesbian scenario. No male figure as such is present. The scissors are the explicit phallic presence (*vagina* means sheath). The scissors are poised near the entrance to the vagina, as the comb, also a phallic object, is poised above it. Pressed against the skin, the scissors cut the hair so close to the skin that the skin is left bruised or cut. The teeth of the comb suggest vagina dentata. The ivory tooth hanging from the neck of the older woman suggests the same, removed from the genitals and generalized to the whole personality.

The two photographs posit an all-female sadism. The lesbian motif is supposed to mean that the values in the photographs really have to do with women, not men. The threat of the scissors gives testimony to the fact that in the male mind two women cannot be together without a phallic third, but despite this reassuring expression of phallic faith, two women without a man purposefully underlines the femaleness of the sexuality pictured. The older woman's cruelty is conveyed especially by the scissors but the younger woman is also cruel, hard, tough. These are the same woman, one younger, one older, one white, one of color. They are the shameless women of sex, the whores whose carnality is assaultive in its arrogance. They are lesbian—purely female—bitches. They are lesbian—purely masculine—bitches. The scissors suggest or promise phallic penetration but they also suggest or promise castration, women with scissors aimed at the genitals. Female genital mutilation (practiced widely, mother to daughter, in sections of the Third World) and the castrating phallic woman (fantasized so energetically in this world) are conjured up simultaneously. The V shape of the hair that is left suggests vulva, vagina, and also victory. The victory of the vagina over the male is a castrating victory. These are the cruel women.

The absence of men from the photographs encourages the belief that men are seeing women as they really are, in private, with each other—a pure female sexuality, a basic carnality usually hidden by the dull conventions of civilization, that tamer of the female. The underlying message is that the female in her pure sexuality is sadistic, a conviction articulated not only by the pornographers but also by the enlightened philosophers of sex on all levels. The Christians called women carnal and evil and killed nine million as witches. The enlightened thinkers secularize the conviction, turn faith to idea. According to women's best friend, Havelock Ellis, in his classic *Studies in the Psychology of Sex*, female sadism is a biologically evident norm, while male sadism is abnormal, unnatural, manifesting in civilization:

> In that abnormal sadism which appears from time to time among civilized human beings it is nearly always the female who becomes the victim of the male. But in the normal sadism which occurs throughout a large part of nature it is nearly always the male who is the victim of the female. It is the male spider who impregnates the female at the risk of his life and sometimes perishes in the attempt; it is the male bee who, after intercourse with the queen, falls dead from that fatal embrace, leaving her to fling aside his entrails and calmly pursue her course. *If it may seem to some that the course of our inquiry leads us to contemplate with equanimity, as a natural phenomenon, a certain semblance of cruelty in man in his relation to woman, they may, if they will, reflect that this phenomenon is but a very slight counterpoise to that cruelty which has been naturally exerted by the female on the male long even before man began to be.*[1] [Italics mine]

Ellis, like so many other male thinkers contemplating the human female, looks to various insects and eight-legged things. Here he has contradicted his main thesis, which is that natural (biological) human sex requires a forceful or cruel male and a woman who pretends to resist or does resist and must be conquered. But he contradicts himself for a purpose: to justify the male force used against women in sex by positing a more fundamental female sadism.

Robert Briffault, author of *The Mothers: The Matriarchal Theory of Social Origins* and another best friend of women, turns to camels and crabs to posit an equality of sexual sadism in male and female:

> With both the male and the female, "love," or sexual attraction, is originally and preëminently "sadic"; it is positively gratified by the infliction of pain; it is as cruel as hunger. That is the direct, fundamental, and longest established sentiment connected with the sexual impulse. The male animal captures, mauls and bites the female, who in turn uses her teeth and claws freely, and the "lovers" issue from the sexual combat bleeding and mangled. Crustaceans usually lose a limb or two in the encounter. All mammals without exception use their teeth on these occasions. Pallas describes the mating of camels: as soon as impregnation has taken place, the female, with a vicious snarl, turns round and attacks the male with her teeth, and the latter is driven away in terror.[2]

The equality of sadism here is patently false: the male animal does the capturing; the poor female camel is a bit late in terrorizing the male—she is already pregnant and barefoot, as it were. But a basis is clearly established for fearing the sexual sadism of the female. The hit-and-run sexuality of the human male seems, in this context, a reasonable attempt to save life and limb from the sadistic treachery of the female. Of course, it would make more sense if he were attempting to fuck a camel.

The more contemporary advocates of crawling, swimming, and flying things as illuminators of human sexual and social behavior take an unambiguous stand in favor of the male as the consummate biological sadist: naturally, they pick bugs, fish, and fowl appropriate to their point of view. Essentially, they maintain that the women's movement is biologically deviant: if women were capable of *taking* power (taking power seen exclusively as a function of inherent sexual sadism), then perhaps women might even be capable of using and maintaining power. Since this idea is repugnant, the strategy of this particular male-supremacist clique is to assert that it is a biological impossibility for females to use sexual force, that is, to be sexually controlling or dominant. In *Sexual Politics*, Kate Millett gave a representative example of this way of thinking. She described the so-called cichlid effect, ". . . a theory of human sexuality modeled on the reactions of a prehistoric fish whom Konrad Lorenz examined to conclude that male cichlids failed to find the courage to mate unless the female of their species responded with 'awe.'" Millett notes that "[h]ow one measures 'awe' in a fish is a question perhaps better left unanswered . . ."[3] The use of the cichlid to buttress male sexual supremacy—not to mention the multitudes of insects that people Edward O. Wilson's *Sociobiology: The New Synthesis*—may be seen to indicate either a new militancy or a new desperation on the part of those who look to other species to justify male domination.

Psychiatrists and psychologists, however, still postulate a basic female sadism. Their proof is clinical, that is, deduced or imagined from what they observe in patients. Bruno Bettelheim suggests that in females sexual sadism would naturally lead to self-mutilation:

> The desires of our little boys indeed suggest that some men would excise part of the female sex organs if not prevented. But the example of the girl who had to take special precautions to prevent herself from tearing off her own clitoris raises a doubt as to whether this far-reaching mutilation also may not be re-enforced at least in part by desires that spring up autonomously in women.[4]

Bettelheim's generalization from the behavior of one disturbed girl expresses a wish, one also expressed in the photographs, scissors in the hand of a woman aimed at the genitals of a woman.

Robert Stoller, concerned ultimately with the paradisical heterosexual adjustment of angry women, posits, much as Briffault did, a sexual sadism that manifests in both males and females. He is particularly contemptuous of women who fail to meet elementary standards of humanism because they think that males alone are sadistic:

> Belle [Stoller's prototypical female] suffered endlessly from her anger at males and envy at their happier lot, without hope that she could move from her inferior position and ashamed that she mismanaged these issues. Yet she discovered that knowing men to be sadists (she did not make that up), she was using that knowledge to read sadism into all our acts. And that

> is propaganda, whether used for social causes or for masturbation.
>
> Women, too, are sadists; she ignored that. Humans, whether by nature or nurture, are often villains. Big news.[5]

Actually, this is "big news" to women whose lives are circumscribed by the sexual sadism of males; but it is good news to those males who justify their abuse of women by believing that women are sexually sadistic at heart and that the sadism of women is formidable despite the fact that it is not socially or historically self-evident. The cage is justified because the animal inside it is wild and dangerous. The sexual philosophers, like the pornographers, need to believe that women are more dangerous than men or as dangerous as men so as to be justified in their social and sexual domination of them. As long as this alleged female sadism is controlled by men, it can be manipulated to give men pleasure: dominance in the male system is pleasure.

At the same time, essential to this gratification on some level is the illusion that the women are not controlled by men but are acting freely. The photographs of the two women are a peek through a keyhole. The conceit is that since the male is not in the photographs, the women are doing what they want to do willfully and for themselves: "When Katherina was asked why she was having her pubic hair styled, she told us that it was purely for her own self." What women in private want to do just happens to be what men want them to do. This is the meanest theme of pornography: the elucidation of what men insist is the secret, hidden, true carnality of women, free women. When the secret is revealed, the whore is exposed. The woman in private (female privacy as a state of being that is emphasized when two females are pictured together without a male) is, in fact, the shameless slut, all life and value in the vagina, all pride in the genitals, the scissors the appropriate tool of entry. Cut the castrating woman before she cuts. Coleridge's "willing suspension of disbelief" operates more consistently in the viewing of pornography than it ever has in the reading of literature. The willing suspension of disbelief is crucial. Without it, one might remember that this rendition of women in private is not women in private at all, but women in makeup and costumes under hot lights in uncomfortable positions posed before a camera behind which is a photographer behind whom is a publisher behind whom is a multibillion-dollar industry behind which are rich lawyers claiming that the photographs are constitutionally protected speech essential to human freedom behind whom are intellectuals who find all of this revolutionary behind all of whom—except the models—are women who launder their underwear and clean their toilets. Indeed, to be a consumer of pornography one must be adept at suspending disbelief. Should disbelief prove stubborn and not easy to suspend, the knowledge that the models posed for money provides confirmation that they are whores and then the photographs are a simple expression of a general truth. For the viewer who remembers that the photographs are artificial constructs, the photographs prove what the photographs show: that women are whores, dumb and evil whores at that; that women like to whore; that women choose to whore. The harlot nature of women is authenticated by the very existence of the photographs. *Harlot* as an adjective means "not subject to control."[6] The imperative is clear: the harlot nature of women must be controlled or the castrating potential of these wild women might run amok. The scissors might be pointed in another direction. The very illusion that these are free women doing what they want creates an inevitable necessity: these females, basically cruel, must be controlled, and any strategy that effectively controls them is warranted because they have no recognizable civilized sensibility or intellectual capacity—they are wild. Finally, of course, the male can relax: the photographs themselves are his proof that male control has fully contained and subdued any authentic female sexuality.

The photographs also document a rape, a rape first enacted when the women were set up and used; a rape repeated each time the viewer consumes the photographs. As described by Elizabeth Janeway, ". . . one of the charms of pornography is that it records session after session of guiltless rape in which the powerful are licensed to have their will of the weak because the weak 'really like it that way.'"[7] The weak are women as a class—economically, socially, and sexually degraded as a given condition of birth: and the women in these photographs graphically embody devotion to the male sexual system that uses them. "Really liking it that way" is the ultimate survival necessity of women raped as a matter of course—women who exist to be used by men, as these models do. "The essence of rape," as Suzanne Brøgger wrote, ". . . lies not in the degree of psychological and physical force . . . but in the very *attitude* toward women that makes disguised or undisguised rape possible. The same attitude that requires a woman to be dead, or at least a bloody mess, before she has earned the right to be considered a victim at all."[8] The essence of rape, then, is in the conviction that no woman, however clearly degraded by what she does, is a victim. If the harlot nature of the female is her true nature, then nothing that signifies or reveals that nature is either violating or victimizing. The essence of rape is in the conviction that such photographs—in any way, to any degree—show a female sexuality independent of male power, outside the bounds of male supremacy, uncontaminated by male force. The rape of women who appear to "really like it that way" by camera is the first definition of the female as victim in contemporary society—not dead, not a bloody mess. Not yet.

There are two photographs, part of a four-picture, two-page layout with text. In the first photograph, a woman stands upright. The front of her body faces the camera directly. Her head is tilted slightly backwards and turned to the left, so that she is looking up. Her eyes are black. Her eye makeup is thick and black, emphasizing the blackness of her eyes. Her hair is black, thick, and wavy. Her lips are full. Her skin is olive in some places, brown in others, depending on how the light falls. Her nipples are dark and so is her pubic hair which is abundant. Her breasts are full. She wears black high heels, spiked, that appear to be open at the toes, and black gloves that extend slightly past the elbows. Her arms are raised above her head. Her hands are chained together at the wrists and attached to a horizontal pole. Her body is bound in black straps: a V opening up from her crotch, wrapped around her waist, an upside-down V that crisscrosses between her breasts to form another V that disappears behind her neck. Zigzagged across her body, in front and behind, are bluish white laser beams. The woman is held stationary by the laser beams that cut across and behind her body. A second photograph shows the woman's naked ass and legs. The top border of the photograph is cropped just below the woman's waist. She is standing. Her legs are spread. She is wearing black spiked heels. Her ankles are manacled. The manacles are fastened by chains to a pole that runs across the top part of the photograph, blocked from view only where the woman's ass blocks it. The chains that fasten the woman to the pole are attached to the outside of each ankle and run perpendicular to the pole without any slack. The woman's skin is brown. Several laser beams appear to penetrate her vagina from behind. The rays of laser light converge from below at what appears to be the point of entry into the woman. It is as if the woman were hoisted on laser beams going into her vagina. The text explains that *Playboy* has eight foreign editions and that the favorite of the editors in the United States is the German one: when they pass the German edition on to their Porsche mechanic, "our car will—inexplicably—run that much better." *Playboy* editors in Munich "have a slightly different approach to eroticism, one that is a refreshing break from the home-grown variety. As you can see from these pictures, their taste runs to the technological." The woman is called "an exquisite volunteer."

The laser promises burning. The word "laser" is an acronym for *l*ight *a*mplification by *s*timulated *e*mission of *r*adiation. Laser light is atomic light. Alex Mallow and Leon Chabot, in the *Laser Safety Handbook*, explain: "Light is produced by internal atomic actions, and a particular form of these internal actions generates laser light."[9] Laser light is especially distinguished from "regular" light—for instance, the light emitted from a light bulb—by its incredible intensity, the fact that it is light of a very pure color, that it manifests as a straight-arrow beam that can be directed with nearly absolute accuracy at any target near or far (for instance, according to *The New York Times*, March 3, 1980, the Pentagon is already developing laser weapons that can destroy tanks, aircraft, missiles, and orbiting satellites). The intensity of light emitted by a laser means that it also generates incredible heat. Laser light is burning light. In *The War of the Worlds*, H. G. Wells, with characteristic prescience, wrote of a ray that caused whatever it touched to burn. He called it "that pitiless sword of heat,"[10] a fairly good description of the modern laser. In popular culture, especially in science fiction and futuristic adventure films, a laser beam, emitted from a gun, will cause a person or thing to vaporize. Scientists have already acknowledged the laser as a potential antipersonnel weapon of astonishing destructive capability. Nehrich, Voran, and Dessel, in their basic book *Atomic Light: Lasers—What They Are and How They Work*, write that "[t]he use of the laser for a death ray cannot be avoided as a possibility. It stands to reason that a light ray powerful enough to penetrate steel could also burn through a nice soft human being."[11]

The amount of energy used in a laser does not indicate its power. In *Lasers: Tools of Modern Technology*, Ronald Brown explains: "A pulse from a ruby laser, focused by a lens, can blast a hole in steel plate a third of a centimeter thick, yet it does not contain enough energy to boil an egg. There is no contradiction here: although the total energy in a pulse is not very great, it is very highly concentrated."[12] According to O. S. Heavens in *Lasers:*

> The hazard of the high-power carbon dioxide laser—which will burn a hole through a firebrick in seconds—is an obvious one so far as danger to humans is concerned. Less obvious is the potential harm that can result from looking at say, a helium-neon laser beam of only *one thousandth of a watt*. Because the lens of the eye focuses the beam on to a minute spot on the retina, the intensity of illumination on the retinal cells could easily be high enough to cause damage.[13] [Italics mine]

In 1964, the United States Navy issued a report on hazards to laser personnel:

> Whether the laser is used in the laboratory as a research tool, in the field as a simulator or as a weapon, or in a space vehicle as a means of communication, its property of generating intense

> light, and therefore heat, constitutes a potential hazard to the personnel who use it.[14]

No reference is made, of course, to the use of the laser in pornography, but one must assume that the hazards are not mitigated by the fun factor.

O. S. Heavens summarizes the dangers of the laser as they are widely recognized by authorities in the field:

> What are the ways in which laser radiation will affect biological material? . . . First, the high intensity in a laser beam may produce heating, so producing a burn or even complete volatilisation of the material. Secondly, the laser beam may generate high-intensity acoustic (sound or ultrasonic) waves which may . . . damage material in the neighbourhood of the laser shot . . . Thirdly, the large electric field associated with the intense beam may affect the biological material. Fourthly, a pressure wave may spread out from the point of impact. Our present understanding of many of these effects is at a very primitive level . . .[15]

Nehrich, Voran, and Dessel stress the foolishness involved in underestimating the danger of any laser, however weak:

> It cannot be emphasized too strongly that there are many dangers in laser operations. Even the least powerful laser beam must be treated as potentially dangerous. It is not necessary, for example, to look directly into the laser beam in order to sustain eye damage. Accidental reflections from such things as wristwatch crystals, metal watch bands, buttons, jewels, or even a glossy enamelled surface may reflect a portion of the beam into someone's eye.[16]

Mallow and Chabot emphasize that "[e]lectrocution is a real possibility. Indeed, four documented electrocutions from laser-related activities have occurred in the United States."[17] In addition to citing dangers to eyes and skin and the possibility of electrical accidents, John F. Ready warns against another threat commonly mentioned in the literature on lasers: "there are hazards . . . from the poisonous materials which are used in many lasers and in laser-associated equipment. These potential dangers have to be balanced against the benefits to be gained from the use of lasers."[18] Mr. Ready, like the U.S. Navy in its report on the hazards of lasers, did not anticipate *Playboy*. Perhaps in science and warfare one must balance dangers against benefits, but in pornography there is no viable argument against whatever works in exciting the male. The importance of pornography to the human male is counted in gold; danger to the female is counted in feathers. After all, the use of laser beams to restrain and then apparently penetrate a woman is "a refreshing break from the home-grown variety" of pornography, and once the mechanic sees the photographs, "our car will—inexplicably—run that much better." Should one—inexplicably—argue that the use of the laser was both hazardous and gratuitous—and therefore too dangerous to be warranted—one would be wrong. It was only hazardous. It was not gratuitous.

The laser beams promise burning. The taste of some Germans has indeed run to the technological: ovens in which masses of Jews were exterminated. There was no laser in Hitler's time, but he and his men pioneered the field of technologically proficient mass extermination. The ethnic or racial identity of the model in this context becomes clear: she is a Jewish physical type. A racial as well as a sexual stereotype is exploited: she walks willingly into the oven. The technological dimension, according to the text, distinguishes the photographs as German; the technological dimension distinguished the German slaughter of the Jews from all other mass slaughters of the Jews. The technology used to kill is what made the numbers possible. The ambition of the Germans to exterminate the Jews was realized to such a staggering extent because of a commitment on the part of the Germans to a technology of extermination. The mention of the Porsche—apparently gratuitous—which "inexplicably" functions better, conjures up the German transport of the Jews.* She is the Jew, the willing victim:

*Ferdinand Porsche and his son Ferry developed assorted tanks for Hitler as well as a champion racing car and the Volkswagen. The Porsches worked for Krupp.

the Jews walked willingly into the ovens. She is the woman, the volunteer for bondage. Women, too, were burned en masse in Germany: the witchcraft persecutions. The manual character of those burnings meant that killing was slower. As described by Pennethorne Hughes in *Witchcraft:* "In almost every province of Germany the persecution raged with increasing intensity. Six hundred were said to have been burned by a single bishopric in Bamberg, where the special witch jail was kept fully packed. Nine hundred were destroyed in a single year in the bishopric of Würzburg, and in Nuremberg and other great cities there were one or two hundred burnings a year."[19] All Western Europe participated in the witch killings, but the mass slaughters were horribly fierce in Germany. For the most part, the witches were burned. The laser promises burning. The photographs reprinted from the German *Playboy*, like all pieces of pornography, do not exist in a historical vacuum. On the contrary, they exploit history—especially historical hatreds and historical suffering. The witches were burned. The Jews were burned. The laser burns. Jew and woman, *Playboy*'s model is captive, bound, in danger of burning.

The sexualization of "the Jewess" in cultures that abhor the Jew—subtly or overtly—is the paradigm for the sexualization of all racially or ethnically degraded women. As Sartre wrote in his classic *Anti-Semite and Jew:*

> There is in the words "a beautiful Jewess" a very special sexual signification . . . This phrase carries an aura of rape and massacre. The "beautiful Jewess" is she whom the Cossacks under the czars dragged by her hair through the streets of her burning village. And the special works which are given over to accounts of flagellation reserve a place of honor for the Jewess. But it is not necessary to look into esoteric [pornographic] literature. . . . the Jewess has a well-defined function in even the most serious novels. Frequently violated or beaten, she sometimes succeeds in escaping dishonor by means of death, but that is a form of justice.[20]

Building on Sartre's insight, Susan Brownmiller, in *Against Our*

Will, linked the experience of black women in the United States with that of the sexualized Jewess:

> It is reasonable to conjecture that the reputation for unbridled sensuality that has followed Jewish woman throughout history . . . has its origins in the Jewish woman's historical experience of forcible rape, and is a projection onto them of male sex fantasies. In this respect, Jewish women and black women have a common bond: the reputation of lasciviousness and promiscuity that haunts black women in America today may be attributed to the same high degree of historical forcible rape.[21]

In this context, "forcible rape" (the word "forcible" underscoring the reality of rape) does not mean the rape of Jew by Jew or black by black or wife by husband or child by father or any other tribal or familial forced sex act. In this context "forcible rape" means rape by an outsider who is racially superior in a given social system and who expresses this racial superiority through rape. The same outsider may also rape women in his own group—also forcible rape though less often recognized as such—but racially motivated rape is a discrete historical reality and has meaning as a discrete phenomenon for both rapists and victims.

The beautiful Jewess ravaged and dragged through the streets by her hair is still enticing, still vibrantly alive in the pool of sexual images that mystify the Jewish woman. But the Nazis in reality created a kind of sexual degradation that was—and remains—unspeakable. Even Sade did not dare to imagine what the Nazis created and neither did the Cossacks. And so the sexualization of the Jewish woman took on a new dimension. She became the carrier of a new sexual memory, one so brutal and sadistic that its very existence changed the character of the mainstream sexual imagination. The concentration camp woman, a Jew—emaciated with bulging eyes and sagging breasts and bones sticking out all over and shaved head and covered in her own filth and cut up and whipped and stomped on and punched out and starved—became the hidden sexual secret of our time. The barely faded, easily accessible memory of her sexual degradation is at the heart of the sadism against all women that is now promoted in mainstream sexual propaganda: she in the millions, she naked in the millions, she utterly at the mercy of—in the millions, she to whom anything could be and was done—in the millions, she for whom there will never be any justice or revenge—in the millions. It is her existence that has defined contemporary mass sexuality, given it its distinctly and unabashedly mass-sadistic character. The Germans had her, had the power to make her. The others want her, want the power to make her. And it must be said that the male of a racially despised group suffers because he has been kept from having her, from having the power to make her. He may mourn less what has happened to her than that he did not have the power to do it. When he takes back his manhood, he takes her back, and on her he avenges himself: through rape, prostitution, and forced pregnancy; through despising her, his contempt expressed in art and politics and pleasure. This avenging—the reclamation of masculinity—is evident among Jewish and black males, though it is in no way limited to them. In fact, in creating a female degraded beyond human recognition, the Nazis set a new standard of masculinity, honored especially in the benumbed conscience that does not even notice sadism against women because that sadism is so ordinary.

In his essay "Night Words," literary critic George Steiner has recognized the assimilation of concentration camp values into the present erotic sensibility:

> The novels being produced under the new code of total statement shout at their personages: strip, fornicate, perform this or that act of sexual perversion. So did the S.S. guards at rows of living men and women. The total attitudes are not, I think, entirely distinct. There may be deeper affinities than we as yet understand between the "total freedom" of the uncensored erotic imagination and the total freedom of the sadist. That these two freedoms have emerged in close historical proximity may not be coincidence. Both are exercised at the expense of someone else's humanity, of someone else's most precious right—the right to a private life of feeling.[22]

This cautious statement avoids the two crucial specifics: Jews and women. It is not that only women were sexually abused or that the sadism in every aspect of the camps had only to do with women. On the contrary, men and boys were sexually used and castrated, giving credence to the idea that unrestrained male sadism would not be gender specific. It is not that only Jews were imprisoned and killed: many other groups, including Gypsies, Poles, and homosexuals, were also captured and slaughtered. The importance of the two specifics—Jew and woman—resides in the resonating power of sexual memory. It is her image—hiding, running, captive, dead—that evokes the sexual triumph of the sadist. She is his sexual memory and he lives in all men. But this memory is not recognized as a sexual fact, nor is it acknowledged as male desire: it is too horrible. Instead, she wants it, they all do. The Jews went voluntarily to the ovens.

The central question is not: what is force and what is freedom? That is a good question, but in the realm of human cruelty—the realm of history—it is utterly abstract. The central question is: why is force never acknowledged as such when used against the racially or sexually despised? Nazi terror used against the Jews is not in dispute. Still, there is an almost universal—and intrinsically anti-Semitic—conviction that the Jews went voluntarily to the ovens. Rational discourse on how the Jews were terrorized does not displace or transform this irrational conviction. And similarly, no matter what force is used against women as a class or as individuals, the universal conviction is that women want (either seek out or assent to) whatever happens to them, however awful, dangerous, destructive, painful, or humiliating. A statement is made about the nature of the Jew, the nature of the woman. The nature of each and both is to be a victim. A metaphysical victim is never forced, only actualized.

The ideology that justifies force against the metaphysical victim and then renders it invisible appears to be contradictory, whereas in fact it is all-encompassing. Hitler painted the Jewish male as a rapist, a despoiler of Aryan women. He painted the Jewish female as a harlot, wild, promiscuous, the sensuous antithesis of the Aryan female, who was blond and pure. Both male and female Jews were characterized as bestial in their sexuality. The wild animal is dangerous and must be caged. Hitler's first and most basic anti-Semitic appeal was not economic, that is, the Jews control the money; it was sexual—and it was the sexuality of the Jews, as portrayed by Hitler, that provoked the German response. Real manhood demanded that the sexual beasts be tamed so that pure Aryan women would not be ravished by the lustful Jew, and Aryan sperm, lured by the lascivious Jewess, would not be misspent in producing half-breeds. This is the paradigm of racist sexual ideology—every racially despised group is invested with a bestial sexual nature. So the force is marshaled and the terror is executed. The men are conquered, castrated, killed. The women are raped, sterilized, tortured, killed. When the terror subsides, the survivors are reevaluated: previously seen as animals, now they are not recognizable as animal or human. They are garbage, remains, degraded beyond recognition. They are seen as compliant, submissive, passive. They did not have to be conquered or tamed or terrorized: they are too pitiful, too ruined. The use of force is erased—it has no meaning—because these battered survivors must have complied, consented: how else could they have been degraded to such an appalling degree? The sexual nature of the metaphysical victim—rapist or harlot—provokes force. The sexual nature of the metaphysical victim—passive, submissive—erases force as the authentic reason for compliance or submission.

The same sexual ideology that both justifies force and makes it invisible is applied to all women, without reference to race, because women are metaphysical victims: actualized, not forced.

The female is seen as sexual provocateur (harlot) or sexual submissive or combinations thereof. "Good woman/bad woman" or "Madonna/whore" as catchwords do not accurately describe the male conceptualization of female nature(s), though each is popular as a coded reference to the female dilemma. Each phrase denotes a conceptual polarity, commonly thought of as "two sides of the same coin." But in male ideology, the elements of harlot and submissive are not really distinct because they are applied simultaneously or sequentially in any proportions to any woman in any circumstance. Rather than being "two sides of the same coin," the harlot-submissive elements are more like the elements in an hourglass: always the same, always present, yet the proportions shift relative to each other, the shifts being manipulated by the one who manipulates the hourglass.

Havelock Ellis maintained that ". . . the primary part of the female in courtship is the playful, yet serious, assumption of the role of a hunted animal who lures on the pursuer, not with the object of escaping, but with the object of being finally caught."[23] Here her resistance is a form of provocation that enables her to submit. Ellis considered "modesty" the single most important defining characteristic of the female. In his world view, which is so significant because his study is the first modern codification of male sexual values, force is required to conquer modesty: "Force is the foundation of virility, and its psychic manifestation is courage. In the struggle for life violence is the first virtue. The modesty of women—in its primordial form consisting in physical resistance, active or passive, to the assaults of the male—aided selection by putting to the test man's most important quality, force. Thus it is that when choosing among rivals for her favors a woman attributes value to violence."[24] This view of sex exists with or without reference to genes, hormones, and the like. It is old and it is new. It is male. It means that a woman naturally resists force because she wants to be conquered by it. It means that the violence she resists is ultimately what she values. It means that she is responsible for giving violence its sexual value by selecting the violent male. It demands that one believe that once the violent male has captured her, it is she who has selected, she who has made the choice. This is the fate of the metaphysical victim: to be seen as responsible for the violence used against her. She wants it, they all do. The violence used against her is never a measure of her authentic resistance. Her final submission is not seen as the triumph of terrorism; it is seen as her nature, her choice—her design all along. The simple, self-evident equation between the force of the aggressor and the will of the victim—that force means a violation of will—is never plausible when the one violated is a woman. Given the premises of this utterly irrational belief system, it is then easy to assert, as Ellis does, that women like the pain inevitably inflicted on them by the sexual violence of men: "While in men it is possible to trace a tendency to inflict pain, or the simulacrum of pain, on the women they love, it is still easier to trace in women a delight in experiencing physical pain when inflicted by a lover, and an eagerness to accept subjection to his will. Such a tendency is certainly normal."[25]

Masochism, then, is defined as synonymous with normal femininity as it manifests in normal women. As expressed so gracelessly by Theodor Reik in *Of Love and Lust:* "Feminine masochism of the woman? Sounds like a pleonasm. It is comparable to an expression like, 'the Negro has dark skin.' But the color of the skin is defined simply by the term Negro; a white Negro is no Negro."[26] For a white in a white-supremacist society, the color of the skin determines race; it is an oppressor's criterion, not authentically derived from the experiences of those measured by it. The white determines that the color of the skin is the measure of identity, whether or not the color of the skin corresponds to racial, social, cultural, or familial history or experience of the ones defined from the outside. The essence of oppression is that one is defined from the outside by those who define themselves as superior by criteria of their own choice. That is why women are defined—from the outside, by men—as masochistic. Masochism is intrinsically both provocation and submission. The ideology that justifies force against women, and at the same time makes that force invisible, requires that masochism be the normal female state: she wants it, they all do. But since masochism defined more specifically as sexual gratification that is derived from pain manifests in some few men, the masochism of the female—even that—must be seen as inferior to the masochism of men. The fictive dichotomy of absolute male and female sexual natures rooted in anatomical differences must be maintained; otherwise—especially when it is acknowledged that the male is capable of masochism—male sexual supremacy might be perceived as delusional. Reik's solution is dazzlingly simple:

> But how does it happen that in female masochism the ferocity and resoluteness, the aggressiveness and the vigor of the male masochism is missing? I believe personally that the anatomical situation does not permit the cultivation of a strong sadism within the woman. The prerequisite of the penis as the carrier of aggression is missing.[27]

Masochism in the male is transformed into a form of sadism. He suffers to conquer; she suffers to submit.

In *Sexual Excitement*, Robert Stoller psychoanalyzes his pseudonymous but eloquently named patient, Belle. Interpreting Belle's sexual fantasy life, Stoller discovers that female suffering is an occasion for female triumph:

> Secreted in the apparent suffering is the triumph. The way is open to full pleasure. What better disguise than to display publicly the opposite—suffering—of what one is secretly or unconsciously experiencing: revenge, undoing, triumph. She has even more control than all these brutal, powerful men. They try to dominate her, but nothing they can do . . . enslaves her. Instead, she belongs to herself, ultimately at the mercy only of her own oversexed nature.[28]

The ideological commitment on the part of the male thinker here is clear: Belle chooses to suffer and the "brutal, powerful men" do what she wants. Stoller's vehicle for his ideology is so-called fantasy: he is describing and analyzing Belle's sexual fantasy which she "authored"; so the concept of choice is particularly underscored. Rather than seeing the sexual images in Belle's inner life as symbolic images—symbolic of a sexual reality in which she is used, trapped, humiliated, angry, powerless to change the values of the men who devalue her—Stoller attributes her sexual masochism as expressed in her inner life to her own free choice. The conceit, popular with psychiatrists and psychologists, is that a free mind can exist within a colonialized body. According to Stoller, Belle chooses sexual masochism because through it she triumphs over men whom ultimately she controls because she is the provocation to which they respond. This is an expression "of her own oversexed nature." She wants it, they all do.

The limitless possibilities of female choice are articulated with slightly different emphasis by Georges Bataille:

> . . . prostitution is the logical consequence of the feminine attitude. In so far as she is attractive, a woman is a prey to men's desire. Unless she refuses completely because she is determined to remain chaste, the question is at what price and under what circumstances will she yield. But if the conditions are fulfilied she always offers herself as an object. Prostitution proper only brings in a commercial element.[29]

Bataille introduces the all-or-nothing variant: she can choose to be chaste or she can choose to be whore. The assertion that she has even this choice—that she can choose chastity—ignores the whole history of the world, in which rape is the perpetual sexual motion of the male. Any so-called choice for sex is a choice for prostitution. Since she is prey "in so far as she is attractive," she can choose chastity only insofar as she is not attractive. Once raped she is, ipso facto, attractive because she has attracted a predator. Once raped, retroactively speaking, she has chosen—chosen her prostitute nature. Since she is prey "in so far as she is attractive," forced sex reveals the prostitute nature that is her true nature "in so far as she is attractive." If a man wants her and takes her, she is a whore and has made a choice. No matter what is done to or with her, the idea is that she has chosen her "price" and "circumstances."

The meaning of force is also obscured by the liberal view, which grants that there is a social tendency to degrade women but assumes that women who want to resist can do so successfully. This means that women who are in fact mercilessly degraded bring it on themselves. In *The Homosexual Matrix*, a book saturated with misogyny and condescension toward all women, homosexual or not, C. A. Tripp insists that ". . . a woman's status is highly variable. It is determined more by how she conducts herself than by other people's predispositions toward her."[30] If she does not want it, she does not get it. If she gets it, she wants it. Tripp describes a woman's rugged, willful descent to the bottom: "To take an extreme example, not even in the most chauvinistic societies is a wife a drudge on her wedding day, or for some time following. It is as if she only slowly works her way down to this level (admittedly with the help of social pressures) . . ."[31] Requisite to this view is Tripp's conviction, based on faith, not fact: "Nor in any era has the individual woman suffered low status whenever she has been 'willful' or has simply had the power—be it political, financial, or social—to express her independence or even her own choices."[32] A simple exercise of individual will can supposedly establish a woman as an exception to what is acknowledged as the generally demoralized status of her kind. A failure to exercise this will is a bona fide choice: since one can, if one does not, then one has chosen not to. The use of the exception (with reference to women more imagined than not) to reconcile all the rest to the rule is clearly shown for what it is in this resourceful example from R. H. Tawney's *Equality*, an analysis of class oppression in England:

> It is possible that intelligent tadpoles reconcile themselves to the inconveniences of their position, by reflecting that, though most of them will live and die as tadpoles and nothing more, the more fortunate of the species will one day shed their tails, distend their mouths and stomachs, hop nimbly on to dry land, and croak addresses to their former friends on the virtues by means of which tadpoles of character and capacity can rise to be frogs. This conception of society may be described, perhaps, as the Tadpole Philosophy, since the consolation which it offers for social evils consists in the statement that exceptional individuals can succeed in evading them.[33]

Women, alas, become Mrs. Frog or frog's girl. Should the female aspire to be a frog in her own right—as an intellectual or artist or lawyer or anything outside the realm of femininity (harlotry and submission)—she will be, as Mary Wollstonecraft described, "hunted out of society as masculine."[34] The force of the hunt, the violence intrinsic to it, is justified by the deviance of the one hunted.

And so there is a woman, tied with black rope, hands chained together at the wrists above her head, her body constrained by laser beams that crisscross in front of and behind her body. She is "an exquisite volunteer." And so there is a woman, her ankles manacled, laser beams appearing to penetrate her vagina. The laser cuts as well as burns. The laser is used in surgery. The laser functions as a knife. *Vagina* means sheath. She is "an exquisite volunteer." She volunteers to be what she is, what all women are: harlot and submissive in one, her presence and representation an affirmation and an echo of her essence as a woman—she wants it, they all do. In describing the laser, one pioneer in the field said that "[l]ight has become something not only to look with, but also a palpable force to be reckoned with."[35] Used as a sadistic weapon against a woman in pornography, a laser cannot be regarded as a palpable force or any force at all because force has no reality when used against a metaphysical victim: she is always "an exquisite volunteer"—expressing her own free will and/or actualizing her own true nature. She wants it, they all do.

The scene is a Mexican jail.

First photograph, two full pages: A Mexican policeman holds a rifle butt in the back of a Mexican woman. The rifle butt pushes her up against the bars of a cell. An Anglo man in the cell is holding the woman around the waist with one hand, lifting her T-shirt to reveal her breasts with the other.

Second photograph, one full page: The woman is on her knees. Her denim shorts are pulled down to her ankles. Her T-shirt is raised above her breasts. Her hands are brought together as if in prayer. The policeman is sitting, his uniform open to reveal a hairy chest, balls, and semierect cock. In one hand he holds the keys to the jail cell. With the other hand, he points to his penis.

Third photograph, one full page: The woman is supporting herself on her hands, she is on all fours except that her knees are raised slightly off the floor. The policeman, sitting, is apparently fucking her in the ass.

Fourth, fifth, and sixth photographs, two full pages: In the fourth photograph, the policeman sits drinking tequila from a bottle. The woman sits on the floor masturbating. The man in the cell holds the arm of the woman and watches her masturbate. He and the woman hold the keys to the cell. In the fifth photograph, the woman is naked. Her arms are stretched to hold the top crossbar of the doorway of the now open cell. The Anglo man holds her from behind around the waist. He appears to be fucking her. In the sixth photograph, the Anglo man is sitting on the bed in the cell. His hands are embracing the woman's back. The woman is on her knees. Her ass is in the forefront of the photograph. Labia hang between her legs.

Seventh photograph, two full pages: The woman is on the bed in the cell, legs spread, vulva bright pink, masturbating. The skin just below her knee is badly bruised. The Anglo man is on his knees on the floor. His ass is emphasized by his position. His mouth is approaching her breast. In the background, through the bars of the cell, the policeman is sleeping, his rifle upright beside him.

Eighth photograph, one full page: The Anglo man and the woman are on the bed. Her vulva, painted pink, is exposed by the spread of her legs. His hand is on the inside of her thigh. Her hand is just above his balls.

Ninth photograph, one full page: The woman is on top, the man is under her, they appear to be fucking, he appears to be completely inside her.

Tenth photograph, two full pages: The woman lies in the forefront masturbating, her vulva is extremely pink, the man reclines behind her. The bruises on the woman's leg are in the forefront of the photograph.

According to the text, printed within the photographic frames, the woman is named Consuela ("consolation"). Consuela has a Yankee boyfriend. He got into a fight in a bar and was arrested. Consuela cannot bear to be without him; so, "driven by passion, she bribes her way past her lover's jailer. The guard has no trouble getting it up for the hot-blooded senorita, but he's a mite greedy. Finally, he OD's on lust (and tequila)." The boyfriend "has had to watch and now he's a little greedy himself." The moral of the story is that "[a] spell in jail doesn't seem such a terrible fate after all."

Everyone's skin is approximately the same color, a light brown. Consuela and the policeman have black hair. The policeman has a black mustache. The boyfriend has lighter hair, still brown, and he too has a mustache with stubble making a dark, shadowy beard. Consuela's lips are painted a glossy pinkish red, her nails are a duller red, her vulva is pink. She wears a bright red flower behind one ear. Consuela's facial expressions indicate rapture, except in the photograph in which she is being fucked in the ass by the policeman—there her expression indicates pain and rapture. Her boyfriend's expressions indicate rapture. The policeman's face is hard and indifferent. One never sees his eyes. They are always either blocked by the visor on his policeman's cap, which he wears throughout, or they are closed. Consuela is "the hot-blooded senorita," the ethnic slur cast so as to be both specific (she is Mexican) and evocative (she is the hot-blooded Latin or Hispanic woman, the hot woman of the south, Carmen Miranda or D. H. Lawrence's mythic Etruscan female). She is the woman sexed by the climate. The color of her skin signals the climate. The climate signals the color of her skin. The text refers to "Siesta time" and "the sticky heat" and the cockroaches in the cell, so that the heat of the climate is part of the sexual imagery. The heat of the climate heats the blood of "the hot-blooded senorita," heats her skin, heats her sex. She happily offers herself to the policeman because she must be fucked by her boyfriend. In the Anglo-Amerikan sexual lexicon, the Latin or Hispanic woman is the woman who cannot do without it. She begs for it. With Mexicans and Puerto Ricans among the poorest of the poor in the United States and with Mexicans particularly despised and exploited as aliens, the photographs have a cruel immediacy. The depiction of "the hot-blooded senorita" who is willing to do anything—even to submit sexually to one of her own kind—in order to be fucked by her Anglo boyfriend embodies an imperial malice. She is used by the Mexican policeman but she belongs to the Anglo boyfriend. She prostitutes herself for him, not because he wants it, but because she wants it.

Once the male figure enters the pornographic picture, he himself is not enough. The paraphernalia of manhood must enter with him: especially uniforms and guns. His sexual force must be emphasized through reiteration: the jail bars (especially when her body is stretched up against them), the rifle (especially when it is pushed against her from behind), the policeman as a figure of brute force, even huge cacti drawn to look like phalluslike growths outside the windows throughout the photographs. The presence of two males is in and of itself a reiteration of male sexual force, even though each male figure has a different racial* significance. The pictorial center is the woman: she is visually lush; she is sexually used. But the drama, such as it is, is in the racial and sexual tension between the two men.

The Mexican male is the figure of overt force and brute sexuality. Every aspect of his stance expresses the brutality of the fuck and a corresponding incapacity to feel. He is the insensitive brute. He fucks the woman without taking off his pants or hat or shirt. When he is finished with her, he drinks tequila from a bottle. The Anglo boyfriend, by contrast, is presented as a sensitive figure: he is, in contrast, the delicate lover. His face always expresses rapture. He is slighter in build than the Mexican male, taller, even more delicate in his physique. A basic opposition of light and dark is established, even though the skin colors of the two males are approximately the same: the Anglo's hair is lighter, he has less chest hair—even the relative delicacy of build contributes to the stereotypical light-dark

*The power relationship is racist, even though the literal distinction between the two men is ethnic. Racism is not comprehensible as a phenomenon based on color of skin alone: for instance, anti-Semitism is a form of racism regardless of whether Jews are noticeably darker than the non-Jewish population and regardless of whether the Jewish genetic pool in question forms a distinct and verifiable race. The perception of a group as not-white and an actual history of contempt, exploitation, and abuse based on that perception mark as racist the relationship of a white-superior group to any other group not perceived as part of that white-superior group.

contrast. The Anglo does more than fuck the woman; he touches her, approaches her nipple, puts his hand on her thigh, sleeps peacefully while she—never having enough—masturbates. Compared with the Mexican male, he expresses a delicacy of feeling as well as a delicacy of touch. This, indeed, is basic to racist sexual ideology: the white male is the civilized male, the bearer of a civilized sexuality. The darker male, the inferior male, has a brute sexual nature. Yet the white male is in Mexico, in a Mexican jail. The power relationship between the two men puts the Mexican on top: it is the white male who, without the woman present, is endangered by the brute sexuality of the Mexican. The danger is most clearly conveyed in the two-page photograph in which the woman masturbates as the white male approaches her nipple; he is down on his knees on the floor as she lies legs spread on the bed, his ass is prominently displayed, behind his ass is the sleeping policeman with his rifle upright beside him. The white male, as the delicate male, is the sexually endangered male. The rifle is the phallic presence, near entry to the vulnerable ass of the white male. The white male is captive; the Mexican male is captor. The sexuality of the white male is depicted as superior in sensitivity. The sexuality of the Mexican male is depicted as superior in terms of brute sexual force. The racially degraded male is, in fact, consistently depicted in this fashion: his alleged sexual nature, being brute and thus bestial, is precisely what licenses violence against him in a racist value system. His sexuality is a savage masculinity, while the phallus of the white carries civilization to the dark places. This is the nexus of sex and race. If women really amount to nothing, are worth nothing, then the conquest of them—except for the momentary pleasure of it—means nothing, proves nothing. It is not sustaining. It cannot sustain a sense of masculine superiority because the conquest of nothing is nothing. But the conquest of other men, especially men with a more massive, more brute sexuality, does amount to something. It is sustaining because the conquest of bigger, better cock is the ultimate conquest. And here one finds the bribe. The racially degraded male collaborates in the degradation of women—all women—because he is offered something important for his complicity: an acknowledgment of a sexuality of which the racially superior male is envious. There is praise in the insult, so much praise, or such essential praise, that the racially degraded male is mesmerized by the myth of his own masculinity, mesmerized into accepting the ideology that posits the force of his sex as his identity, even though this myth often costs him his life. The solution then seems simple: he will avenge himself on the women of the racially superior group through taboo sexual relations or he will take back his own women using his sexuality against them. He cannot see his way clear to making an alliance with women—even the women of his peer group—based on sexual justice because he has accepted the bribe: masculinity belongs to him; he brings it to its purest expression; to contaminate it through empathy with the female would mean weakening or losing it, the one thing he has, masculinity. And so, in Hispanic communities in the United States, one sees the cult of machismo, the cult of masculine suicide, lived to its fullest: gang warfare, the organized supermasculine packs that maim and kill each other because masculine pride depends on it. The bribe, once accepted by the racially degraded male of any group, insures that if the racially superior male does not kill him, he will kill himself. The triumph of masculinity is realized in the triumph of male over male, whether the sphere of conflict for dominance is intraracial or interracial. The genius of the bribe is in the fact that, metaphorically speaking, no matter which gang wins the battle, the white man wins the war. The sexuality of the racially degraded male—the only capacity allowed him—becomes both jusification for taming or colonializing or castrating him and the mechanism by which he destroys himself, because he honors masculinity as authentic identity.

The essential sexual antagonism that is basic to racism is expressed as if the possession of women were the issue, but fundamentally the antagonism is homoerotic. Antagonism is established in male sexual thought as a key element in sexual excitement. The importance of antagonism, proclaimed with trumpets and fanfare by sexual philosophers when the conflict is male-female, is understated when applied to race because its fascist content is more easily perceived. For instance, Tripp consistently maintains that wife beating is an expression of an erotic, exciting sexual antagonism. So did Havelock Ellis, and this assertion is common in the ruminations of the male sexual philosophers. In describing the systematic devaluing of the female, Tripp can point to the sexual benefits of this devaluing. It increases sexual antagonism, which increases sexual pleasure:

> From this vantage point it is evident that the many derogations of women are more than merely the incidental offshoots of male supremacy and female "inferiority." They also qualify as contrivances that sharpen the breach between the sexes, increase the tension (resistance) between them, and add spice to their relations.[36]

Has a liberal, serious thinker ever postulated that racial insults or the violence of white supremacy adds "spice" to race relations? Instead, the thinker (in this case Tripp) is more circumspect: "The clash between social levels, between races, between partners who are dispositionally mismatched can all lead to arousing situations as easily, or more easily, than contacts between conventionally compatible partners."[37]

Stoller carries the notion of antagonism, which he calls hostility or resistance, into the realm of danger:

> To me, "excitement" implies anticipation in which one alternates with extreme rapidity between expectation of danger and just about equal expectation of avoidance of danger, and in some cases, such as in eroticism, of replacing danger with pleasure.[38]

The heightening of sexual pleasure in the male system demands a heightening of antagonism, an intensification of danger—and in a racist society, racial conflict represents the most keenly felt, the most dangerous, form of antagonism: this alone is enough to give it its sexual value in the male system. In rigid class societies, class has the same value. Possession of the woman is presented as the reason for the antagonism, whereas in fact it is the antagonism that gives value to possession of the woman. The antagonism that counts in the sexual sphere is the antagonism between male and male because it is between two real (that is, phallic) beings. A racist male hierarchy heightens this antagonism and further sexualizes the male-male interactions that take place over and through women's bodies. This sexualization occurs both in men elevated and in men demeaned by the racist system. But the elevated male tells a lie: he claims that he is afraid that the brute sexuality of the racially degraded male will be used against "his" women. In fact, he is afraid that this sexuality will be used against him. This is the meaning of the pornographic depiction of the Anglo in a Mexican jail, his ass exposed and highlighted next to the erect rifle of a Mexican policeman—this depiction published in the United States, where the power relationship in reality is precisely the opposite. Since sexual force used against the white male is recognized as force, it need only be suggested to provoke racial hatreds—one of the main functions of pornography since these hatreds are highly sexualized. To make the sexual tension pleasurable, a resolution is provided. The woman is the resolution. The sexual use of the racially degraded female, common usage, allows the male viewer, whatever his background or ethnic values, to experience the male-male sexual antagonism not as anguish but as pleasure: she can be fucked by both of them, used by both of them, because she begs for it, she cannot do without it. Her usage protects—in this case—the white male from violation by the Mexican male. Neither male violates her because she cannot do without it. She is not forced; she begs for it.

The feature is called "The Art of Dominating Women." It consists of four black-and-white photographs and a "case history" with an introduction by a "Dr." The first photograph is a full page. A white woman, very white skin, dark hair, gagged, her wrists bound together by rope, hangs suspended by her bound wrists from a light fixture. Her legs are spread. Each ankle is tied by rope to the thigh of the same leg. She is wearing sheer black tights that cover the legs and stop at the waist. She is wearing black high heels. A workman dressed in overalls is squeezing one of her breasts apparently to pulp. The next three photographs are all three inches by two and a half inches. They are the middle column of a page, with the print of the accompanying story on each side. The second photograph, the first of the small ones, shows the woman on her back, her legs spread open, her knees flexed. She wears a black corset that goes from her waist to just below her nipples, apparently squeezing the breasts tightly. She is gagged and the gag is reinforced with some kind of metal contraption that fastens behind her neck. Her hands, raised above her head, are fastened by white chains that are wrapped around her arms and around her neck. Her legs, flexed at the knees, are bound, thigh to calf of each separate leg, by various metal contraptions and straps. There are so many metal or leather constraints on each leg that flesh is barely visible, except right between her legs, the pubic area. Her ankles are manacled. The third photograph, the second small one, shows the woman tied at her wrists and above her elbows by white rope, arms raised over her head, gagged. The workman in overalls is grabbing her breast. He is approaching the breast with pliers. The fourth photograph, the third small one, shows the gagged woman to just below her breasts. The hand with the pliers is also in the picture. The pliers appear to be cutting her breast. The feature promises "[i]ntimate details of a thoroughly submissive female and the incredible excesses she requires for total satisfaction." The doctor explains that all relationships are really sadomasochistic. The doctor explains that the sadist is a leader, a guide, and that this role properly falls to the male. The doctor explains that with the growth of the women's movement more men than usual seem to be sexually submissive but, never fear, the male will never give up or lose his role of leadership. The doctor explains that most men remain interested in the genuinely submissive woman. The doctor explains that in his private practice as a sexologist he has met many such women and he is now going to open up his private files so that the reader can delve, be edified, and masturbate. The "case history" is as follows. She finds her life confusing. She is without purpose. She needs guidance. Also, she remembers her father squeezing her when she was a child. For these reasons, she likes to be bound, gagged, humiliated, and badly hurt: "nothing will get my snatch drippier." She can manage to get off while being beaten with a hairbrush if she is handcuffed. The most extreme bondage she experienced almost killed her. She was bound at the feet and wrists and hung by the neck until she began suffocating. She prefers being tied to a footstool, each of her arms and legs bound separately to separate legs of the stool while she is in a nylon straitjacket. The best fun she ever had was with a man who owned a complete supply of bondage equipment of a certain brand: she lists the items in two separate paragraphs of considerable length. As much as she enjoys all of this for its own sake, she also enjoys the thrill of finding the man who will do all these things to her. She takes to the streets and finds Puerto Ricans. She explains Puerto Rico's commonwealth status, explains that the island of Puerto Rico is in the Caribbean, explains that Puerto Rican males are to be found in large numbers in urban areas of the United States. She explains that Puerto Rican men have huge cocks and a peculiar view of maleness called machismo. She found Carlos on a street corner. He was drinking rum from a bottle. He had a huge bulge in his pants. She told him in Spanish that she was a witch and wanted him to fuck her. They took a cab to her house, petted in the traffic. He was wearing bikini underpants, which she claims is another thing one can count on with Puerto Ricans. They reached her home, smoked a joint, put on a disco record. The hair on his body was cinnamon. She is very white, twenty-two years old, very thin, with big breasts and a big ass, "the kind that begs to be spanked." Her pussy smells sweet, has a good grip, and the hair on her head, under her armpits, and in the pubic area all matches. Carlos sucked her tits, they kissed and smeared saliva all over. He whispered in her ear a lot. She could not wait any longer. She grabbed his cock. It was *incredible*! She sucked on it and then he took over. He grabbed her neck, shoved his fingers into her vagina, then into her ass, shoved his cock down her throat, hit her in the eye, smacked her a few times. She pushed his cock into her pussy:

"It was so painful. If *[sic]* felt like a hot poker was being shoved into my body." This was because it was so big. She wanted them both to experience the rapture of bondage simultaneously but seriously doubted that Carlos had the temperament for this. He agreed to handcuff her wrists behind her back, so she had to make do with imagining Carlos "restrained against Gothic pillars" as she was "trussed up and hogtied for his pleasure." Then he fucked her in the ass and spanked her at the same time. Then he took off her handcuffs and put a noose around her neck that was attached to a dog collar. Then he ordered her to lick his ass clean, which she then did. Then he fucked her some more. Then he tied her to a Parsons table and gagged her with a leather belt. Then he fucked her in the ass. When he stopped she farted so he punished her for this breach of manners by biting her tits and ears until they bled. Then he beat her across the face with his cock. She kept trying to cry out "Fuck me. Fuck . . Fuck!!Fuck!!FUCK ME!" but the gag prevented her. So he just kept beating her face with his cock, which she compares to the Chrysler Building. She was certain that he would piss in her mouth but he did not, which disappointed her. Instead, he fucked her for a half hour: "[s]uch a sensation one gets only once in a lifetime, and I was lucky." She knew the experience of total submission to a man: "being tied down, beaten to a pulp, and fucked with a big dick until there was hardly a hole left . . ." This was a "mystic" revelation "which spelled out in neon: 'Woman, you are *alive*!'" She then explains that for Carlos too this was the supreme experience of life. Finally Carlos came. Carlos collapsed over her body for nearly an hour. She was still tied to the Parsons table and gagged. She had to pee. Carlos untied her. She gave him a joint and some orange juice. They left her apartment together. She kissed him good-bye at the subway. On her way home she saw a beautiful Dominican man who asked her if she was the witch. She took him home. She concludes that having a reputation is a wonderful thing.

Force here is acknowledged. The form the acknowledgment takes is celebration. Force, rendered invisible or insignificant in other instances of female degradation, is here the point and purpose of sex. Force is sex. The woman who wants sex wants force. Every possible emphasis on force is encouraged through violence against the woman's body and through concentration on the mechanics and artifacts of bondage. The conceit is that this is a woman's story told in a woman's voice, a woman's celebration of the force she seeks out so that she can submit to it, be hurt by it, and experience her transcendent femininity. This transcendent femininity is supposed to be the exclusive province of white women, sheltered, protected, spoiled, bossy. The white woman actively recruits the Puerto Rican male because of his huge cock and his "peculiar view" of masculinity called machismo. The white woman, the totally submissive woman, demands total force, total pain, total humiliation, at the hands of a male racially stereotyped as a sexual brute. She is the woman who demands it. The two poles of her existence as a white woman are underscored: she is boss; she is total submissive. The violence she requires is the measure of her need to submit. Her appetite for pain is insatiable. Short of death, which would not offend her if it were cruel enough, nothing done to her can harm her sufficiently to stop her from demanding it from the next (Hispanic) man and the next (Hispanic) man and the next (Hispanic) man, so great is her need to submit. This is the particular erotic significance given to white skin as a sexual symbol in the women of pornography: she is the boss who demands servicing, who demands force and violence and pain; she is insatiable; she is the unquenchable submissive whose femininity is fulfilled in the most abject degradation. The force is recognized as real because she demands it. In this context, rape or battery cannot exist as violations of female will because they are viewed as expressions of female will. It is through the celebration of force—supposedly her celebration of it—that rape becomes just a better-quality fuck and battery becomes excellent foreplay. The white woman uses her racial superiority to demand rape, to demand battery, to demand humiliation, to demand pain. She wills these experiences and revels in them. The male complies. He is going his own way when she intervenes and demands. She is the initiator. She sets the terms. It is this sexualization of the white woman that is used as the standard sexuality of all women, unless specific racial characteristics are exploited to indicate particular modulations of sexuality. As many black feminists have pointed out, "women" almost always means "white women." So all women are saddled with the supposed sexual nature of white women, while women of color have added onto that nature the sexual attributes imposed as a consequence of color in a society in which color is seen as deviant from the norm. Conversely and at the same time, sexual philosophers in white-supremacist societies search so-called primitive tribes, subcultures of persons of color, and societies in which persons of color are the majority for endless examples of wife beating and other sexual violence against women to demonstrate that such violence is natural (the natural will of women), not culture-bound. The sexuality of the woman of color is supposedly outside the constraints of civilization, that is, natural. The sexuality of the white woman is the norm of civilized sexuality. In both circumstances, the violence women experience is postulated as being the will of the women; in both circumstances, she wants it, they all do. The degree of force (force perceived as such) used against the white woman establishes the norm of force acceptable in sex in white-supremacist civilization. The degree of force, then, is without limit because she wants it to be. Nothing done to the female can possibly violate her because the white woman demands violence and pain; her demand gives force its sexual value. The white woman, the civilized woman, whose transcendent femininity is realized through submission, requires force. Force to exist as such requires violence. Violence inevitably means the infliction of pain. The norm of femininity as it manifests in normal women is masochism. Force actualizes femininity. Violence is sex. Pain is pleasure for the woman. The pornographic conceit is that the normal female demands the force, the violence, the pain. This pornographic conceit is precisely reiterated in the works of the most distinguished sexual philosophers, who as purveyors of male supremacy necessarily share the values implicit in it. This pornographic conceit accounts for the fact that men in general do not believe that rape or battery are violations of female will. Film critic Molly Haskell, at the end of a decade of vigorous feminism in the

United States, expressed the weary anger and astonishment of women who keep knocking their heads against this particular brick wall:

> If we think talking it all out has brought us [men and women] closer together in the last few years, we have only to broach the subject of rape. Men seem incapable of understanding what rape means to a woman—the sense of total violation, or the mere threat of rape as a lifelong shadow over her freedom of movement. . . .
>
> The central division is between the sense of rape as an act of hostility and aggression, as women see and know and experience it, and rape as an erotic act, as fantasized by men.[39]

Men do not believe that rape or battery are violations of female will in part because men of influence have consumed pornography in the private world of men for centuries. Men of sensibility and intelligence and cultural achievement have always incorporated its values into their mainstream cultural work in art, religion, law,* literature, philosophy, and now psychology, films, and so forth. In many cases, these otherwise thoughtful men have been educated about women and sex through pornography, which they see as hidden, forbidden sexual truth. The most enduring sexual truth in pornography—widely articulated by men to the utter bewilderment of women throughout the ages—is that sexual violence is desired by the normal female, needed by her, suggested or demanded by her. She—perpetually coy or repressed—denies the truth that pornography reveals. It is either/or. Either the truth is in the pornography or she tells the truth. But men are the tellers of truth and men are the creators of and believers in pornography. She is silenced altogether—she is not a voice in the cultural dialogue, except as an annoying or exceptional whisper—and when she speaks, she lies. She hides and denies what pornography reveals and affirms: that she wants it, they all do. He has the power of naming and in

*The harlot nature of women is a premise of law relating to sexual violence against women. That is why it is nearly impossible for a woman to prove that she has been forced.

pornography he uses it to name her slut: a lewd, dissolute, brazen thing, a whore always soliciting—begging or demanding to be used for what she is. Women, for centuries not having access to pornography and now unable to bear looking at the muck on the supermarket shelves, are astonished. Women do not believe that men believe what pornography says about women. But they do. From the worst to the best of them, they do.

Story of the Eye by Georges Bataille was originally published in France in 1928. Jean-Paul Sartre, Michel Foucault, Peter Brook, and Susan Sontag among others have proclaimed it profound. Some call it "erotic" to distinguish it from the general pornographic sludge. Others, Sontag foremost among them, use it to argue that pornography of high quality—gracefully conceived and written—is art. This book—like *Story of O*, *The Image*, and the works of Sade—has the weight of intellectual adulation behind it.

The story is told by a narrator in the first person. He grew up alone and was frightened of the sexual. When he was sixteen he met Simone, the same age. Three days after they met they were alone at her villa. Simone was wearing a black pinafore. They were both anxious. He wanted her to be naked under her pinafore. She wore black silk stockings. He wanted to pick up her pinafore from behind to see her cunt, the word he considers the most beautiful one for vagina. There was a saucer of milk in a hallway for the cat. Simone put the saucer on a bench and sat down on it. He was transfixed. He was erect. He lay down at her feet. She stayed still. He saw her cunt in the milk. They were both overwhelmed. She stood up. He saw the milk dripping. She wiped herself with a handkerchief. He masturbated and writhed on the floor. They had simultaneous orgasm without touching each other. When Simone's mother came home and Simone was snuggled in her mother's arm, he lifted her pinafore from behind and thrust his hand between her legs. He hurried home to jerk off more. The next day he was so tired from masturbating that Simone told him not to masturbate without her anymore. They were intimate and driven. They never talked about it. They were in a car speeding and they crashed into a very young and very pretty girl on a bicycle, which nearly severed the girl's head. They parked near the corpse and reacted to it as they always did to each other: orgasmically. The narrator recalls that they waited a long time before copulating. Instead they indulged in unusual acts. He recalls that when Simone asked him not to masturbate alone, she told him to lie down on the ground, pulled down his pants, mounted his belly with her back toward his face, while he put his fingers into her cunt. Then she, still with her back toward him, put her head between his legs and raised her cunt up, and asked him to pee up into her cunt. He pointed out that the urine would get on her face and dress. That was what she wanted, so first he peed all over her, then he came all over her. They lay together for a long time. Then they heard a noise. They saw Marcelle, who collapsed and cried. They tore themselves away from each other to descend on her. Together they generally maul her, a thunderstorm begins, Simone smears herself with mud, Simone forces herself between Marcelle's thighs. Then Simone developed a craving for breaking eggs with her ass. The mother comes upon Simone performing for the narrator, but pretends she does not see. Days later, however, Simone, who was hoisted in the rafters of a garage with the narrator, pissed on her mother, who was walking underneath. Simone laughs and the narrator uncovers Simone's cunt completely and jerks off. They run into Marcelle on the street one day. Marcelle is blond, shy, pious, innocent. Marcelle blushed. Simone begged her forgiveness and promised that they would never lay a hand on her again. Marcelle agrees to have tea with them with other friends. Instead, they have champagne. Marcelle's blushing has completely enthralled them. Simone and he had a common purpose and nothing would stop them. There was Marcelle, three other pretty girls and two boys. The oldest was not yet seventeen. They all got drunk, but were not sufficiently excited. Simone put on a record and danced the Charleston by herself. She showed her legs up to her cunt. The other girls did the same. They had panties on. Marcelle refused to dance. Simone picks up a tablecloth and bets that she can pee into it in front of all of them. A boy dared her to do so. Since she immediately did, she won, at which point she pulled down the pants of the boy who had dared her. She also took off his shirt. Simone touched the boy, but she was obsessed with Marcelle, who was begging to leave. Simone fell on the floor, had a sexual fit, and kept telling the undressed boy to piss on her. Marcelle blushed. She said she wanted to take off her dress. The narrator tore it off and fell on her. Marcelle shut herself in a large antique bridal wardrobe in the room. She wanted to masturbate and to be left in peace. Marcelle pissed in the wardrobe. Marcelle cried and cried. The wardrobe was now her prison. Half an hour later, the narrator lets her out. She was feverish. She screamed violently on seeing him. He was smeared with blood because during the orgy shards of glass had cut two of the participants. One of the girls was throwing up. Simone was sleeping peacefully. Marcelle kept screaming horribly. People began coming. Marcelle kept screaming. The police were called. The narrator decides it would be best not to stay with his parents. He steals a gun from them and says he will kill himself and the police if they send the police to look for him. He travels near the seashore. He thinks he might kill himself but then thinks that his life must have some meaning. He slept in the woods during the day and at night he went to Simone's. They went to the beach together. He kept taking hold of her cunt. They did not come that night, but embraced mouth to mouth. He and Simone lived in her room. Her mother accepted the situation. Marcelle had been put in a mental institution. The narrator tried to rape Simone in her bed but she refused to be treated like a housewife. She demands Marcelle. He is disappointed but agrees with her. They think about Marcelle pissing. Simone pisses on him. He pisses on her. He smears semen all over her face. She climaxes. She says that now, with her nose in his ass, he smells like Marcelle. They want to fuck but Marcelle must be there:

> Thus it was that our sexual dream kept changing into a nightmare. Marcelle's smile, her freshness, her sobs, the sense of shame that made her redden and, painfully red, tear off her own clothes and surrender lovely blond buttocks to impure hands, impure mouths, beyond all the tragic delirium that had

> made her lock herself in the wardrobe to jerk off with such abandon that she could not help pissing—all these things warped our desires, so that they endlessly racked us.[40]

The narrator explains that Simone cannot forget that her own obscene behavior provoked Marcelle's orgasm, howls, writhing, and so she needed Marcelle's attitude to exaggerate and fully experience her own brazenness. So Simone's cunt now became, for the narrator, a "profound, subterranean empire of a Marcelle" who was imprisoned:

> There was only one thing I understood: how utterly the orgasms ravaged the girl's face with sobs interrupted by horrible shrieks.
>
> And Simone, for her part, no longer viewed the hot, acrid come that she caused to spurt from my cock without seeing it muck up Marcelle's mouth and cunt.[41]

They could only think of Marcelle, especially hanging herself and dying. They went to the asylum. The wind became violent. A figure hangs a sheet from the window. It has a wet stain. Simone falls to the ground. It was Marcelle at the window. The stain was her urine, the result of jerking off. The narrator entered the asylum. He took off all his clothes. Someone is following him. A naked woman is in the window frame. She jumps down. He still has a gun in his hand. He considers chasing the woman to kill her. He is out of breath. He is excited by the revolver. A hand grabs his cock. Kisses are planted on his ass. He ejaculates into the face of his wonderful Simone. He fires the gun blindly. Simone and he start running. They look up at Marcelle's sheet. One of the bullets had penetrated her window. Marcelle came to the window. They expected to see her fall dead from the bullet. Simone had taken off her clothes. Marcelle disappeared. Marcelle returned. They could see her beautiful body. She saw them. She called. She blushed. Simone jerks off. Marcelle does the same. Simone is wearing a black garter belt and black stockings. Marcelle is wearing a white garter belt and white stockings. The narrator explains certain personal symbols: urine is associated with saltpeter, lightning with an antique ceramic chamber pot that he once saw. Since having been at the asylum, these images were associated with cunt and with Marcelle's facial expressions. Then, his imagination would be saturated by light and blood, because Marcelle could not come without urinating. But back at the asylum, he and Simone had had to flee, both naked, bicycling, exhausted, sweating, but they still kept touching each other, he took off one of her stockings to wipe her body which smelled like debauchery. They kept bicycling. The leather seat stuck to Simone's cunt. The bicycle fork was in the crevice of his ass. It occurred to him that if he and Simone died, it would be cosmic. His penis was absurdly rigid. Simone masturbated with more and more force on the leather seat. She was torn from the bicycle by pure joy and her naked body was hurled. He found her bleeding and unconscious. He threw himself on top of her and came, his teeth bared, his mouth drooling. Simone came to, so he revived from the orgasm over what he had thought was her corpse. He carried her home. Since he had just rescued the person he loved most and since he would see Marcelle soon, he slept. Simone's recovery was slow. It was peaceful for him. The mother would come in to care for Simone and he would step into the bathroom. He would read items about violence to Simone from the newspapers. She was weak. She insisted that he throw hard-boiled eggs into the toilet. She would watch the eggs. He would suck out the insides in varying degrees so that they would sink to varying depths. Simone would sit on the toilet and watch the eggs under her cunt. Then Simone would have him flush the toilet. He would crack fresh eggs on the edge of the bidet and empty them under her. She would piss on them or swallow them from the bottom of the bidet. They imagined Marcelle. They wanted to put her in a bathtub full of fresh eggs. They wanted Marcelle to pee while crushing the eggs. Simone wanted him to hold Marcelle, who would have on garter belt and stockings; Simone, in a bathrobe wet with hot water, would get up on a chair and he would excite her breasts with a revolver that had been loaded and just fired; Simone would pour a jar of fresh cream on Marcelle's anus and urinate on her robe or back or head while he would piss on Marcelle from the other side or on her breasts. Marcelle would also be free to piss. After such wonderful dreams, Simone would ask the narrator to lay her down on blankets by the toilet and she would stare at the eggs. He would lie down next to her. When the toilet was finally flushed, Simone would be happy. Simone was mesmerized when a half-sucked egg was suddenly invaded by water. She climaxed. Simone wanted to urinate but she did not so that she could feel pleasure. Her belly bloated up and her cunt swelled. The word *urinate* reminded her of *terminate*. The narrator continues with associations: eggs, eyes, razor, sun, the white of the eye, the yolk is the eyeball. Simone wants the narrator to promise to shoot eggs with his rifle when they go outside. He refuses. She continues associating: each of her buttocks is a peeled hard-boiled egg, urine is a gunshot, and so on. They decide to send for hot soft-boiled eggs without the shells. The mother brings them. They treat her like a maid. Simone sat on the toilet and they each ate an egg. He rubs the other eggs all over her and slowly drops each into the toilet. Nothing like this ever happened again, *except once*, which will be revealed later. If eggs came up in the conversation, they blushed. He fixes the bicycles and rigs up an attachment for Marcelle. They arrive at the asylum. Marcelle escapes. Marcelle wants to marry the narrator. He kisses her. Marcelle does not understand where she is or who she is with or what she is doing. Marcelle asks the narrator to protect her when the cardinal returns. They were lying in the forest. Simone asked who the cardinal was. Marcelle answers, the man who locked her in the wardrobe. Now the narrator understands why Marcelle was so frightened when he finally let her out of the wardrobe. He had been wearing a red cap and was covered in blood from deep cuts in a girl he had raped. Marcelle's dress was pulled up and Simone and the narrator were so enchanted by the sight that they did not move. Simone urinated and climaxed and the force of this denuded her which then occasioned the narrator's climax. The narrator gives more symbols: milky way, astral sperm, heavenly urine, broken egg, broken eye, rooster, cardinal, red. The narrator discourses on the nature of lewdness: he cares only for the dirty; decent people have "gelded eyes"; people like sexual pleasure only if it is insipid; his kind of debauchery soils everything including the whole universe. More symbols: moon with vaginal blood of mothers and sisters. He loved Marcelle but he did not mourn her. Her death was his fault. He sometimes locked himself up for hours to think about her but he wanted to start all over, for instance, by forcing her head into a toilet bowl. Marcelle hanged herself when she recognized the wardrobe. They cut her down and masturbated over the dead body. They fucked each other for the first time. Simone was still a virgin. The three of them were all calm. Simone pissed on the corpse. Marcelle belonged to them. They ran away to Spain. Simone had a rich English sponsor, Sir Edmond. Simone was indifferent to most things but her orgasms became more violent. Sir Edmond captured a streetwalker and had her locked in a pigsty where she was trampled in liquid manure by the pigs. Simone had the narrator fuck her outside the locked door as Sir Edmond jerked off. They went to numerous bullfights. They fucked in numerous environments, generally surrounded by stink and flies and urine. Simone demands the raw balls of a bull. Sir Edmond provides them. She wants to sit on them but cannot because of all the other people present. Sir Edmond, Simone, and the narrator become horribly excited. Simone bit into one of the raw balls. The bullfighter was killed. As the people screamed in horror, Simone had an orgasm. The bullfighter's eye was dangling from his head. The three of them went to Seville because Simone was in a foul mood. Simone wore a flimsy dress that exposed her. They never stopped having sex. Sir Edmond would follow and masturbate. They go into a church. Don Juan is supposedly buried under the church. They laugh. Simone pisses. The urine makes Simone's dress stick to her body. A woman is confessing in the church. Simone wants to watch. The woman leaves. Simone goes to confess. Simone jerks off as she confesses. Simone confesses that she is jerking off while confessing. Simone exposes herself to the priest. Simone opens the door to the priest. Simone grabs his cock. The priest hissed. Simone sucked his cock. Sir Edmond pulled the priest out of the confessional. They carried him to the vestry. They sat him in a wooden armchair. Simone slapped him, which gave the priest another erection. They stripped him and Simone pissed on his clothes. Simone jerked him off and sucked him while the narrator urinated in his nostrils. Then the narrator fucked Simone in the ass as she sucked the cock of the priest. Sir Edmond found the key to the tabernacle. Simone flagellated the cock of the priest with her teeth and tongue. Sir Edmond found hosts and a consecrated chalice. Sir Edmond lectures on the meaning of the blood of Christ, white wine which really means semen. Simone slammed the chalice against the skull of the priest. Simone sucked the cock of the priest. Simone hit the priest again on the face with the chalice. Simone undressed and the narrator fingerfucked her. The priest peed into the chalice. Sir Edmond then made him drink the urine. Simone jerked him off and sucked his cock. The priest crashed the chalice against a wall. The two men lift the priest up, the priest comes on the hosts that Simone held while jerking him off. They dropped the priest on the floor. They order him to fuck Simone. The priest refuses. Sir Edmond explains that a man hanging dies with an erection. They gag and tie the priest, strangle him as Simone mounts him. The priest comes and dies. The narrator has never been so in love with Simone and so content. Simone wants the priest's eye. Sir Edmond cuts it out for her. Simone caressed the eye. Simone put the eye in her ass. The eye fell out onto the body of the corpse. Sir Edmond undressed the narrator. The narrator pounced on Simone. He fucked her hard while Sir Edmond rolled the eye all over them. Simone tells Sir Edmond to put the eye in her ass. He does. Simone takes the eye and puts it in her cunt. The narrator pulls her legs apart: "in *Simone's* hairy vagina, I saw the wan blue eye of *Marcelle*, gazing at me through tears of urine."[42] Simone climaxes and pees. They leave town to find new adventures with a sailing crew of Negroes on Sir Edmond's new yacht.

In the world of high-class literary pornography, of which *Story of the Eye* is fairly typical, force is imbued with meaning because it is the means to death. Death is the stunning essence of sex. The violence of death is the violence of sex and the beauty of death is the beauty of sex and the meaning of life is only revealed in the meaning of sex which is death. The intellectual who loves this kind of pornography is impressed with death. High-class symbols are also essential to high-class pornography: eggs, eyes, hard-boiled, soft-boiled, the difference between a half-full and a half-empty egg as it sinks into a toilet, an eye in the cunt. Ruminations on the stars in the sky and sudden portentous thunderstorms, abundant in *Story of the Eye*, also help to establish a work of pornography as inordinately meaningful. Religious rebellion—for instance, the torture and rape of a priest—also heralds a class act. The priest as the man in skirts, feminized because he has turned away from masculine sexual action as a way of life, is easily viewed as a symbol of the repression caused by religion, whereas it would be more realistic—but less comfortable—to see him as a substitute woman. His true sexual nature is revealed in his erection and he is punished for having denied it—for his sexual downward mobility as it were. Marcelle is the more conventional victim, anatomically female, passive, shamed by her own sexual desire. Her violation and death are in the normal course of things, in the nature of sex itself. The violation of a priest passes as a rebellious idea.

Force in high-class pornography is romanticized because it leads to death. It is romanticized as if it were dance: ritualized movement intrinsic to sex, leading inevitably to death, which is mysterious and in its mystery sublime. Bataille has outlined a sequel to *Story of the Eye:* Simone ends up in a death camp; she is beaten to death; "[s]he dies as though making love, but in the purity (chaste) and the *imbecility* of death; fever and agony transfigure her."[43] The outline was published in 1967, in the fourth edition of *Story of the Eye*. This makes clear the tally of female deaths: very young girl on bicycle, Marcelle, whore in the pigsty, priest as feminized male, and later—much later because she is so cruel—Simone. The death camp is eroticized in the man of intellect after Auschwitz. Also, Bataille has published a personal essay on his own life, in which he describes some probable origins of the symbols in *Story of the Eye*. The sense of the author's personal anguish also gives the work credibility among intellectuals: he writes of his own dread and obsession and pain, the staples of the male artist as hero. This makes the book by definition brave in its revelations. It allows other intellectuals to see Bataille and themselves in his characters as it suits them: especially not as violators but as sufferers. This, needless to say, is utterly sentimental, but the sentimentality is well hidden in endless abstractions—ponderings on death and sex with no regard for the realities of either. The intellectual claim made for the work is that Bataille has revealed a sexual secret: the authentic nexus between sex and death. Sometimes this revelation is posited as the value of high-class pornography. But in fact, Bataille has obscured more than he has uncovered. He has obscured the meaning of force in sex. He has obscured the fact that there is no male conception of sex without force as the essential dynamic. He has done this by romanticizing death. Force is inconsequential when the cosmic forces move through man in sex. It is plodding and pedestrian to demand that one pay attention to it. What matters is the poetry that is the violence leading to death that is the ecstasy. The language stylizes the violence and denies its fundamental meaning to women, who do in fact end up dead because men believe what Bataille believes and makes pretty: that death is the dirty secret of sex. In some cases, the death is literal. In some cases, it is the annihilation of female will. The grand conceptions—death, angst—cover the grand truth: that force leading to death is what men most secretly, most deeply, and most truly value in sex. Death is the idea behind the action.

Simone exists in the male sexual framework: the sadistic whore whose sexuality is murderous and insatiable; ultimately she is also the exquisite victim, fulfilled through annihilation, Bataille's logical though delayed tribute to the femininity suggested by her anatomy and by the fact that now and then she gets fucked. She is a prototypical figure in the male imagination, the woman who is sexual because her sexuality is male in its values, in its violence. She is the male idea of a woman let loose.

When Simone, Sir Edmond, and the narrator go off on a yacht with a crew of Negroes, an image that appeared earlier in the text is underlined and given new significance: Simone's orgasms after Marcelle's death were

> incomparably more violent than before. These orgasms were as different from normal climaxes as, say, the mirth of savage Africans from that of Occidentals. In fact, though the savages may sometimes laugh as moderately as whites, they also have long-lasting jags, with all parts of the body in violent release, and they go whirling willy-nilly, flailing their arms about wildly, shaking their bellies, necks, and chests, and chortling and gulping horribly.[44]

This wild laughter is then again paralleled to Simone's violent orgasms. The escape with the crew of Negroes promises more savage sexual experiences. The promise is that more force will lead to more death that will be more exciting because the light/dark symbolism—suggested in an all-white environment by Simone and Marcelle (Simone dark, Marcelle blond, Simone dressed in black stockings, Marcelle in white, and so forth)—will provide the context for conquest. In an all-white context, Marcelle was the pale, frail submissive who denied her harlot nature, which provoked Simone to express hers. In an all-white context and also in a white-supremacist context, the dark one is the dangerous one. But in the white-supremacist context, the white one will win, the dark one will be conquered: Simone is white, not black; she is the winner. The challenge of savage sexuality in a black crew in service to a wealthy English aristocrat provides a new context for conquest. Force leading to sex which inevitably means death takes on a new dimension, suggests to the colonializing sexual mentality wilder and wilder sexual possibilities. Conquest, the subterranean theme of both rape and romance, is carried in pornography, at some point of satiation, inevitably into the racial realm. The death of one's own racial kind is not quite enough, and so the romanticization of death which obscures the meaning of force permits the romanticization of racial conquest and racial murder. Force, once perhaps abhorrent to the intellectual in the realm of race, now has an entirely sexual significance which permits its expansion into race without challenging, or even alerting, conscience. The acceptance of force in the sexual realm allows its extension into the racial realm because one is dealing with metaphysical sexual truths, which race does not change and in relation to which justice is both irrelevant and ridiculous. A conscience calloused with regard to force in sex is inevitably rendered insensible to racist force as well.

> And cruelty is an idea in practice.
>
> Antonin Artaud, *Collected Works*

> Woman is made to submit to man and to endure even injustice at his hands.
>
> Jean-Jacques Rousseau, *Émile*

> All the women who copulate to keep peace in the house are the victims of rape. All our grandmothers who just "let it happen" were essentially force-fucked all their lives.
>
> Suzanne Brøgger, *Deliver Us from Love*

The idea of the woman as sexual provocateur or harlot, so consistently postulated in pornography as the first principle of sex, is not, it will be argued, really commonplace or believed. The idea that women do not like or need sex is stronger. Too many headaches over too many centuries have damaged the credibility of both the pornographers and like-minded philosophers of sex. Yes, the idea of the woman as sexual provocateur may rise like the mythical phoenix in rape cases. It may magically manifest in incest cases, where the female who wants it is a prepubescent child. To women, the sudden appearance of this idea when applied to themselves is always incredible and inexplicable, especially because most women encounter the power of this idea when it is they who have been physically abused and then are accused and condemned. Before the woman is actually assaulted, the idea has set limits on her life: she is always trying to retain the status of innocent, one who is not forced because she did not provoke it. But the idea limits her life, innocence demanding ignorance, in such a way that she cannot recognize or be conscious of it. Once attacked, she is accused, and the idea determines the immediate course of her life. Indeed, in rape or incest cases, as in battery, the so-called victim is distinguished from other females by her provocativeness, which accounts for her individual victimization, which is not victimization because she provoked it. There are always those billions of other women who were not raped or beaten at that particular time by that particular man. *They* were passed by, which is the evidence that convicts her. Something in her caused the assault—her sexuality, in fact—and now she must convince strangers not only that it was against her will but also that she did not like it: an indignity beyond imagining and in the male system nearly always impossible. She cannot comprehend what she is up against when she claims that she did not want it. She is up against the whole world of real male belief about her real nature, expressed most purely in pornography.

But still, there is another idea, closer to the surface and in that sense more superficial, that women are inhibited or have a low sex drive or do not want or need sex. Perhaps this is a recognition, however perverse, that no one could possibly like and want what men do to women. This idea, also articulated as a universal truth, appears to contradict the idea that women are by nature whores who beg for it, want it, demand it. But in fact, it is the perfect complement. The whore provokes because she wants to be forced (sex intrinsically defined as conquest). How does one have sex with the real woman who so often expresses reluctance, aversion, boredom, refusal, disdain, or a desire to go back to school instead, especially if she is one's wife, the woman over whom one has legal conjugal rights? One forces her. The system is foolproof. The woman who does want it wants force. She expresses this desire for force by resisting which provokes force which is what she wants. The woman who does not want it must be forced. Once the woman who does not want it has been forced, she is indistinguishable from the woman who resisted because she did want it. Male supremacy is dizzying in its unrelenting circularity.

Kinsey is the sexual philosopher who claimed to quantify and thus accurately describe actual sexual behavior. He and his followers conclude that women have a low sex drive and are defined in their personalities, behaviors, and values by sexual inhibitions. Kinsey's sexual ideology, accepted without significant modification by those who continued his work, used the idea that women have a low sex drive to justify force against the woman who does not want it except in the cases where force is justified because she does want it but does not have the decency to admit it thereby causing tragic problems for the male who forced her because he was not inhibited and did what was natural.

Kinsey counted and classified sexual acts, a technique he described as "taxonomic, in the sense in which modern biologists employ the term. . . . The transfer from insect to human material is not illogical, for it has been a transfer of a method that may be applied to the study of any variable population, in any field."[45] Kinsey had spent a good part of his life as a scientist collecting and classifying gall wasps, called by male scientists "killer wasps." He took the methods he had applied in describing the gall wasp and applied them to human sexuality. Kinsey's first absolute claim was that his method was scientific and objective, uncolored by social prejudices or moral judgments: "That much is expected of the student measuring the lengths of insect wings, recording chemical changes that occur in a test tube, or observing the colors of the stars. It is not too much to expect similar objectivity of the student of human behavior."[46] Kinsey's material on sexual acts was collected through interviews. Challenged on his ability to recognize absolute truth in verbal descriptions of sexual acts, the objective scientist countered : "As well ask a horse trader how he knows when to close a bargain."[47]*

*Kinsey's sources were, in fact, much more unreliable than anyone could deduce from reading either of his volumes on human sexuality. In his biography, *Dr. Kinsey and the Institute for Sex Research* (New York: Harper & Row, Publishers, 1972), p. 122, Wardell B. Pomeroy, a disciple and coresearcher with Kinsey, unselfconsciously tells this story: "We had heard through Dr. Dickinson of a man who had kept an accurate record of a lifetime's sexual behavior. When we got the record after a long drive to take his history, it astounded even us, who had heard everything. This man had had homosexual relations with 600 preadolescent males, heterosexual relations with 200 preadolescent females, intercourse with countless adults

The two volumes written by Kinsey and his associates *(Sexual Behavior in the Human Male, Sexual Behavior in the Human Female)* and the one volume written by his disciples based on his data *(Sex Offenders: An Analysis of Types)* all classify sexual acts of white persons. Kinsey was particularly criticized because the volume on the human female dealt with white, mostly urban, and well-educated women. Actually it deals mostly with insects, animals, and men. According to Arno Karlen, Kinsey

> pointed out that this made less difference than it would in a male sample, for he had enough lower-level female subjects to show that education and parent's occupation were minor influences for females. The various levels had produced very different patterns of aggression and control in males, but girls *[sic]* of all classes got pretty much the same kind and amount of training in restraint.[48]

This is strongly reminiscent of Freud's attitude toward what he called "servant girls *[sic]*": "Fortunately for our therapy, we have previously learned so much from other cases that we can tell these persons their story without having to wait for their contribution. They are willing to confirm what we tell them, but one can learn nothing from them."[49] Scientists tend to be more rigorous and interested in collecting information on insects than on women and Kinsey was no exception. His curiosity about sexual acts committed

---

of both sexes, with animals of many species, and besides had employed elaborate techniques of masturbation. He had set down a family tree going back to his grandparents, and of thirty-three family members he had had sexual contacts with seventeen. His grandmother introduced him to heterosexual intercourse, and his first homosexual experience was with his father. If that sounds like *Tobacco Road* or *God's Little Acre*, I will add that he was a college graduate who held a responsible government job. We had traveled from Indiana to the Southwest to get this single extraordinary history, and felt that it had been worth every mile.

"At the time we saw him, this man was sixty-three years old, quiet, soft-spoken, self-effacing—a rather unobtrusive fellow. It took us seventeen hours to get his history, *which was the basis for a fair part of Chapter Five in the Male volume, concerning child sexuality. Because of these elaborate records, we were able to get data on the behavior of many children, as well as of our subject.*" [Emphasis mine]

by the human female never matched his curiosity about the gall wasp. His main preoccupation, among humans, was with class strata among males. He found distinctly different patterns of sexual interaction in what he called "lower-level" and "upper-level" males. Kinsey's data confirm that these men had mostly female partners. Therefore, the behaviors of the women of the various social strata must have differed. This too is confirmed by the data—the data on males. Kinsey's own attitudes toward the female could not even stand the test of his own data.

Kinsey characterized sexual response as a physiological phenomenon in both males and females in this way: "The closest parallel to the picture of sexual response is found in the known physiology of anger."[50] He claimed that physiological responses in male and female were the same, but that psychological responses were entirely different. He also claimed that female attitudes toward sex (the psychological) have a biological basis, at which point Noah's ark issues forth. He also claimed that while no one knows whether female sexuality is determined by genes, passed from generation to generation (apparently he meant through learning), or by a combination of nature and nurture, one must look to the behavior of other mammals to find what human sexual behavior should be—though he claimed that his method did not allow the intrusion of a *should*. Kinsey strongly believed that human sexual patterns should mimic animal patterns, which were natural, but he never recognized that this constituted a point of view. As an objective scientist, he could say all of the above: his authority forbade notice of his simple self-contradiction and confusion.

In *Sexual Behavior in the Human Male*, Kinsey asserts that male orgasm would occur, at the least, on a daily basis were it not for social restrictions. Under what he calls "optimal conditions,"[51] it would occur more frequently than once a day during adolescence and early adult life. The heterosexual environment, courtship rites, women's provocative clothing, and the depictions of women in films, advertisements, fiction, and so forth, are constantly arousing: "For most males, whether single or married, there are ever-present erotic stimuli, and sexual response is regular and high."[52] The lower-level male wants and gets sexual intercourse. The upper-level male, denied what he really wants (intercourse), must fall back on substitutes, which accounts for the attention the upper-level male pays (relatively speaking, among males) to what women might call lovemaking—kissing, cunnilingus, fondling, and so on:

> The very fact that upper level males fail to get what they want in socio-sexual relations [this is deduced by Kinsey because they have lower rates of premarital and extramarital intercourse] would provide a psychologic explanation of their high degree of erotic responsiveness to stimuli which *fall short of actual coitus*. The fact that the lower level male comes nearer having as much coitus as he wants would make him less susceptible to any stimulus except actual coitus.[53] [Italics mine]

Kinsey then characterizes the coital behavior of the lower-level male as sexual freedom. The criteria Kinsey uses to determine sexual freedom are quantity of sexual interactions that are coital and degree of promiscuity (number of partners). It is a continuing theme in Kinsey that "average frequencies of sexual outlet for the human male are distinctly below those which are normal among some other anthropoids and which would probably be normal in the human animal if there were no restrictions upon his sexual activity."[54] Kinsey's formulation of authentic male sexuality—his speculation, distinct from his stated goal of objectively describing, counting, and classifying actual sexual acts, but not acknowledged as opinion or conjecture—is unequivocal:

> There seems to be no question but that the human male would be promiscuous in his choice of sexual partners throughout the whole of his life if there were no social restrictions. This is the history of unrestrained human males everywhere.[55]

Kinsey considers women responsible for the unnatural social restrictions on men. He condemns social workers, women on parole boards, mothers, schoolteachers, for controlling "moral codes, schedules for sex education, campaigns for law enforcement, and programs for combating what is called juvenile delinquency. It is obviously impossible," he asserts, "for a majority of these women to understand the problem that the boy faces in being constantly aroused and regularly involved with his normal biologic reactions."[56]

Kinsey especially disdained the attitudes of upper-level females. He was most offended by upper-level women in social work who did not understand (condone and support) the male coital imperative. He maintained that the inhibitions of the upper-level female were extreme. The proof was that so many of these women had objected to intercourse when first married or remained apathetic throughout marriage. Some even objected to new techniques tried out on them by their husbands and "charge their husbands with being lewd, lascivious, lacking in consideration, and guilty of sex perversion in general. There are numerous divorces which turn on the wife's refusal to accept some item in coital technique which may in actuality be commonplace in human [male] behavior."[57] To Kinsey, this data did not suggest anything about male sexuality as such; only that women were perpetually messing men up, standing in the way of male sexual release. Kinsey, who did not, in his exhaustive, objective research, uncover marital rape or wife battery, did find "several instances of wives who have murdered their husbands because they insisted on mouth-genital contacts."[58] "Insisted" might perhaps be considered a euphemism. He also found, to his disgust, that divorces had been granted because of "the coital frequencies which the husband had demanded."[59] Even "demanded" might perhaps be considered a euphemism. He saw, in the instances of divorces granted because the woman objected to the husband's sexual use of her, collusion between women and the law, the two great social forces for sexual restriction of the male. Denial of sexual access by women to men is nowhere viewed by Kinsey as a right of women. He consistently sees refusal as sexual inhibition, moralism, or evidence of a low sex drive in the female. He is contemptuous of the Freudian formulation of sexual inhibition, though he maintains that the female is sexually inhibited. To Kinsey, inhibition means refusal on any level for any reason. He particularly undertook to shatter Freud's concept of sublimation by pointing out that the sexual histories of male artists did not confirm that they were sexually inactive, and sexual sublimation—or inhibition or repression—could not be proven by looking to women because the concept does not take into account "the high incidence of relatively unresponsive females who never had any appreciable amount of sexual energy to be diverted."[60] According to Kinsey, psychotherapy is wasted on persons with a low sex drive, and most women are sexually apathetic: "But such inactivity is no more sublimation [or repression or inhibition; Kinsey used the words interchangeably] of sex drive than blindness or deafness or other perceptive defects are sublimation of those capacities."[61] Despite the low sex drive of the female, her resultant moralism, her sexual inhibition here used to mean refusal of sexual access, "we do not find evidence . . . that the individual, rid of her inhibitions, would not be capable of response."[62] All she has to do is to say yes. Mute submission would also pass as "response" in Kinsey's system because

> [i]t cannot be emphasized too often that orgasm cannot be taken as the sole criterion for determining the degree of satisfaction which a female may derive from sexual activity. Considerable pleasure may be found in sexual arousal which does not proceed to the point of orgasm, and in the social aspects of a sexual relationship. Whether or not she herself reaches orgasm, many a female finds satisfaction in knowing that her husband or other sexual partner has enjoyed the contact, and in realizing that she has contributed to the male's pleasure.[63]

At the same time, predictably, "[i]t is inconceivable that males who were not reaching orgasm would continue their marital coitus for any length of time."[64]

The function of the female in the conventional sexual relationship, as described by Kinsey, in which the woman participates not for her sexual benefit but for that of the male and gets a social reward for her compliance is stated clearly by Kinsey: under these circumstances, it is "impossible to draw a line between the most obvious sort of commercialized prostitution and the relationships of every husband and wife."[65] The basic sameness of wife and whore (Kinsey's version of "all women are whores") is the line Kinsey takes in defending prostitution as an institution that must be accepted because the male needs unrestricted sexual outlet, which the wife does not provide because she has a low sex drive and is inhibited and would provide were she not inhibited despite her low sex drive. The purpose of wife and whore is the same. The goal is male sexual expression—mostly in coitus if the male is not frustrated by female noncompliance. The use of the female, whatever her status, by the male for his own genital satisfaction is the substance and near totality of natural human sexuality as described by Kinsey. The so-called low sex drive of the female justifies the use of her without reference to her satisfaction and without cognizance of her sexual integrity, which simply cannot exist in Kinsey's male-supremacist value system. Any refusal on the part of the female to comply with male sexual demands is evidence of incapacity or inhibition. The sexually natural female would never say no precisely because her sexual nature is apathetic. Strong sexual aversion on her part—for instance, aversion to having sex to which she is indifferent because there is no meaning or pleasure in it for her—is by definition inhibition. Since wife and prostitute have the same function, the function is clearly delineated in the analogy: to serve the male in sex. Rape, needless to say, does not have an authentic existence in Kinsey's system, except as a repressive social construct with which women haunt and punish and restrict the male. Anything—law or personal protestation or resistance—that keeps the male from using the female as he wishes is female moralism or sexual repression or social restriction that ignores or violates male sexual nature, which is taking and using at will. Kinsey's philosophy at base is that there is no valid reason for the male not to: not to have coital access to the female at will. He has a great sense of the tragic when needless (all) social restrictions impinge on male sexual nature: "Sexual activities in themselves rarely do physical damage, but disagreements over the significance of sexual behavior may result in personality conflicts, a loss of social standing, imprisonment, disgrace, and the loss of life itself."[66] It is the male who is the victim here: who has personality conflicts, loses social standing, is imprisoned, disgraced, and sometimes killed for raping. The sense of Kinsey's view is that rape, to the extent that it does exist (mostly illusory), would not exist if females would comply, which they would do were they not twisted. It is the female who refuses and then accuses, destroying the natural man who just wants to function in harmony with his authentic sexuality.

In Kinsey's system, charges of rape are almost always false, occasioned by female hysteria, not by male assault. Since he cannot imagine a female sexual will that contradicts the male and at the same time is not warped, he cannot comprehend the meaning, for instance, of child molestation to child or woman—only that the hysteria of women descends once again to punish the male:

> Many small girls reflect the public hysteria over the prospect of "being touched" by a strange person *[sic]*; and many a child, who has no idea at all of the mechanics of intercourse, interprets affection and simple caressing from anyone except her own parents, as attempts at rape. In consequence, not a few older men serve time in penal institutions for attempting to engage in a sexual act which at their age would not interest most of them, and of which many of them are undoubtedly incapable.[67]

Kinsey had no interest in exploring or documenting child abuse because no sexual act desired by the male if properly gratified could be abusive. He could not begin to comprehend the varieties of sexual abuse directed against female children because he had no notion of meaningful consent for any female of any age. The male was always the victim of female refusal or antagonism. The refusal or antagonism was never justified.

In addition, Kinsey saw rape as a female stratagem to hide female participation in sex:

> In both the baboon and the rhesus monkey, females soliciting new sexual partners have been known to utilize a remarkably human procedure to escape the anger of their established mates.

> When the mates discover them in coitus with other males, or seem about to discover them, the females may cease their sexual activities and attack the new male partners. A high proportion of the human "rape" cases which we have had the opportunity to examine involve something of the same motifs.[68]

When not screaming rape to propitiate the angry baboon, the female may scream rape by way of explanation to her parents. In *Sex Offenders*, Kinsey's disciples remember his deep insight into this origin of rape:

> As Dr. Kinsey often said, the difference between a "good time" and a "rape" may hinge on whether the girl's *[sic]* parents were awake when she finally arrived home.[69]

In the main, Kinsey held that it was the social valuation of coitus that turned it into rape—especially the woman's attitude toward an act that was the same whether called coitus or rape; meaning not that coitus as practiced is a form of rape, but that rape is a misrepresentation of coitus. Harm to the female had no significance for Kinsey:

> The disturbances which may sometimes follow coitus rarely depend on the nature of the activity itself, or upon its physical outcome. An occasional unwanted pregnancy, a rare instance of venereal disease, or a very rare instance of physical damage are about the only undesirable physical after-effects.[70]

Harm, like rape, is mostly a figment of the female imagination. Who would compare the inconvenience of unwanted pregnancy (especially at the time of contraband birth control and illegal abortion, when Kinsey wrote) or venereal disease (commonly undiagnosed in the female and thus disabling, when Kinsey wrote) or the maimed and battered bodies of raped or abused women (undiscovered by Kinsey, despite his objective methods and thousands of interviews) to the tragic situation of the male who is disturbed or imprisoned or even killed merely for using his natural sexual capacity? Harm to the female can have an authentic meaning only when the bodily integrity of the female is a premise in the sexual value system. Otherwise, she exists to be used and harm to her in the process of using her is always incidental, usually her own fault, and no cause for mourning or rage or even reevaluation. Once a woman is dead, it is easier to grant that harm was done to her, even that she really was forced; but short of death, harm, like force, is hard to prove and is almost never considered significant.

In *Sex Offenders*, which purports to count and classify the acts of convicted sex offenders, these values are carried forth. The sex offender is distinguished from the normal man who commits a forcible sexual act—like kissing—because he has been convicted: "Once there is a conviction the matter cannot be trivial even though the act may have been."[71] *Sex Offenders* is the great and terrible story of men who suffer imprisonment because they violated meaningless taboos—like all other normal men, except that they were caught. Its great themes are the falsity and hysteria of women and the cruelty of the law. The story is told almost entirely from the point of view of the sex offender himself, except that his voice is given authority by the objective scientists who present his case, his plight, his dilemma. Because the use of force in rape cases where the man has actually been convicted is by definition pronounced, there is, unavoidably, some recognition of force as a reality in the category called "heterosexual aggressor vs. adults," which roughly translates into adult men raping adult women:

> The heterosexual aggressors vs. adults are well aware of public skepticism concerning rape, and make use of it in offering their own versions of their offenses. Perhaps more than any other group they give seemingly plausible accounts of their actions to prove their innocence, and while we are interviewing them it is often quite easy to be persuaded of the validity of their stories. Later, upon examining official records, we may discover that the allegedly willing female had to have five stitches taken in her lip.[72]

This liberality—the credence given to the five stitches—is the exception rather than the rule. In most instances, according to the scientists, that lip was just looking for trouble. Using sophistry and cunning, the scientists dismiss force as a reality in virtually every kind of crime.

The first method of dismissal is implicit in the methodology itself. The normal male, according to *Sex Offenders*, commits sexual acts against the will of the female as a matter of course. To be distinguished as an offender, he must be convicted. It is the conviction, not the offense, that makes his act significant. Someone convicted of burglary who intended to rape is included in the study; someone who actually raped but was not convicted is excluded. In itself, this is unfortunate, "but this is the price we must pay, fortunately very infrequently, in obtaining a workable definition of sex offense."[73] The premise is that the unconvicted rapist is an oddity. Importance is given not to the incidence of actual rape but to "obtaining a workable definition of sex offense."

The sophistry involved in describing or determining the use of force in a sexual act committed by a male convicted of a sex offense is clearest in the attempts to categorize acts against children and minors. "Children" are here defined as female children under the age of twelve, not the daughters of the men convicted. "Minors" are females from twelve to fifteen, not the daughters of the men convicted. The "heterosexual offender" did not use force; the "heterosexual aggressor" did.

In describing sex acts committed against children, the scientists were at pains to establish two categories, one in which force was used and one in which it was not:

> Force ranges from unmitigated violence to, let us say, holding a child by the wrist; threat runs the gamut from specific verbal threat or brandishing a weapon to a subtle implication. In any relationship between a child and an adult there is always in the background an element of duress; the inevitable disparity in strength and social status is an omnipresent factor. A man, even though a stranger, is in an authoritarian superior position. While it was manifestly impossible to cope with these vaguer (but nonetheless effective) forms of force and threat, we were able to exclude from heterosexual offenders vs. children anyone

> who told us of using force or threat or whose official record mentioned its use.[74]

Given the excellence of this description of male force, both brutal and subtle (though it omits the direct power of male over female), it is remarkable that the scientists did indeed isolate a category of male offenders against female children under the age of twelve in which the use of force was not involved. The information on which they based the existence of this extraordinary category was supplied by the offenders themselves or by official records. In these cases, children were not represented by their own counsel, and standards for taking and recording testimony from children varied greatly. In sexual offenses against children, quoted above, the first issue is not the kind or degree of force used, but the fact that force is implicit for the reasons articulated in the description of force with respect to children. In any event, the scientists did not feel obligated to determine from information supplied by the victims whether or not force in any of the senses that it properly pertains had been used. The invisibility of the victim is built into the data by virtue of its sources. No consideration is given to delineating circumstances that would guarantee that force had not been used. The commitment of the scientists here, their sexual imperative as it were, is to create a category in which females under twelve years of age satisfy the male without the use of force on his part. The issue is not whether the satisfaction is coital; it is whether it is sexual in any sense, thus establishing a viable sexual possibility for the adult male in regard to the female child. The category itself—which defies both common sense and the clear description of what constitutes force from male adult to female child—provides a basis for belief that the use of a female child under twelve by an adult male can, under circumstances known only to the authors of *Sex Offenders*, exclude force as a factor.

The philosophy that permits the invisibility of the victim and insists on the accuracy of the category and data arrived at by the objective scientist is more fully explicated in the information on heterosexual offenders versus minors. The category as defined means that force was not used in committing the sexual act. The use of force or its absence is held to be easy to determine because the girl aged twelve to fifteen is seen to have the sexual characteristics and awareness of a well-informed adult woman. These girls "are sufficiently developed physically and sufficiently aware of social attitudes for a man to have to use considerable force or definite threat if the girl objects to sexual contact."[75] The girl is considered knowledgeable of any male's sexual intent. She also "knows that in rejecting a sexual advance society is on her side."[76] Unless formidable force was used against her, she is seen to have consented. Basically, if the girl is short of bruised and maimed, force was not used. All of the data on harm done to her, remember, are either filtered through the criminal justice system or come from the offender. To the scientists, this does not indicate prejudice to her because society is on her side; the only prejudice is to the male. Proof of the girl's essential complicity and compliance is inferred from the source of the report to the police: "Who reported the sexual behavior to the authorities? The girl herself rarely did so directly. Usually the situation was discovered by friends or relatives who thereupon reported it. The suspicious mother and the garrulous girl friend are common sources of the offender's downfall."[77] The tragic figure is the male. He has a "downfall." The females responsible for the "downfall" are interfering, prudish mothers or yacking girlfriends—eternal troublemakers who babble irresponsibly to the police. There is no indication that the objective scientists considered the girl, upset and confused, unable to explain an assault on her, asking for help, or cracking under the stress. Because she is viewed by the objective scientists as an adult woman, even though socially she is a child and even though all females are characteristically kept ignorant of sex and male genital goals, she has not been misused because misuse is implicitly impossible when a sexually viable female is used by a male exercising natural sexuality. The presumption is that the girl aged twelve to fifteen fully and knowledgeably consented to the sexual act after which her mother or another troublesome female intruded, causing the "downfall" of a blameless male.

Confronting the high incidence of pair and multiple sexual attacks on girls aged twelve to fifteen, the scientists still have a category called "heterosexual offenders," meaning that no force was involved meaning that the male was convicted for having sex with a consenting female—or even for just being nearby:

> At first one wonders why females aged twelve to fifteen should be particularly subject to such polyandrous attention, but a simple explanation exists: when society learns that a young girl has had some sort of sexual relationship with an adult male, not only that male, but any other adult male who was within a radius of one hundred feet is apt to be convicted. If there were copartners in the offense, there was usually one, less often two, and only rarely more. The traditional "line-up" or "gang-bang" is essentially absent in the offenders vs. minors, but there does seem to have been a considerable amount of double-dating and of pairs of males hunting for girls.[78]

Convicted offenders against girls aged twelve to fifteen are judged by the objective scientists to be, on the whole, a very healthy group with excellent parental relationships: but then, they were not accused of molesting their parents. Scientists, of course, are experts on health, and the behavior, for instance, of adult males hunting for girls aged twelve to fifteen is no less healthy than adult males similarly hunting for adult women. If sex is the hunt and sex is health, then the hunt is health. The problem is not that males abuse a female, but that society—according to Kinsey controlled by the sexually apathetic or inhibited female—collects the males in a hundred-foot radius when a female aged twelve to fifteen is sexually used. Two or more adult males hunting a girl aged twelve to fifteen does not, for the scientists, constitute the use of force. What, then, does constitute the use of force against a girl aged twelve to fifteen? The scientists have a category, "heterosexual aggressors vs. minors," in which the use of force is recognized as such even by the rather dense authors of *Sex Offenders*. The plight of the poor male is still the dramatic issue:

> The male who realizes too late that what he interpreted as

> encouragement was nothing of the sort is in real danger if he attempts, by physical force, to detain a frightened girl in order to calm her and make his apologies. Assault with intent to rape is a charge that requires very little in the way of physical contact, and judges and juries are apt to be cynical toward the man who disclaims any intention to rape. Men, knowing themselves, are prone to assume the worst about another man charged with a sex offense.[79]

The authority of the scientist, which is the authority of the male, permits this astonishing somersault. Suddenly, the male, recognizing his own desire to rape, will attribute an intention to rape to other males, virtually without evidence. The male, convicted for using force (an astonishment in and of itself), might well have been attempting to comfort a hysterical female whom he innocently misunderstood—probable because the provocative behavior of the female is so misleading. The projection of the male judge or juror (a necessary construct, since it is hard to blame the female directly when she is not allowed on juries nor is she on the bench; women were systematically excluded from serving on juries until recently, women are still systematically excluded from the judiciary) is used to posit the essential blamelessness of the man whose use of force was in fact so gross that not only was he convicted of a sex offense but even the authors of *Sex Offenders* had to create a category for him in which the use of force established the parameters of the category.

Needless to say, if one has managed to obscure the meaning of force when used by adult men against females under the age of twelve and females aged twelve to fifteen, it is unlikely that the use of force in sex against adult women will be a compelling issue.

In the category called "heterosexual offenders vs. adults," the use of force is excluded by definition. This is a remarkable category because the scientists basically conclude that the men in this category were convicted for having consensual coitus with females who were adult—by their definition, over the age of fifteen. This conclusion is in part held to be self-evident because three-quarters of the females attacked were friends of the offenders and the sexual act at issue occurred in a residence.

According to the scientists, in the category "heterosexual offenders vs. adults," only 16 out of 183 females resisted the commission of the sex act, but even in these cases "her resistance and his persistence did not exceed the bounds of the customary male vs. female contest. There was no threat and no violence. Included are a few cases where female consent was completely absent, but force or duress were absent also."[80] The situations in which consent was absent but force or duress were not used are cases in which the men use "surprise or stealth."[81] The example given is the instance of a man who when he was drunk surprised a girl *(sic)* by hugging her. The authors point out that the girl *(sic)* thought she was being grabbed. "Hugging" is the neutral term used by the authors in describing the act; "grabbing," as the female point of view, is put in quotes. Or, in another example, a man "could not resist touching females' legs even in inappropriate situations."[82] The essential information in these two examples, from the authors' perspective, is that "there was nothing especially antisocial in the behavior per se, but the circumstances of the situation (particularly the fact that the men were not known to the females) constituted grounds for punitive action."[83] The presumption is that access to the female body is a male right, and that even in the absence of consent the presumption of a right to access is not antisocial. Surprise and stealth do not constitute force. There are also cases where, according to the scientists, consent was given, then withdrawn. One case cited as an example of consent given, then withdrawn, is that of a twenty-year-old man who had on other occasions had coitus with his seventeen-year-old girlfriend *(sic)*. One night he was drunk, she resisted him, he hit her, she called the police, and he was arrested and convicted of rape. Fortunately, the court "recognized some of the essentials of the situation"[84] and sentenced the man to ninety days and payment of court costs. Apparently, to the objective scientists, consent once given is eternally given. Battery is not an issue of force. Previous coitus negates the validity of any charge of rape, since consent is inferred from previous sexual contact.

In 91 percent of the cases in the category "heterosexual offenders vs. adults," the sexual act was premeditated by the male. Premeditation also does not indicate force because, of course, in the normal male "interest, hope, and premeditation are inextricably fused when he is confronted with a socially suitable female . . ."[85] Two or more males aligned against a single female also is not necessarily forcible sex: these are "polyandrous situations."[86]

In creating the category "heterosexual offenders vs adults," meaning a category in which men were convicted for having consensual relations, usually coital, with adult females, the criterion was that the use of force not be *substantial*, that is, outside the bounds of what is socially acceptable:

> Our society expects the male to be the aggressor in heterosexual relationships, and a certain amount of physical force and duress is consequently acceptable and perhaps even socially necessary. Girls *[sic]* are frequently subjected to rather intense and effective duress which takes many forms: threats not to date them again, threats to impair their popularity through adverse comments, even threats to make them walk home—all these are not only common but are accepted as a part of social living. The same is true with physical force, but here a delicacy of judgment is necessary.[87]

The delicacy of judgment shown by the scientists is truly overwhelming in its delicacy: "Concerning force, we would retain the case [in the offender's category in which, by definition, no force was used] where a male touched, or briefly held, or pulled an unwilling female, but we would exclude cases where she was struck or physically overpowered."[88] The acknowledged unwillingness of the female is not relevant because it is commonplace for a female to be unwilling and at the same time touched, held, or pulled despite or because of her unwillingness.

In the hope that at least when the female is struck or physically overpowered, the use of force is clearly delineated and left unjustified by the objective scientists, one might turn to the category called "heterosexual aggressors vs. adults," meaning that by definition in this category force was used. There all hope is shattered by a return to first principles. In the category "heterosexual aggressors vs. adults," where force was undoubtedly and absolutely used, one finds that

> [t]he phenomenon of force or threat in sexual relations between adults is beclouded by various things. In the first place, there may be the ambivalence of the female who is sexually aroused but who for moral or other reasons does not wish to have coitus. She is struggling not only against the male but against herself, and in retrospect it is exceedingly easy for her to convince herself that she yielded to force rather than to persuasion. This delusion is facilitated by the socially approved pattern for feminine behavior, according to which the woman is supposed to put up at least token resistance, murmuring, "No, no" or "We mustn't!" Any reasonably experienced male has learned to disregard such minor protestations, and the naive male who obeys his partner's injunction to cease and desist is often puzzled when she seems inexplicably irritated by his compliance.[89]

Not only did she probably want it all along—being unwilling only for moral reasons, which do not count, or because she is inhibited, which does not count—but an accusation against the male—where force was clearly used—indicates her struggle with herself. The presumption is that the woman will refuse and that the man will, as a matter of course, use force, and that her resistance and her unwillingness are meaningless except insofar as they indicate moralistic values without which she would not object or a hidden, internal struggle because she really wants to do what she resists doing.

Also, the use of force against the adult female, even where the use of force is acknowledged by definition of the category, is "beclouded" by the inherent, never-dormant masochism of women:

> . . . there is a certain masochistic streak in many women: they occasionally desire to be overpowered and treated a little roughly. It is, after all, very ego-satisfying for a female to feel she is so sexually attractive that the male cannot maintain social restraints and reverts to "caveman" tactics. Indeed, some women complain that their partners are too gentle: "Why do you always ask me, why don't you just take me sometimes?"[90]

In a study specifically of force used against adult females by males, the objective scientists introduce the female put off by gentleness, the female who wants to be "treated a little roughly," the female who cannot be satisfied without the use of force. Since "[a] standard gambit in feminine flirtation is to irritate the male and provoke him into physical contact . . . ,"[91] it is hard to blame the male even for using gross force against the female—hurting her, hitting her, physically overpowering her: nonobjective persons not scientists sometimes call it "rape." So the scientists do not blame him or even hold him responsible for his own behavior. The masochistic female with her low sex drive or inhibitions or morals who pretends to resist or is actually but unjustifiably unwilling is in fact the one responsible for the harm done to her, which is not really harm, since she is used in an appropriate way because she is female.

The destiny of the woman who does not want it—moralistic or inhibited or with a low sex drive—is the familiar female destiny because underneath is the masochist who does want it, with force. The destiny of the woman who does not want it—a superficial characterization of her, since underneath she does want it or would if she were not moralistic or inhibited—is precisely the same as the destiny of the harlot who provokes in order to be forced. The female is never entitled not to want sex. Force used against her when she refuses is always warranted because she is never either justified or serious in not wanting sex. No authentic idea of bodily integrity is ever hers to claim or to have. Force does not violate her or victimize her because force is nature's way of giving her what she really wants. Force is nature's victory over the constraints of civilization. Force is intrinsic to male sexuality and force used against her does not victimize her; it actualizes her. The objective scientists and the pornographers agree: she wants it hard, she wants it rough, she provokes it because she likes it; and even the sexual apathy posited by Kinsey simply establishes another reason to disregard her will because an assertion of will on her part—by definition, refusal—is a misrepresentation of her own sexual nature, which is fulfilled when she is sexually used by the male to satisfy him, especially in coitus.

6

Pornography

> Consider also our spirits that break a little each time we see ourselves in chains or full labial display for the conquering male viewer, bruised or on our knees, screaming a real or pretended pain to delight the sadist, pretending to enjoy what we don't enjoy, to be blind to the images of our sisters that really haunt us—humiliated often enough ourselves by the truly obscene idea that sex and the domination of women must be combined.
>
> Gloria Steinem, "Erotica and Pornography"

> Somehow every indignity the female suffers ultimately comes to be symbolized in a sexuality that is held to be her responsibility, her shame. Even the self-denigration required of the prostitute is an emotion urged upon all women, but rarely with as much success: not as frankly, not as openly, not as efficiently. It can be summarized in one four-letter word. And the word is not *fuck*, it's *cunt*. Our self-contempt originates in this: in knowing we are cunt. This is what we are supposed to be about—our essence, our offense.
>
> Kate Millett, *The Prostitution Papers*

> I can never have my fill of killing whores.
>
> Euripides' Orestes, in *Orestes*

The word *pornography*, derived from the ancient Greek *pornē* and *graphos*, means "writing about whores." *Pornē* means "whore," specifically and exclusively the lowest class of whore, which in ancient Greece was the brothel slut available to all male citizens.

The *pornē* was the cheapest (in the literal sense), least regarded, least protected of all women, including slaves. She was, simply and clearly and absolutely, a sexual slave. *Graphos* means "writing, etching, or drawing."

The word *pornography* does not mean "writing about sex" or "depictions of the erotic" or "depictions of sexual acts" or "depictions of nude bodies" or "sexual representations" or any other such euphemism. It means the graphic depiction of women as vile whores. In ancient Greece, not all prostitutes were considered vile: only the *porneia*.

Contemporary pornography strictly and literally conforms to the word's root meaning: the graphic depiction of vile whores, or, in our language, sluts, cows (as in: sexual cattle, sexual chattel), cunts. The word has not changed its meaning and the genre is not misnamed. The only change in the meaning of the word is with respect to its second part, *graphos:* now there are cameras—there is still photography, film, video. The methods of graphic depiction have increased in number and in kind: the content is the same; the meaning is the same; the purpose is the same; the status of the women depicted is the same; the sexuality of the women depicted is the same; the value of the women depicted is the same. With the technologically advanced methods of graphic depiction, real women are required for the depiction as such to exist.

The word *pornography* does not have any other meaning than the one cited here, the graphic depiction of the lowest whores. Whores exist to serve men sexually. Whores exist only within a framework of male sexual domination. Indeed, outside that framework the notion of whores would be absurd and the usage of women as whores would be impossible. The word *whore* is incomprehensible unless one is immersed in the lexicon of male domination. Men have created the group, the type, the concept, the epithet, the insult, the industry, the trade, the commodity, the reality of woman as whore. Woman as whore exists within the objective and real system of male sexual domination. The pornography itself is objective and real and central to the male sexual system. The valuation of women's sexuality in pornography is objective and real because women are so regarded and so valued. The force depicted in pornography is objective and real because force is so used against women. The debasing of women depicted in pornography and intrinsic to it is objective and real in that women are so debased. The uses of women depicted in pornography are objective and real because women are so used. The women used in pornography are used in pornography. The definition of women articulated systematically and consistently in pornography is objective and real in that real women exist within and must live with constant reference to the boundaries of this definition. The fact that pornography is widely believed to be "sexual representations" or "depictions of sex" emphasizes only that the valuation of women as low whores is widespread and that the sexuality of women is perceived as low and whorish in and of itself. The fact that pornography is widely believed to be "depictions of the erotic" means only that the debasing of women is held to be the real pleasure of sex. As Kate Millett wrote, women's sexuality is reduced to the one essential: "cunt . . . our essence, our offense."[1] The idea that pornography is "dirty" originates in the conviction that the sexuality of women is dirty and is actually portrayed in pornography; that women's bodies (especially women's genitals) are dirty and lewd in themselves. Pornography does not, as some claim, refute the idea that female sexuality is dirty: instead, pornography embodies and exploits this idea; pornography sells and promotes it.

In the United States, the pornography industry is larger than the record and film industries combined. In a time of widespread economic impoverishment, it is growing: more and more male consumers are eager to spend more and more money on pornography—on depictions of women as vile whores. Pornography is now carried by cable television; it is now being marketed for home use in video machines. The technology itself demands the creation of more and more *porneia* to meet the market opened up by the technology. Real women are tied up, stretched, hanged, fucked, gang-banged, whipped, beaten, and begging for more. In the photographs and films, real women are used as *porneia* and real women are depicted as *porneia*. To profit, the pimps must supply the *porneia* as the technology widens the market for the visual consumption of women being brutalized and loving it. One picture is worth a thousand words. The number of pictures required to meet the demands of the marketplace determines the number of *porneia* required to meet the demands of graphic depiction. The numbers grow as the technology and its accessibility grow. The technology by its very nature encourages more and more passive acquiescence to the graphic depictions. Passivity makes the already credulous consumer more credulous. He comes to the pornography a believer; he goes away from it a missionary. The technology itself legitimizes the uses of women conveyed by it.

In the male system, women are sex; sex is the whore. The whore is *pornē*, the lowest whore, the whore who belongs to *all* male citizens: the slut, the cunt. Buying her is buying pornography. Having her is having pornography. Seeing her is seeing pornography. Seeing her sex, especially her genitals, is seeing pornography. Seeing her in sex is seeing the whore in sex. Using her is using pornography. Wanting her means wanting pornography. Being her means being pornography.

7

Whores

> The best houses do not exhibit the women in cages.
>
> *The Nightless City or the History of the Yoshiwara Yukwaku*, 1899 report on a red-light district in Japan

Male sexual domination is a material system with an ideology and a metaphysics. The sexual colonialization of women's bodies is a material reality: men control the sexual and reproductive uses of women's bodies. The institutions of control include law, marriage, prostitution, pornography, health care, the economy, organized religion, and systematized physical aggression against women (for instance, in rape and battery). Male domination of the female body is the basic material reality of women's lives; and all struggle for dignity and self-determination is rooted in the struggle for actual control of one's own body, especially control over physical access to one's own body. The ideology of male sexual domination posits that men are superior to women by virtue of their penises; that physical possession of the female is a natural right of the male; that sex is, in fact, conquest and possession of the female, especially but not exclusively phallic conquest and phallic possession; that the use of the female body for sexual or reproductive purposes is a natural right of men; that the sexual will of men properly and naturally defines the parameters of a woman's sexual being, which is her whole identity. The metaphysics of male sexual domination is that women are whores. This basic truth transcends all lesser truths in the male system. One does not violate something by using it for what it is: neither rape nor prostitution is an abuse of the female because in both the female is fulfilling her natural function; that is why rape is absurd and incomprehensible as an abusive phenomenon in the male system, and so is prostitution, which is held to be voluntary even when the prostitute is hit, threatened, drugged, or locked in. The woman's effort to stay innocent, her effort to prove innocence, her effort to prove in any instance of sexual use that she was used against her will, is always and unequivocably an effort to prove that she is not a whore. The presumption that she is a whore is a metaphysical presumption: a presumption that underlies the system of reality in which she lives. A whore cannot be raped, only used. A whore by nature cannot be forced to whore—only revealed through circumstance to be the whore she is. The point is her nature, which is a whore's nature. The word *whore* can be construed to mean that she is a cunt with enough gross intelligence to manipulate, barter, or sell. The cunt wants it; the whore knows enough to use it. *Cunt* is the most reductive word; *whore* adds the dimension of character—greedy, manipulative, not nice. The word *whore* reveals her sensual nature (cunt) and her natural character.

"No prostitute of anything resembling intelligence," writes Mencken, "is under the slightest duress . . ."[1] "What is a prostitute?" asks William Acton in his classic work on prostitution. "She is a woman who gives for money that which she ought to give only for love . . ."[2] Jane Addams, who worked against the so-called white slave trade, noted that "[t]he one impression which the trial [of procurers] left upon our minds was that all the men concerned in the prosecution felt a keen sense of outrage against the method employed to secure the girl [kidnapping], but took for granted that the life she was about to lead was in the established order of things, if she had chosen it voluntarily."[3] Only the maternal can mitigate the whorish, an opposition more conceptual than real, based on the assumption that the maternal or older woman is no longer desired. Freud writes Jung that a son approaching adulthood naturally loses his incestuous desires for the mother "with her sagging belly and varicose veins."[4] René Guyon, who argued for male-defined sexual liberation, writes that "[w]oman ages much sooner. Much earlier in life she loses her freshness, her charm, and begins to look withered or over-ripe. She ceases to be an object of desire."[5] The mother is not the whore only when men have stopped desiring her.

Guyon, in whose name societies for sexual freedom exist today, held that women were defined exclusively by their sexuality, which was essentially and intrinsically the sexuality of the prostitute. "Women's sexual parasitism," writes Guyon, "is innate. She has a congenital tendency to rely on man for support, availing herself of her sexual arts, offering in return for maintenance (and more, if she can get it) the partial or complete possession of her person."[6] This propensity for exchanging her body for material goods is her sexuality, her purpose, her passion, and consequently "[s]ale or contract, monogamy or harem—these words mean little to her in comparison with the goal."[7] For this reason, Guyon contends that even the so-called white slave trade—the organized abduction of lone or young or destitute women for the purposes of prostitution—cannot be construed as forcible prostitution:

> How hypocritical it is to speak of the White *[sic]* Slave Trade only as a means for recruiting the ranks of prostitution. The White *[sic]* Slave Trade is universal, being carried on with the consent of the "slaves," since every woman has a specific sexual value. She must sell herself to the highest bidder, even though she cheat as to the quality of the goods.[8]

Like most male advocates of sexual freedom (the unrestrained expression of male sexuality), Guyon theoretically and repeatedly deplores the use of force; he simply never recognizes its existence in the sexual use of women.

Typically, every charge by women that force is used to violate women—in rape, battery, or prostitution—is dismissed by positing a female nature that is essentially fulfilled by the act of violation, which in turn transforms violation into merely using a thing for what it is and blames the thing if it is not womanly enough to enjoy what is done to it.

Sometimes "consent" is construed to exist. More often, the woman is perceived to have an active desire to be used by the male on his terms. Great Britain's Wolfenden Report, renowned for its recommendation that legal persecution of consenting male homosexuals cease, was also a report on female prostitution. The Wolfenden Report stressed that "there are women who, even when there is no economic need to do so, choose this form of livelihood."[9] The Wolfenden Report recommended increasing legal penalties against prostitutes and argued for more stringent enforcement of laws aimed at prostitutes. Male sexual privilege was affirmed both in the vindication of consensual male homosexuality and in the advocacy of greater persecution of female prostitutes. At the same time, women's degraded status was affirmed. The whore has a nature that chooses prostitution. She should be punished for her nature, which determines her choice and which exists independent of any social or economic necessity. The male homosexual also has a nature, for which he should not be punished.

This desire of the woman to prostitute herself is often portrayed as greed for money or pleasure or both. The natural woman is a whore, but the professional prostitute is a greedy whore: greedy for sensation, pleasure, money, men. Novelist Alberto Moravia, like many leftist writers seemingly obsessed with the prostituted woman, writes in an assumed first-person-female voice to convey the woman's pleasure in prostitution:

> The feeling I experienced at that moment bewildered me and, no matter how or when I have received money from men since, I have never again experienced it so clearly and so intensely. It was a feeling of complicity and sensual conspiracy . . . It was a feeling of inevitable subjection which showed me in a flash an aspect of my own nature I had ignored until then. I knew, of course, that I ought to refuse the money, but at the same time I wanted to accept. And not so much from greed, as from a new kind of pleasure which this offering had afforded me.[10]

The pleasure of the prostitute is the pleasure of any woman used in sex—but heightened. The specific—the professional whore—exists in the context of the general—women who are whores by nature. There is additional pleasure in being bought because money fixes her status as one who is for sex, not just woman but essence of woman or double-woman. The professional prostitute is distinguished from other women not in kind but by degree. "There are certainly no women absolutely devoid of the prostitute instinct to covet being sexually excited by any stranger,"[11] writes Weininger, emphasizing both pleasure and vanity. "If a woman hasn't got a tiny streak of a harlot in her," writes D. H. Lawrence, "she's a dry stick as a rule."[12] The tininess of Lawrence's "streak" should not be misunderstood: "really, most wives sold themselves, in the past, and plenty of harlots gave themselves, when they felt like it, for nothing."[13] The "tiny streak" is her sexual nature: without a streak of whore, "she's a dry stick as a rule."

There is a right-wing ideology and a left-wing ideology. The right-wing ideology claims that the division of mother and whore is phenomenologically real. The virgin is the potential mother. The left-wing ideology claims that sexual freedom is in the unrestrained use of women, the use of women as a collective natural resource, not privatized, not owned by one man but instead used by many. The metaphysics is the same on the Left and on the Right: the sexuality of the woman actualized is the sexuality of the whore; desire on her part is the slut's lust; once sexually available, it does not matter how she is used, why, by whom, by how many, or how often. Her sexual will can exist only as a will to be used. Whatever happens to her, it is all the same. If she loathes it, it is not wrong, she is.

Within this system, the only choice for the woman has been to embrace herself as whore, as sexual wanton or sexual commodity within phallic boundaries, or to disavow desire, disavow her body. The most cynical use of women has been on the Left—cynical because the word *freedom* is used to capture the loyalties of women who want, more than anything, to be free and who are then valued and used as left-wing whores: collectivized cunts. The most cynical use of women has been on the Right—cynical because the word *good* is used to capture the loyalties of women who want, more than anything, to be good and who are then valued and used as right-wing whores: wives, the whores who breed. As Kate Millett writes: ". . . the great mass of women throughout history have been confined to the cultural level of animal life in providing the male with sexual outlet and exercising the animal functions of reproduction and care of the young."[14]

Men of the Right and men of the Left have an undying allegiance to prostitution as such, regardless of their theoretical relationship to marriage. The Left sees the prostitute as the free, public woman of sex, exciting because she flaunts it, because of her brazen availability. The Right sees in the prostitute the power of the bad woman of sex, the male's use of her being his dirty little secret. The old pornography industry was a right-wing industry: secret money, secret sin, secret sex, secret promiscuity, secret buying and selling of women, secret profit, secret pleasure not only from sex but also from the buying and selling. The new pornography industry is a left-wing industry: promoted especially by the boys of the sixties as simple pleasure, lusty fun, public sex, the whore brought out of the bourgeois *(sic)* home into the streets for the democratic consumption of all men; her freedom, her free sexuality, is as his whore—and she likes it. It is her political will as well as her sexual will; it is liberation. The dirty little secret of the left-wing pornography industry is not sex but commerce.

The new pornography industry is held, by leftist males, to be inherently radical. Sex is claimed by the Left as a leftist phenomenon; the trade in women is most of sex. The politics of liberation are claimed as indigenous to the Left by the Left; central to the politics of liberation is the mass-marketing of material that depicts women being used as whores. The pimps of pornography are hailed by leftists as saviors and savants. Larry Flynt has been proclaimed a savior of the counterculture, a working-class hero, and even, in a full-page advertisement in *The New York Times* signed by distinguished leftist literati, an "American Dissident" persecuted as Soviet dissidents are. Hugh Hefner is viewed as a pioneer of sexual freedom who showed, in the words of columnist Max Lerner, "how the legislating of sexuality could be fought, how the absurd anti-play and anti-pleasure ethic could be turned into a stylish hedonism and a lifeway which includes play and playfulness along with work."[15] Lerner also credits Hefner with being a precursor of the women's movement.

On the Left, the sexually liberated woman is the woman of pornography. Free male sexuality wants, has a right to, produces, and consumes pornography because pornography is pleasure. Leftist sensibility promotes and protects pornography because pornography is freedom. The pornography glut is bread and roses for the masses. Freedom is the mass-marketing of woman as whore. Free sexuality for the woman is in being massively consumed, denied an individual nature, denied any sexual sensibility other than that which serves the male. Capitalism is not wicked or cruel when the commodity is the whore; profit is not wicked or cruel when the alienated worker is a female piece of meat; corporate bloodsucking is not wicked or cruel when the corporations in question, organized crime syndicates, sell cunt; racism is not wicked or cruel when the black cunt or yellow cunt or red cunt or Hispanic cunt or Jewish cunt has her legs splayed for any man's pleasure; poverty is not wicked or cruel when it is the poverty of dispossessed women who have only themselves to sell; violence by the powerful against the powerless is not wicked or cruel when it is called sex; slavery is not wicked or cruel when it is sexual slavery; torture is not wicked or cruel when the tormented are women, whores, cunts. The new pornography is left-wing; and the new pornography is a vast graveyard where the Left has gone to die. The Left cannot have its whores and its politics too.

> But the example of Bluebeard should give us pause. For years he has been, for one reason or another, killing off his wives. Now, finding his life disgusting, devoid of sense, he searches his experience for pattern, sees that he has regularly murdered his wives, and asserts that next time he will do it on purpose. *Voilà!*
>
> John Gardner, *On Moral Fiction*

In the introduction to *Black Fashion Model*, a book, the reader is warned that this story "was tempered by the fire of experience, molded in the cauldron of intense, adult desire . . ." Those who are shy or those who want to see the world through rose-colored glasses are advised not to read the book. Watergate has shaken public confidence in the president and elected officials. *Black Fashion Model* will scrutinize "the possibilities for tragedy when public power becomes a tool for private use." Another major theme in the story is "the simple unalterable fact of [the main character's] color—she is a Negress, a young, beautiful black woman." The abuse of power and the fact of prejudice are in the center of her life. Her name is Kelly Morris. She moves like a bird or snake. When she was five, she won a dance contest in the ghetto. She started studying dance when she was eight. Kelly's mother wanted her to be a professional dancer but she had ideas of her own since she was "one of the most physically charming black women ever to leave the streets of the ghetto." Her body is long, her breasts are big. Her features show "a perfect, savage beauty." She has dark, thick lips, a wide and slightly squashed nose. She is beautiful and innocent. Her skin is "dark mellow cocoa" and deep brown. Kelly walks down the street in high heels and her tightest skirt. Men talk about how they want a piece of her, but how she will be famous one day. Kelly tires of dance. When she was seventeen, she allowed someone to take photographs of her. The savage beauty of her face became important in front of the camera. Men respected her for her innocence but the camera made Kelly "into a wanton, lusty *woman*!" Kelly became one of the most famous models in the country and the most famous black model. She remained innocent, a savage beauty, a black diamond. Robert Grey watches Kelly posing. Robert Grey imagines her on her knees between his white thighs. Robert Grey imagines her touching his cock. Robert Grey imagines her pink tongue sucking his cock. Robert Grey imagines her two hot red nipples. Robert Grey imagines her two black naked breasts and his pink hardening cock. Robert Grey imagines her saying: "I like a big stiff cock like that, Mr. Robert Grey. I really do . . ." Kelly stops posing. Kelly has a weakness for men like

Robert Grey who look so helpless. Kelly thinks of her love, Doug, who is white. Robert Grey tells Kelly that Doug has been arrested on a morals charge. Robert Grey watches her breasts shimmer. Doug did something to a little girl. Robert Grey wonders what it would be like to be a photographer and take pictures of naked girls all day long. Robert Grey asks the photographer if he ever got the chance to—ah, ah—Eric, the photographer, blushes. Kelly returns wearing a fur coat and a bikini. Kelly thinks Robert Grey is a policeman. She follows him to his car to go to Doug in jail. Robert Grey abducts Kelly. Robert Grey pushes Kelly into a run-down house. A white woman is in the room. She is holding wet, glossy photographs in her hands. She calls Kelly a bitch. Kelly demands an explanation. The white girl winks at Robert Grey. The white girl tells Kelly she will explain. She shows Kelly pictures of Doug with a child, then another child, then another child. Kelly is sick. Robert Grey closes the blinds and double-locks the door. Robert Grey calls Kelly "little black girl." Her black breasts shimmer. The white woman is going to take photographs of Kelly. Kelly's breasts are exposed. The white female fingers are on her big black breasts. She gets upset. She struggles free. Robert Grey hits her. He hits her again. She cries and feels "pain and humiliating submissiveness." She falls into a heap of "half-naked black flesh," her thighs undulate. Robert Grey undoes his pants. Robert Grey says: we know you want it. Angela, the white girl, is naked too. Angela mimics black slang. Kelly says that she always tried to be nice to white people. Angela tells her that this has nothing to do with race. Angela wants to use the photographs she is going to take of Kelly to make a career for herself, but she gets pleasure too from having Kelly there naked. Robert Grey's prick is getting even harder. Robert Grey takes off Kelly's bikini bottom. He sees the young black girl's black hips. He wants to get his mouth around her black nipples. His hand touches her black breast. She squirms like a black snake. She is like an animal in a zoo. Angela takes photographs. Robert Grey's fingers are on her black ankles and his soft white lips are on her thick black mouth. His cock rubs against her black thigh. Angela tells him to get Kelly in the cunt. Robert Grey fingerfucks her between her black loins. She screams. Robert Grey lets her go and watches her anus, which is in the middle of her black buttocks. He calls her "my little brown butterfly." He grabs her and pulls her humiliatingly downward. Kelly tells them that what they are doing is not right. The white girl says: "you'd think this was a convention for the promotion of black-white relations the way she talks." The white girl wants Kelly tied up. The white man ties up "the young pretty Negress." She is tied spread-eagle. "Her naked black flesh shimmered . . ." Angela kisses her and touches her all over. Robert Grey takes photographs. A chill goes up Kelly's "small, black spine." Angela kisses the black girl's dark flesh. She arrives at "the Negress's black nipple." Angela sucks the black girl's vagina. Kelly moans: do it, do it. Angela's hand slides down the black girl's belly and her dark hip. Angela's hand holds her black breast. Angela takes her tongue away from "Kelly's black cuntal lips" and calls Kelly her little black princess. Robert Grey gets excited. Kelly is "beginning to go out of her mind with the powerful affects *[sic]* of cunt-licking lust!" Angela continues to kiss the environs of Kelly's cunt as Kelly wonders how she could have been a fashion model for a national magazine only a few hours ago and now she is in the middle of a nightmare with an ambitious lesbian photographer. Robert Grey now wants his. Angela tells him to give our little black friend a rest. Robert Grey demands that Angela suck him. Kelly looks on, despite herself. Angela sucks his cock. Angela wonders if our little black bitch can suck cock as well as she can. Angela keeps sucking. Kelly is disgusted to have to watch a white couple performing oral sex while she is tied like an animal. But an inner voice with masochistic urges is telling her that she loves being forced. Angela keeps sucking. Robert Grey begins to play with her vagina with his fingers. Robert Grey can see the black girl with her black thighs. Angela keeps sucking. Angela keeps sucking. Robert Grey looks at Angela's vicious face. Angela sucks "with wanton frenzy." Kelly is disgusted. Kelly feels an erotic thrill. Kelly keeps watching. Angela keeps sucking. Angela's cheeks bloat. Angela has become a wild animal in heat, a bitch. Angela keeps sucking. Robert Grey jams his fingers into her cunt. Angela sucks harder.

The cum pours out of Robert Grey's prick. Kelly tries to turn away but it is too late. Angela keeps sucking. Robert Grey rams his cock deep into her throat. Robert Grey says that he should have saved all that for our little black girl. Kelly tries not to think. Robert Grey decides to fuck the black girl. He licks her black breasts and her black lips. Robert Grey gloats that she is the wealthiest, most famous black fashion girl in the world. She struggles as he violates her black flesh. He climbs between her legs. He has never really looked at the vagina of a black girl before. It is just like his wife's cunt except that his wife is an old hag. He sucks her. She has chills in her black loins. His penis touches her young black leg. She prays. His lips clamp down on her clitoris. She experiences erotic excitement and moral frustration. She prays. Robert Grey sucks. He looks at her cunt. Her skin and hair are deeply black. Her pubic hair is black fleece. He likes the deep crimson of "the inner cuntal area." He sucks. Robert Grey extracts his tongue to say that "times like this I wish I was a black man." He chomps on his lips. His lips and tongue are wanton and lewd. He sucks. She begs him to stop. She is hot. Robert Grey tells her to "grin and bear it like a good little nigger girl." Kelly is hurt. She is being defiled physically and her self-respect is also being defiled. She is being made to enjoy it. She cries. He keeps calling her "little nigger girl." He starts putting his fingers in her cunt. He calls her a dumb bitch. She is feeling the hot passions of arousal. Robert Grey is hurting her with his fingers. Kelly prays. Kelly thinks she will be torn. Kelly thinks she will faint. Robert Grey is sadistic and blushing. He makes her smell his fingers. She licks his fingers. She begs him to stop. He asks her what she would rather he do. He asks if he should ram her pussy with his fist or use a big rhino dildo or get the Great Dane that fucks women to come fuck her. She asks where Doug is. Robert Grey has a plan. Kelly looks up. She sees her smooth black belly. Robert Grey fingerfucks her. He keeps withdrawing. He spreads the fluid from her cunt on his cock with his fingers. He tells her it excites her. His monstrous white shaft is between her black thighs. His fingers pinch her clitoris. He puts his finger in her. Robert Grey's "blood-filled cock would soon be ramming into her body."

Robert Grey does not want to hurt her by forcing his cock in too fast. He wants her to like it too. But Kelly is so excited she can't wait. When his cock is buried in her belly she feels as though she is being stretched apart. She loves it. Robert Grey keeps fucking her. Kelly tries to resist wanting it but she can't. Robert Grey is twice as excited because she is black and he is white! Robert Grey thrusts harder. She is hopelessly impaled. Angela comes from the darkroom with new photos. She laughs as she sees Kelly's "writhing body welcoming the forceful thrusts of Robert Grey's driving cock. The young black girl's hot little gash seemed to gape in greedy desire." Angela gets excited. Kelly feels ashamed and excited. Kelly starts screaming: Fuck me, fuck me, fuck me. Robert Grey sadistically stops. Robert Grey sadistically begins again. He keeps fucking her until she finally goes limp. "Her body was beaten and bruised and satiated from the ravishment, but she slowly but surely remembered who she was and who the man was she was with." The camera is clicking. Angela shows her the photographs of her being fucked by Robert Grey. Kelly asks for Doug. They call Bart, Kelly's former boyfriend. Bart is going to be the third person. Bart Kurtis stands above her. He undresses. He is a policeman with a detective's .38. He has had Doug arrested. He wants revenge on Kelly. They untie her. Her breasts hang like wild black fruits. Angela sucks Bart. He wants Kelly to suck him. She is lust-wracked. He makes her suck. Her black lips suck. His prick is too big for any natural orifice. His cock keeps sticking at the bottom of her throat. She feels lust. She considers herself "the worst little nigger girl in the entire city." Bart lunges viciously in her throat but she is sucking with a wild abandon. Her pain is horrible but her lust is overwhelming. She pulls away and manages to stop Bart from coming in her mouth. The white lavalike cum erupts. He tries to get it on her black cheek. She wonders how it is that a black man's cum and a white man's cum are the same color. Robert Grey gets her on top of him. Bart's long, thick cock is getting ripe again. It is too big to fit in her cunt. Angela puts Robert Grey's cock in Kelly's cunt. Bart says: "Okay now, you little black whore, what about some brown-eye . . . just to let you feel how good it is to be home again, eh? I bet you'd really like to have my cock up your tail, hey?" She screams. Bart has a huge, meaty erection. Bart pushes and pushes and pushes in. She realizes with terror that Bart's cock is not even nearly in her yet. He keeps going in farther and farther. It is like a crucifixion, "the nail pounding into her . . . defiling her asshole." Then she starts to get excited and like it. She screams, fuck me, fuck me, fuck me, hurt me, fuck my ass my lover. Robert Grey fucks harder. Angela makes Kelly eat her cunt while the two men are fucking Kelly. Bart cums. Kelly cums and cums and cums. Her cumming makes the two men hard again. The four continue their lusty, wild abandonment. Kelly returns to work the next day. She tries to keep the secret of her "molestation and the horrible agony of her ultimate defilement and humiliation." A national newspaper prints one of the lascivious photos and Kelly is ruined forever. The once most famous black fashion model retires to anonymity with Doug, the white lover she tried to protect.

The relationship of all this to Watergate is not entirely clear.

At the heart of the story, however, is indeed "the simple unalterable fact of her color."

All the sex in *Black Fashion Model* is the standard stuff of pornography: rape, bondage, humiliation, pain, fucking, assfucking, fingerfucking, cocksucking, cuntsucking, kidnapping, hitting, the sexual cruelty of one woman toward another, pair sex, gang sex.

All the values are the standard values of pornography: the excitement of humiliation, the joy of pain, the pleasure of abuse, the magnificence of cock, the woman who resists only to discover that she loves it and wants more.

The valuation of the woman is the standard valuation ("a wanton, lusty *woman*!"), except that her main sexual part is her skin, its color. Her skin with its color is her sex with its nature. She is punished in sex by sex and she is punished as a consequence of sex: she loses her status. All this punishment is deserved, owing to her sex, which is her skin. The genital shame of any woman is transferred to the black woman's skin. The shame of sex is the shame of her skin. The stigma of sex is the stigma of her skin. The use of her sex is the use of her skin. The violence against her sex is violence against her skin. The excitement of torturing her sex is the excitement of torturing her skin. The hatred of her sex is the hatred of her skin. Her sex is stretched over her like a glove and when he touches her skin he puts on that glove. She models her skin, her sex. Her sex is as close, as available, as her skin. Her sex is as dark as her skin. The black model need not model naked to be sex; any display of her skin is sex. Her sex is right on the surface—her essence, her offense.

Bart, the black male policeman with a gun, punishes her for leaving him, leaving home, leaving by moving up and out. His race is first made clear in a description of the size of his cock. Later the text reveals that he is a black man; but the reader, having encountered the size of his cock ("His prick is too big for any natural orifice"), is presumed to know already. He is the boss. The white folks are under his orders and doing what he wants. He is on top; he is the meanest; he fucks the black woman in the ass to hurt her the worst. These are all reasons to fear him, especially to fear his sex. He avenges his masculinity and his race on her—by using his huge cock. She ends up calling him her lover and begging him to hurt her: with each other, race is neutralized—they are just male and female after all.

Kelly is a good girl *(sic)*. Only in front of the camera is she wanton, lewd, lusty—a woman! Her sexual nature is in what the camera captures—her skin. Once actually used—revealed in sex to be what she is in skin—she loses everything. The camera captures her skin in sexual action, her skin actualized, being used for what it is. The huge cock reveals the black man. The black female's skin reveals her: her skin is cunt; it has that sexual value in and of itself. Her face is savage beauty, savage cunt. She has no part that is not cunt. One wants her; one wants her skin. One has her; one has her skin. One rapes her; one rapes her skin. One humiliates her; one humiliates her skin. As long as her skin shows, her cunt shows. This is the specific sexual value of the black woman in pornography in the United States, a race-bound society fanatically committed to the sexual devaluing of black skin perceived as a sex organ and a sexual nature. No woman of any other race bears this specific burden in this country. In no other woman is skin sex, cunt in and of itself—her essence, her offense. This meaning of the black woman's skin is revealed in the historical usage of her, even as it developed from the historical usage of her. This valuation of the black woman is real, especially vivid in urban areas where she is used as a street whore extravagantly and without conscience. Poverty forces her; but it is the sexual valuation of her skin that predetermines her poverty and permits the simple, righteous use of her as a whore.

How, then, does one fight racism and jerk off to it at the same time? The Left cannot have its whores and its politics too. The imperial United States cannot maintain its racist system without its black whores, its bottom, the carnal underclass. The sexualization of race within a racist system is a prime purpose and consequence of pornography. In using the black woman, pornography depicts the whore by depicting her skin; in using the pornography, men spit on her sex and her skin. Here the relationship of sex and death could not be clearer: this sexual use of the black woman is the death of freedom, the death of justice, the death of equality.

GENA COREA: Are you saying that some doctors are now feeling that in order to preserve the birth canal, they should do cesarean sections?

DR. HERBERT RATNER: There are some doctors who have taken that position—that this is an improvement on nature. I think that, deep down, this is the way doctors are really thinking, although they don't articulate it. They somehow think they are preserving the birth canal, not only claiming that it protects against later pathology like cystocele and prolapse, which has never really been demonstrated—but they also think, though they probably don't articulate it, they really think it's a contribution to lovemaking. . . . Deep down, the American physician thinks he's doing a woman a favor in preserving her vagina for sexual activities. He can't sew back the

> hymen *[laughs]* so he can't take it back to a real virginal state, but if he could do that, he'd probably do it.
> GENA COREA: Are they doing her a favor or her husband a favor, do you think?
> DR. HERBERT RATNER: I think they're doing this in good part for the husband but behind it is that if the wife can function better for the husband, she's happier too. They're doing it for both.
>
> Unpublished interview by Gena Corea,
> September 20, 1979

The magazine is called *Mom*. It is subtitled "Big Bellied Mamas." The model on the cover is white and great with child. She is fingering her huge belly. Her fingernails are painted purple. She is naked except for a garter belt that hangs unfastened, framing her huge belly. Inside, this model is called Anna. There are twenty-three pages of photographs of Anna, some in color, some black and white. In most of the photographs, Anna is displaying her huge belly as if it were—in the visual vocabulary of pornography—her breasts or ass or cunt. In the rest of the photographs, Anna is fingering other parts of her body, especially her genitals, or she is displaying her genitals. In many of the photographs Anna has on pieces of underwear—garter belt, bra, stockings, robe. In every case, the positioning of the underwear on and around her body suggests bondage. In two photographs Anna has a stethoscope: in one, it is on her belly, her legs spread, her underwear suggesting bondage; in the other it is approaching her vagina, her legs spread, her underwear suggesting bondage. In three photographs, Anna is shown being sprayed with a shower of water. The source of the water is not clear; the photographs suggest "water sports," urine. In one photograph, there is the belly, in between her legs, her vaginal opening above her belly, her ass at the top of the frame. In other words, the model is on her stomach, with her legs spread, her vagina on display, shot from behind so that only her belly, vaginal opening, ass, and thighs are shown. Her garter belt, which must be around her waist, is shown as if it were a rope tied around her belly. In one photograph Anna stands, belly in profile, looking at several large dildoes. The accompanying text explains that while most pregnancies cause no trouble, there are some exceptions. Anna has had a lot of trouble with endrocrine gland disorders. Diseases of the thyroid are listed. Anna started getting awful pains in her back and stomach. This was the pituitary gland "out of order," the "master gland" that produces "about six known hormones." Anna told her doctor but he only nodded his head and took her temperature, which she thought was unprofessional. In her fourth month she felt the baby move. The doctor explained that the embryo was now a fetus and that it was "stretching itself in its bag of water." Anna, being inquisitive, wanted to investigate. Could she X-ray the fetus? No. Anna had to look at pictures in medical books. Anna, like other women going through pregnancy, developed a philosophy. Before she had been fatalistic. Now she decided that she did have control over her life. Anna used to be morbid but now she is not. She is not concerned with failing anymore because she has succeeded in being pregnant. Anna "commands a new kind of attention now. She can tell by looking in a man's eyes exactly what he is thinking. Her motherhood has awakened deep maternal instincts. He would never have had these same emotions if her stomach were flat." Soon Anna will give birth. She has been warned by other women. She could have metabolic problems causing toxemia. "And then there is the struggle for the balance of power between the estrin and progestin hormones." This struggle for the balance of power "irritates" the uterus and causes labor. Although Anna is usually concerned with warnings, she is determined to listen to advice but to maintain calm in the face of "these dire premonitions." Anna's outlook is completely positive. She gets unexpected heartbeats at unexpected times and she has difficulty catching her breath. For several weeks she was worried because a close friend had a hemorrhage and almost died from internal bleeding: "From her doctor she discovered that there were two kinds of hemorrhage: antepartum, meaning the kind that comes before the baby is born and postpartum, which comes afterwards." A ruptured uterus is also a grim possibility. Anna cannot stop thinking about this. But since Anna has been meditating, she is good at taking naps. Because the enlarged uterus displaces the rest of the abdomen, there can be frequent urination. Anna does not want to have to get up in the middle of the night and go all the way to the bathroom. She has wanted "a portable receptacle" on wheels. But she hasn't found a store that sells one. Anna is very curious about men's reactions to her pregnancy. She approaches strangers and asks them. The answers vary but most of the men were intrigued by her shape and size. Anna so far hasn't had morning sickness. She is having trouble judging time. "All of this is part of being pregnant, of course." Anna's story is followed by twenty-two pages of photographs of Abbey, a white woman with big breasts distinguished by particularly large, dark aureoles around her nipples. Abbey's belly, big but not so big as Anna's, is the center of attention, unless she is masturbating or her legs are spread to show her genitals. The photographs are in color and in black and white. Abbey could not believe she was pregnant. She had been swallowing fertility pills like mad. Abbey ovulated fourteen days before her menstrual period. Abbey could not see this miracle directly but her instincts told her it was happening: "In her mind she was right there watching this particle of herself begin an incredible cycle." The life of the ovum is explained. The male ejaculate ("approximately one teaspoonful of fluid") is explained. Abbey remembers the ejaculation and looks forward to it each time. The "male sperm" are "eel-like with arrow-shaped heads and they know exactly what they are and what is expected of them." Their journey is described. Abbey is dizzy just thinking "that she is the container for all that running about." The sperm mostly die but one doesn't. It finds a bed. Once Abbey was told that she had a small tumor in her uterus that meant she couldn't conceive. But the "obstacle dissolved away" and "there was no blockage in the junction to her Fallopian tubes." Abbey could not believe she was pregnant. "And then Boom!" Abbey had taken the air insufflation test to see whether her Fallopian tubes were clear. The tubes were clear but still she had "to submit to postcoital scrutiny." The examination was to see whether there were secretions in the vagina that were destroying the sperm—Abbey feared this was the case—or whether there were not enough sperm. During the tests Abbey could not have intercourse. Smears would show whether the sperm was viable or not when in touch "with the vaginal contents." Abbey worried. She had "strange erotic dreams." She dreamed that her limbs were separated from her body. Once she knew she was pregnant she became strong. All the trials of the past were erased. She could not dress with her former style but she knew a designer who made maternity clothes that would accentuate her femininity. She had to adjust to a new schedule. She couldn't get up early and take a walk. Moving around wasn't so simple. Abbey had to adjust to a new response to her body. Before she had had a stunning body and had gotten attention wherever she went. She wouldn't wear a bra because she wanted her breasts to have freedom. "And, of course, her sleek, long legs were accustomed to stretching out and allowing her full buns all the liberty they desired." Sometimes the wind would raise her skirt and her silk panties would show: "It didn't take much imagination to visualize her perky pussy enclosed within that tiny strip of fabric." Now all that "street fun" is gone. But Abbey will someday be "strutting her stuff" again. Abbey has no regrets. Being pregnant is so exciting that "[s]ince changes are occurring so rapidly inside of her now she hardly has time to talk about it to anyone." Before she was always on the telephone chatting with old lovers. Now she hasn't the time. Pregnancy has stopped her informal communication: "Abbey is limited by her condition . . . even dialing can become a chore when a girl is carrying around all that added weight." Abbey still has an active mind, however. She can imagine herself doing all the things she used to be able to do when she was lighter. Abbey has pointers for women who are afraid of pregnancy. Abbey has even written these down "because she wants to pass them on to all future mothers." Abbey must spread her joy. Anyone who looks at her expression will conclude that "[t]his girl loves being pregnant!" Because her metabolism has changed, she has changed her eating habits. She eats pickles and ice cream and still gets the necessary twenty-five hundred calories a day, which is what counts.

The pornography of pregnancy—the graphic depiction of mothers as whores—completes the picture. The maternal does not exclude the whorish; rather, the maternal is included in the whorish as long as the male wants to use the woman. The malevolence of the woman's body is stressed: its danger to sperm and especially its danger to the woman herself. Her glands, metabolism, hormones, tubes, ovaries, "the vaginal contents"—all are potentially or actually malevolent. It is as if she is swollen and bound to explode from inside.

The sperm are male. The vagina will destroy them. Pregnancy is the triumph of the phallus over the death-dealing vagina.

The women display themselves, display their sex, display their bellies. The huge belly is fetishized but the whore behind it stays the same: the cunt showing herself.

The pregnancy is seen as a condition of both bondage and humiliation: her difficulty in moving is dwelled on with transparent delight and so is bladder irritation.

The men who discuss sex say that there are two conflicting sides: those who believe only in reproductive sex versus those who believe in sex for pleasure not connected to reproduction. But there are not two sides: there is a continuum of phallic control. In the male system, reproductive and nonreproductive sex are both phallic sex, use of the whore for male pleasure. The woman great with child is the woman whose sex is ready to burst, who has taken so much of the male into her that now he is growing there.

The pornography of pregnancy, as of now, is right-wing pornography: kept secret, a hidden trade in the sluts who get knocked up. The emphasis on pregnancy is, in terms of sexual values, distinctly right-wing. This pornography is kept hidden to hide the truth it tells. Women are not cleansed or purified or made good by pregnancy. Pregnancy is confirmation that the woman has been fucked: it is confirmation that she is a cunt. In the male sexual system, the pregnant woman is a particular sexual object: she shows her sexuality through her pregnancy. The display marks her as a whore. Her belly is her sex. Her belly is proof that she has been used. Her belly is his phallic triumph. One does not abort his victory. The right wing must have its proof, its triumph; she, a woman of sex, must be marked. The pregnant woman is the sexual obsession of the right-wing male sexual mentality: that obsession kept secret but acted on in public policy that forbids abortion. The pregnancy is punishment for her participation in sex. She will get sick, her body will go wrong in a thousand different ways, she will die. The sexual excitement is in her possible death—her body that tried to kill the sperm being killed by it. Even in pregnancy, the possibility of her death is the excitement of sex. And now, the doctors have added more sex—to birth itself. *Vagina* means sheath. They cut directly into the uterus with a knife—a surgical fuck. She is tied down—literally cuffed and tied, immobilized by bondage, the bondage of birth, her legs spread; they pour drugs into her to induce labor; their bondage and their drugs cause intense and unbearable pain; she cannot have natural labor; she is drugged and sliced into, surgically fucked. The epidemic of cesarean sections in this country is a sexual, not a medical, phenomenon. The doctors save the vagina—the birth canal of old—for the husband; they fuck the uterus directly, with a knife. Modern childbirth—surgical childbirth—comes from the metaphysics of male sexual domination: she is a whore, there to be used, the uterus of the whore entered directly by the new rapist, the surgeon, the vagina saved to serve the husband.

IN THE SYSTEM of male sexual domination explicated in pornography, there is no way out, no redemption: not through desire, not through reproduction.

The woman's sex is appropriated, her body is possessed, she is used and she is despised: the pornography does it and the pornography proves it.

The power of men in pornography is imperial power, the power of the sovereigns who are cruel and arrogant, who keep taking and conquering for the pleasure of power and the power of pleasure.

Women are the land, as Marcuse wrote. He did not write the rest: men are the army; penises and their symbolic representations are the weapons; terror is the means; violence is the so-called sex.

And inside this system, women are *porneia,* in our real live bodies the graphic depictions of whores, used as whores are used, valued as whores are valued.

WE WILL KNOW that we are free when the pornography no longer exists. As long as it does exist, we must understand that we are the women in it: used by the same power, subject to the same valuation, as the vile whores who beg for more.

The boys are betting on our compliance, our ignorance, our fear. We have always refused to face the worst that men have done to us. The boys count on it. The boys are betting that we cannot face the horror of their sexual system and survive. The boys are betting that their depictions of us as whores will beat us down and stop our hearts. The boys are betting that their penises and fists and knives and fucks and rapes will turn us into what they say we are—the compliant women of sex, the voracious cunts of pornography, the masochistic sluts who resist because we really want more. The boys are betting. The boys are wrong.

Acknowledgments

The difficulties involved in writing and publishing this book were enormous. The pornography that I had to study became a central part of my life and caused me great personal anguish. I had a very hard time making a living while writing this book, partly because magazines and newspapers, with few exceptions, refused to publish my work. Book publishers did not want to publish this book. The completion of this book is for me a triumph of survival as a writer. Many people helped me and I will never forget them. It is both fair and true to say that I would have gone under without them.

John Stoltenberg and Elaine Markson: I can never express what I owe them.

During the time I wrote this book all of these people helped me substantially: Kathleen Barry, Raymond Bongiovanni, Gena Corea, John Corwin, Sheryl Dare, Margaret Desmond, Wendi Dragonfire, Joanne Edgar, Sandra Elkin, Ellen Frankfort, Leah Fritz, Robert Gurland, Susan Hester, Lin Hill, Shere Hite, Patricia Hynes, Karla Jay, Eleanor Johnson, Judah Kataloni, Barbara Levy, Catharine MacKinnon, Donna Mages, Julie Melrose, Robin Morgan, Bert Pogrebin, Letty Cottin Pogrebin, Janice Raymond, Adrienne Rich, Florence Rush, Anne Simon, Gloria Steinem, Margaret Stoltenberg, Vincent Stoltenberg, Geri Thoma, Laurie Woods and her colleagues at the National Center on Women and Family Law.

Women's groups all over the country also helped me—their activism was a constant support. I thank Women Against Pornography, Women Against Violence in Pornography and Media, Women Against Violence Against Women, Women Against Pornography, People Against Pornography, Feminists Against Pornography,

Women Against Sexist Violence in Pornography and Media, and all the feminist activists with whom I have had the honor to march, to plan, to picket, to talk, and to do other things. And I thank those who have organized and sponsored lectures, conferences, and seminars on issues of violence against women in which I have participated.

I owe very special thanks to Gena Corea for her contribution to my understanding of the pornography of pregnancy.

I also thank the hundreds of women, perhaps over a thousand, who have told me their experiences of rape and battery over these last years. They are written into every page of this book and they were with me in memory as I wrote. I am particularly grateful to the women who told me about the use of pornography by their husbands, fathers, sons, brothers, and lovers, and about the use of pornography in acts of sexual abuse that these women experienced. I thank the feminist workers in the areas of rape and battery who have shared their knowledge and experience with me. I thank, always and forever, the feminist writers who have written on violence against women. I thank the many readers of my work who communicated encouragement to me during the course of writing this book. I thank the many individuals who have read this book or parts of it in manuscript and in proof.

I also thank Linda Marchiano, who in the last months of my writing this book has been an inspiration and an example.

And finally I thank Sam Mitnick, who had the courage to publish this book, and the people at Perigee.

ANDREA DWORKIN
New York City

Notes

Preface

1. Christabel Pankhurst, "The Government and White Slavery," pamphlet reprinted from *The Suffragette*, April 18, April 25, 1913, p. 11.

Chapter 1: Power

1. Mary Daly, *Beyond God the Father* (Boston: Beacon Press, 1974), p. 8.
2. Daly, *Beyond God the Father*, p. 8.
3. Phyllis Chesler and Emily Jane Goodman, *Women, Money and Power* (New York: William Morrow & Co., 1976), p. 31.
4. Virginia Woolf, *A Room of One's Own* (New York: Harcourt, Brace & World, 1957), p. 36.
5. Arthur Rimbaud, "A Season in Hell," in *A Season in Hell and The Drunken Boat*, trans. Louise Varèse, bilingual ed. (Norfolk, Conn.: New Directions Books, 1961), p. 3.
6. Jil Clark, "Circulating Information," interview with Allen Young, *Gay Community News*, May 12, 1979, p. 9.

Chapter 2: Men and Boys

1. Virginia Woolf, *The Pargiters: The Novel-Essay Portion of THE YEARS*, ed. Mitchell A. Leaska (New York: New York Public Library & Readex Books, 1977), p. 164.
2. Bruno Bettelheim, *The Uses of Enchantment: The Meaning and Importance of Fairy Tales* (New York: Alfred A. Knopf, 1976), p. 46.

3. John Stoltenberg, "Eroticism and Violence in the Father-Son Relationship," in *For Men Against Sexism*, ed. Jon Snodgrass (Albion, Calif.: Times Change Press, 1977), p. 106.
4. Norman O. Brown, *Love's Body* (New York: Random House, 1966), p. 180.
5. Brown, *Love's Body*, p. 244.
6. Paul H. Gebhard, John H. Gagnon, Wardell B. Pomeroy, and Cornelia V. Christenson, *Sex Offenders: An Analysis of Types* (New York: Harper & Row, Publishers, and Paul B. Hoeber, 1965), p. 6.
7. R. D. Laing, *The Facts of Life* (New York: Pantheon Books, 1976), p. 65.
8. Martin Luther, cited by Margaret Sanger, *Margaret Sanger: An Autobiography* (New York: Dover Publications, 1971), p. 210.
9. Norman Mailer, *The Prisoner of Sex* (Boston: Little, Brown & Co., 1971), p. 126.
10. Havelock Ellis, *Studies in the Psychology of Sex*, vol. 2, pt. 2 (New York: Random House, 1937), p. 194.
11. T. E. Lawrence, in a letter to Charlotte Shaw, March 26, 1924, British Museum, Department of Western Manuscripts, Additional Manuscripts, cited by John E. Mack, *A Prince of Our Disorder: The Life of T. E. Lawrence* (Boston: Little, Brown & Co., 1976), pp. 419–20.
12. Giacomo Casanova, *History of My Life*, vol. 11, trans. Willard R. Trask (New York: Harcourt Brace Jovanovich, 1971), p. 15.
13. Laing, *Facts of Life*, p. 3.
14. D. H. Lawrence, *Sex, Literature and Censorship*, ed. Harry T. Moore (New York: Twayne Publishers, 1953), p. 49.
15. Ellis, *Psychology of Sex*, vol. 2, pt. 3, p. 21.
16. Georges-Michel Sarotte, *Like a Brother, Like a Lover*, trans. Richard Miller (Garden City, N.Y.: Doubleday & Co., Anchor Press, 1977), p. 165.
17. Jeffrey Klein, "Born Again Porn," *Mother Jones*, February–March 1978, p. 14.
18. Virginia Woolf, *A Room of One's Own* (New York: Harcourt, Brace & World, 1957), p. 29.

CHAPTER 3: THE MARQUIS DE SADE (1740–1814)

1. Albert Camus, *The Rebel*, trans. Anthony Bower (New York: Random House, Vintage Books, 1954), p. 35.
2. Camus, *The Rebel*, p. 36.

3. Cited by Ronald Hayman, *De Sade: A Critical Biography* (New York: Thomas Y. Crowell Co., 1978), p. 81.
4. Georges Bataille, *Death and Sensuality* (New York: Ballantine Books, 1969), p. 163.
5. Donald Thomas, *The Marquis de Sade* (Boston: Little, Brown & Co., 1976), p. 103.
6. Thomas, *Marquis de Sade*, p. 104.
7. Ibid., p. 7.
8. Simone de Beauvoir, "Must We Burn Sade?" trans. Annette Michelson, in *The 120 Days of Sodom and Other Writings*, Donatien-Alphonse-François de Sade, trans. Austryn Wainhouse and Richard Seaver (New York: Grove Press, 1967), p. 8.
9. Richard Seaver and Austryn Wainhouse, Foreword, *Justine; Philosophy in the Bedroom; Eugénie de Franval, and Other Writings*, Donatien-Alphonse-François de Sade, trans. Richard Seaver and Austryn Wainhouse (New York: Grove Press, 1966), p. ix.
10. Norman Gear, *The Divine Demon: A Portrait of the Marquis de Sade* (London: Frederick Muller, 1963), p. 135.
11. Jean Paulhan, "The Marquis de Sade and His Accomplice," in *Justine; Philosophy in the Bedroom; Eugénie de Franval, and Other Writings*, p. 7.
12. Hobart Ryland, Introduction, *Adelaide of Brunswick*, Donatien-Alphonse-François de Sade, trans. Hobart Ryland (Washington, D.C.: Scarecrow Press, 1954), p. 6.
13. Geoffrey Gorer, *The Life and Ideas of the Marquis de Sade* (London: Peter Owen, 1953), p. 28.
14. Thomas, *Marquis de Sade*, p. 47.
15. Ibid.
16. Ibid., p. 66.
17. Hayman, *De Sade*, p. 50.
18. Angela Carter, *The Sadeian Woman and the Ideology of Pornography* (New York: Pantheon Books, 1979), p. 29.
19. Carter, *Sadeian Woman*, p. 29.
20. Hayman, *De Sade*, p. 49.
21. Roland Barthes, *Sade/Fourier/Loyola*, trans. Richard Miller (New York: Hill & Wang, 1976), p. 8.
22. Gear, *Divine Demon*, p. 60.
23. Thomas, *Marquis de Sade*, p. 76.
24. Hayman, *De Sade*, p. 64.
25. Edmund Wilson, "The Vogue of the Marquis de Sade," in *The Bit Between My Teeth: A Literary Chronicle of 1950–1965* (New York: Farrar, Straus & Giroux, 1965), p. 162.

26. Gorer, *Life and Ideas*, p. 37.
27. Ibid., p. 23.
28. Wilson, "The Vogue of the Marquis de Sade," p. 163.
29. Camus, *The Rebel*, p. 36.
30. Apollinaire, Preface to the 1949 edition of *Juliette* (Pauvert), cited by Austryn Wainhouse, Foreword to *Juliette*, Donatien-Alphonse-François de Sade, trans. Austryn Wainhouse (New York: Grove Press, 1976), p. ix.
31. Donatien-Alphonse-François de Sade, *Selected Letters*, ed. Margaret Crosland, trans. W. J. Strachan (New York: October House, 1966), p. 65.
32. Sade, *Selected Letters*, p. 66.
33. Ibid., p. 74.
34. Ibid., p. 70.
35. Ibid., pp. 78–79.
36. George Steiner, *Language and Silence* (New York: Atheneum Publishers, 1977), p. 69.
37. Ibid.
38. Barthes, *Sade/Fourier/Loyola*, p. 143.
39. Apollinaire, cited by Wainhouse, Foreword to *Juliette*, p. ix.
40. Sade, *Juliette*, p. 991.
41. John T. Noonan, Jr., "An Almost Absolute Value in History," in *The Morality of Abortion*, ed. John T. Noonan, Jr. (Cambridge: Harvard University Press, 1970), p. 37.
42. Linda Bird Francke, *The Ambivalence of Abortion* (New York: Random House, 1978), p. 14.
43. Gorer, *Life and Ideas*, p. 174.
44. Sade, *Philosophy in the Bedroom*, in *Justine; Philosophy in the Bedroom; Eugénie de Franval, and Other Writings*, p. 207.
45. Sade, "The 120 Days of Sodom," *120 Days of Sodom*, p. 293.
46. Sade, *Philosophy in the Bedroom*, p. 267.
47. Sade, "Yet Another Effort, Frenchmen, If You Would Become Republicans," in *Philosophy in the Bedroom*, p. 319.
48. Peter Weiss, *The Persecution and Assassination of Jean-Paul Marat As Performed by the Inmates of the Asylum of Charenton Under the Direction of the Marquis de Sade*, trans. Geoffrey Skelton (New York: Atheneum Publishers, 1967), p. 92.
49. Christopher Lasch, *The Culture of Narcissism* (New York: Warner Books, 1979), p. 132.
50. Lasch, *Narcissism*, p. 133.
51. Gerald and Caroline Greene, *S-M: The Last Taboo* (New York: Grove Press, 1974), p. 64.

52. De Beauvoir, "Must We Burn Sade?" p. 20.
53. Camus, *The Rebel*, p. 47.
54. Sade, "Oxtiern," in *120 Days of Sodom*, p. 701.
55. Sade, *Juliette*, p. 269.
56. Richard Gilman, *Decadence: The Strange Life of an Epithet* (New York: Farrar, Straus & Giroux, 1980), p. 81.

Chapter 4: Objects

1. Sylvia Pankhurst, *The Suffragette Movement* (London: Virago, 1978), p. 95.
2. Ernest Becker, *The Structure of Evil* (New York: Free Press, 1976), p. 158.
3. Ernest Becker, *The Revolution in Psychiatry* (London: Collier-Macmillan, 1964), p. 19.
4. Becker, *Revolution in Psychiatry*, p. 19.
5. Christopher Lasch, *The Culture of Narcissism* (New York: Warner Books, 1979), p. 81.
6. Margaret S. Mahler, Fred Pine, and Anni Bergman, *The Psychological Birth of the Human Infant* (New York: Basic Books, 1975), p. 109.
7. Mahler, Pine, and Bergman, *Psychological Birth*, p. 12.
8. Becker, *Revolution in Psychiatry*, pp. 32–33.
9. Bruno Bettelheim, *The Uses of Enchantment: The Meaning and Importance of Fairy Tales* (New York: Alfred A. Knopf, 1976), p. 134.
10. Havelock Ellis, *Studies in the Psychology of Sex*, vol. 2, pt. 3 (New York: Random House, 1937), p. 539.
11. Ferdinand Lundberg and Marynia F. Farnham, *Modern Woman: The Lost Sex* (New York: Harper & Brothers, Publishers, 1947), p. 275.
12. Becker, *Revolution in Psychiatry*, p. 52.
13. Hannah Tillich, *From Time to Time* (Briarcliff Manor, N.Y.: Stein & Day, 1974), p. 176.
14. Théophile Gautier, *Mademoiselle de Maupin* (New York: Ives Washburn, 1929), p. 200.
15. Gautier, *Mademoiselle de Maupin*, p. 194.
16. Anthony Storr, *Sexual Deviation* (Harmondsworth, England: Penguin Books, 1964), pp. 44–45.
17. Anthony M. Ludovici, *Woman* (London: Constable & Co., 1926), p. 25.

18. Otto Weininger, *Sex and Character* (New York: G. P. Putnam's Sons, 1975), p. 299.
19. Weininger, *Sex and Character*, p. 92.
20. Leopold von Sacher-Masoch, diary, April 15, 1872, cited by James Cleugh, *The First Masochist: A Biography of Leopold von Sacher-Masoch (1836–1895)* (London: Anthony Blond, 1967), p. 96.
21. Roland Barthes, *A Lover's Discourse*, trans. Richard Howard (New York: Hill & Wang, 1979), p. 31.
22. H. L. Mencken, *In Defense of Women* (Garden City, N.Y.: Garden City Publishing Co., 1922), pp. 135–36.
23. James Lewton Brain, *The Last Taboo: Sex and the Fear of Death* (Garden City, N.Y.: Doubleday, Anchor Press, 1979), p. 55.
24. Brain, *Last Taboo*, p. 46.
25. Norman Mailer, *The Prisoner of Sex* (Boston: Little, Brown & Co., 1971), pp. 117–18; also in his *Genius and Lust: A Journey Through the Major Writings of Henry Miller* (New York: Grove Press, 1976), p. 94.
26. Thomas Hardy, *The Well-Beloved* (London: Macmillan London, 1978), p. 34.
27. Mary Welsh Hemingway, *How It Was* (New York: Alfred A. Knopf, 1976), p. 170.
28. Robert J. Stoller, *Sexual Excitement: Dynamics of Erotic Life* (New York: Pantheon Books, 1979), p. 8.
29. Jean-Paul Sartre, *Anti-Semite and Jew*, trans. George J. Becker (New York: Schocken Books, 1970), pp. 10–11.
30. John Keats, "Ode on a Grecian Urn," in *John Keats and Percy Bysshe Shelley: Complete Poetical Works* (New York: Modern Library, n.d.), p. 185.
31. George Sand, *My Life*, ed. and trans. Dan Hofstadter (New York: Harper & Row, Publishers, 1979), p. 25.
32. Herbert Marcuse, *An Essay on Liberation* (Boston: Beacon Press, 1969), pp. 26–27.
33. Edgar Allan Poe, "The Philosophy of Composition," in *Literary Criticism of Edgar Allan Poe*, ed. Robert L. Hough (Lincoln: University of Nebraska Press, 1965), p. 26.
34. Georges Bataille, *Death and Sensuality* (New York: Ballantine Books, 1969), p. 140.
35. Edmond and Jules de Goncourt, *The Woman of the Eighteenth Century*, trans. Jacques Le Clercq and Ralph Roeder (New York: Minton, Balch & Co., 1927), pp. 10–11.

36. Charles Baudelaire, *Journaux Complètes* (Paris, 1963), p. 1272, cited by Alex de Jonge, *Baudelaire: Prince of Clouds* (New York: Paddington Press, 1976), p. 5.
37. Flaubert, in a letter to Louise Colet, June 1853, *Correspondance*, vol. 3, p. 216, cited by Enid Starkie, *Flaubert: The Making of the Master* (London: Weidenfeld & Nicolson, 1967), p. 74.
38. Gustave Flaubert, *Sentimental Education*, trans. Robert Baldick (Harmondsworth, England: Penguin Books, 1974), p. 419.
39. Flaubert, *Sentimental Education*, p. 419.
40. Havelock Ellis, *Sex and Marriage* (Westport, Conn.: Greenwood Press, Publishers, 1977), p. 42.
41. Becker, *Structure of Evil*, p. 177.
42. Richard Freiherr von Krafft-Ebing, *Psychopathia Sexualis*, trans. Harry E. Wedeck (New York: G. P. Putnam's Sons, 1965), pp. 244–45.
43. C. A. Tripp, *The Homosexual Matrix* (New York: New American Library, 1976), p. 19.
44. Tripp, *Homosexual Matrix*, p. 142.
45. Ibid., p. 17.
46. Ibid.
47. Maurice North, *The Outer Fringe of Sex* (London: Odyssey Press, 1970), p. 61.
48. Krafft-Ebing, *Psychopathia Sexualis*, p. 246.
49. Becker, *Structure of Evil*, p. 179.
50. Sigmund Freud, "Fetishism," in *The Future of Illusion; Civilization and Its Discontents; and Other Works*, eds. and trans. James Strachey and Anna Freud, *The Standard Edition of the Complete Psychological Works of Sigmund Freud*, vol. 21 (London: Hogarth Press and Institute of Psycho-Analysis, 1968), pp. 152–53.
51. Storr, *Sexual Deviation*, pp. 55–56.
52. Ibid., p. 54.
53. Ibid., p. 56.
54. Alfred C. Kinsey, Wardell B. Pomeroy, Clyde E. Martin, and Paul H. Gebhard, *Sexual Behavior in the Human Female* (Philadelphia: W. B. Saunders Co., 1953), pp. 678–79.
55. Charles Winick, "A Neuter and Desexualized Society?" in *The New Sexual Revolution*, eds. Lester A. Kirkendall and Robert N. Whitehurst (New York: Donald W. Brown, 1971), p. 99.
56. Lars Ullerstam, *The Erotic Minorities*, trans. Anselm Hollo (London: Calder & Boyars, 1967), p. 103.
57. Tillich, *From Time to Time*, p. 87.

58. Ibid., p. 14.
59. Herbert Marcuse, *Negations* (Boston: Beacon Press, 1968), p. 242.
60. Adrienne Rich, "Twenty-one Love Poems," I, *The Dream of a Common Language* (New York: W. W. Norton & Co., 1978), p. 25.

Chapter 5: Force

1. Havelock Ellis, *Studies in the Psychology of Sex*, vol. 1, pt. 2 (New York: Random House, 1936), p. 128.
2. Robert Briffault, *The Mothers: The Matriarchal Theory of Social Origins* (New York: Macmillan Co., 1931), p. 48.
3. Kate Millett, *Sexual Politics* (New York: Avon Books, 1971), p. 209.
4. Bruno Bettelheim, *Symbolic Wounds* (Glencoe, Ill.: Free Press, 1954), pp. 64–65.
5. Robert J. Stoller, *Sexual Excitement: Dynamics of Erotic Life* (New York: Pantheon Books, 1979), p. 161.
6. A. Merriam-Webster, *Webster's Third New International Dictionary of the English Language Unabridged*, ed. Philip Babcock Gove (Springfield, Mass.: G. & C. Merriam Co., 1976), p. 1034.
7. Elizabeth Janeway, *Between Myth and Morning: Women Awakening* (New York: William Morrow & Co., 1974), pp. 197–98.
8. Suzanne Brøgger, *Deliver Us from Love*, trans. Thomas Teal (New York: Delacorte Press, Seymour Lawrence, 1976), p. 113.
9. Alex Mallow and Leon Chabot, *Laser Safety Handbook* (New York: Van Nostrand Reinhold Co., 1978), p. 4.
10. H. G. Wells, *The War of the Worlds* in *The Invisible Man; The War of the Worlds; A Dream of Armageddon* (London: T. Fisher Unwin, 1924), p. 247.
11. Richard B. Nehrich, Jr., Glenn I. Voran, and Norman F. Dessel, *Atomic Light: Lasers—What They Are and How They Work* (New York: Sterling Publishing Co., 1967), p. 101.
12. Ronald Brown, *Lasers: Tools of Modern Technology* (Garden City, N.Y.: Doubleday & Co., 1968), p. 26.
13. O. S. Heavens, *Lasers* (New York: Charles Scribner's Sons, 1971), p. 140.
14. P. A. Cirincione, "Biological Effects of Lasers: Safety Recommendations," in *Laser Technology and Applications*, ed. Samuel

L. Marshall (New York: McGraw-Hill Book Co., 1968), p. 251.
15. Heavens, *Lasers*, pp. 140–41.
16. Nehrich, Voran, and Dessel, *Atomic Light*, p. 94.
17. Mallow and Chabot, *Laser Safety Handbook*, p. 26.
18. John F. Ready, *Effects of High-Power Laser Radiation* (New York: Academic Press, 1971), p. 345.
19. Pennethorne Hughes, *Witchcraft* (Harmondsworth, England: Penguin Books, 1971), p. 183.
20. Jean-Paul Sartre, *Anti-Semite and Jew*, trans. George J. Becker (New York: Schocken Books, 1970), pp. 48–49.
21. Susan Brownmiller, *Against Our Will: Men, Women and Rape* (New York: Simon & Schuster, 1975), p. 124.
22. George Steiner, *Language and Silence* (New York: Atheneum Publishers, 1977), p. 76.
23. Ellis, *Studies in the Psychology of Sex*, vol. 1, pt. 2, pp. 68–69.
24. Ibid., pp. 32–33.
25. Ibid., p. 89.
26. Theodor Reik, *Of Love and Lust* (New York: Farrar, Straus & Co., 1957), p. 341.
27. Reik, *Of Love and Lust*, pp. 346–47.
28. Stoller, *Sexual Excitement*, p. 79.
29. Georges Bataille, *Death and Sensuality* (New York: Ballantine Books, 1969), p. 126.
30. C. A. Tripp, *The Homosexual Matrix* (New York: New American Library, 1976), p. 56.
31. Tripp, *Homosexual Matrix*, p. 56.
32. Ibid.
33. R. H. Tawney, *Equality* (London: Unwin Books, 1964), p. 105.
34. Mary Wollstonecraft, *A Vindication of the Rights of Woman* (New York: W. W. Norton & Co., 1967), p. 69.
35. A. Schawlow, cited by Nehrich, Voran, and Dessel, *Atomic Light*, p. 102.
36. Tripp, *Homosexual Matrix*, p. 56.
37. Ibid., p. 110.
38. Stoller, *Sexual Excitement*, p. 4.
39. Molly Haskell, "Rape in the Movies: Update on an Ancient War," *The Village Voice*, October 8, 1979, p. 45.
40. Georges Bataille, *Story of the Eye*, trans. Joachim Neugroschel (New York: Urizen Books, 1977), pp. 24–25.
41. Bataille, *Story of the Eye*, p. 26.
42. Ibid., p. 98.

43. Ibid., p. 120.
44. Ibid., p. 63.
45. Alfred C. Kinsey, Wardell B. Pomeroy, and Clyde E. Martin, *Sexual Behavior in the Human Male* (Philadelphia: W. B. Saunders Co., 1948), p. 9.
46. Kinsey et al., *Sexual Behavior in the Human Male*, pp. 41–42.
47. Ibid., p. 43.
48. Arno Karlen, *Sexuality and Homosexuality* (New York: W. W. Norton & Co., 1971), p. 443.
49. Sigmund Freud, *The Freud/Jung Letters: The Correspondence Between Sigmund Freud and C. G. Jung*, ed. William McGuire, trans. Ralph Manheim and R. F. C. Hull (Princeton, N.J.: Princeton University Press, 1974), p. 64.
50. Alfred C. Kinsey, Wardell B. Pomeroy, Clyde E. Martin, and Paul H. Gebhard, *Sexual Behavior in the Human Female* (Philadelphia: W. B. Saunders Co., 1953), p. 705.
51. Kinsey et al., *Sexual Behavior in the Human Male*, p. 205.
52. Ibid., p. 217.
53. Ibid., p. 363.
54. Ibid., p. 468.
55. Ibid., p. 589.
56. Ibid., p. 223.
57. Ibid., p. 545.
58. Ibid., p. 578.
59. Kinsey et al., *Sexual Behavior in the Human Female*, p. 369.
60. Kinsey et al., *Sexual Behavior in the Human Male*, p. 207.
61. Ibid., p. 209.
62. Kinsey et al., *Sexual Behavior in the Human Female*, p. 374.
63. Ibid., p. 371.
64. Ibid.
65. Kinsey et al., *Sexual Behavior in the Human Male*, p. 595.
66. Ibid., pp. 385–86.
67. Ibid., p. 238.
68. Kinsey et al., *Sexual Behavior in the Human Female*, p. 410.
69. Paul H. Gebhard, John H. Gagnon, Wardell B. Pomeroy, and Cornelia V. Christenson, *Sex Offenders: An Analysis of Types* (New York: Harper & Row, Publishers, and Paul B. Hoeber, 1965), p. 178.
70. Kinsey et al., *Sexual Behavior in the Human Female*, p. 320.
71. Gebhard et al., *Sex Offenders*, p. 6.
72. Ibid., p. 178.
73. Ibid., p. 9.

74. Ibid., p. 54.
75. Ibid., pp. 84–85.
76. Ibid., p. 85.
77. Ibid., p. 101.
78. Ibid.
79. Ibid., p. 156.
80. Ibid., pp. 128–29.
81. Ibid., p. 129.
82. Ibid.
83. Ibid.
84. Ibid.
85. Ibid., p. 128.
86. Ibid., p. 129.
87. Ibid., pp. 108–9.
88. Ibid., p. 109.
89. Ibid., p. 177.
90. Ibid.
91. Ibid., p. 178.

Chapter 6: Pornography

1. Kate Millett, *The Prostitution Papers* (New York: Avon Books, 1973), p. 95.

Chapter 7: Whores

1. H. L. Mencken, *In Defense of Women* (Garden City, N.Y.: Garden City Publishing Co., 1922), p. 187.
2. William Acton, *Prostitution* (New York: Frederick A. Praeger, Publishers, 1969), p. 118.
3. Jane Addams, *A New Conscience and an Ancient Evil* (New York: Macmillan Co., 1914), p. 40.
4. Sigmund Freud, *The Freud/Jung Letters: The Correspondence Between Sigmund Freud and C. G. Jung*, ed. William McGuire, trans. Ralph Manheim and R. F. C. Hull (Princeton, N.J.: Princeton University Press, 1974), p. 503.
5. René Guyon, *Sexual Freedom*, trans. Eden and Cedar Paul (New York: Alfred A. Knopf, 1958), p. 239.
6. Guyon, *Sexual Freedom*, p. 198.
7. Ibid., p. 200.
8. Ibid., p. 204.

9. John Wolfenden, *Report of the Committee on Homosexual Offences and Prostitution* (London: Her Majesty's Stationery Office, 1957), p. 80.
10. Alberto Moravia, *The Woman of Rome*, trans. Lydia Holland (New York: Manor Books, 1974), p. 88.
11. Otto Weininger, *Sex and Character* (New York: G. P. Putnam's Sons, 1975), p. 219.
12. D. H. Lawrence, *Sex, Literature and Censorship*, ed. Harry T. Moore (New York: Twayne Publishers, 1953), p. 69.
13. Lawrence, *Sex, Literature and Censorship*, p. 69.
14. Kate Millett, *Sexual Politics* (New York: Avon Books, 1971), p. 119.
15. Max Lerner, "Playboy: An American Revolution of Morality," *New York Post*, January 10, 1979.

Bibliography

Works of Pornography Analyzed in This Book

Anderson, Greg. *I Love a Laddie.* United States: Continental Classics, 1970.
"Barbered Pole." *Cavalier*, December 1978, pp. 7–11.
Bataille, Georges. *Story of the Eye.* Translated by Joachim Neugroschel. New York: Urizen Books, 1977.
"Beaver Hunters." *Hustler*, December 1978, p. 18.
Guber, Dr. Fritz. "The Art of Dominating Women." *He & She*, January 1979, p. 46.
"Last Tango in Tijuana." *Hustler*, December 1978, pp. 73–84.
"Les Girls." *Swank*, June 1979, pp. 27–33.
Miller, Jessie. *Whip Chick.* New York: Bee-Line Books, 1972.
Mom, no. 1.
"Playboy's Roving Eye." *Playboy*, July 1979, pp. 246–47.
Sade, Marquis de, works of (see full Bibliography).
Wilson, John. *Black Fashion Model.* California: Publisher's Consultants, 1978.

In addition to the works listed above, I have read or looked at thousands of pieces of pornography: photographs, books, magazines, and films.

Books

Abbott, Sidney, and Barbara Love, *Sappho Was a Right-On Woman.* New York: Stein & Day, 1973.
Acton, William. *Prostitution.* New York: Frederick A. Praeger, Publishers, 1969.

Addams, Jane. *A New Conscience and an Ancient Evil.* New York: Macmillan Co., 1914.

Alcott, Louisa May. *Behind a Mask: The Unknown Thrillers of Louisa May Alcott.* Edited by Madeleine Stern. New York: Bantam Books, 1978.

Alcott, William A. *The Young Woman's Guide to Excellence.* Boston: George W. Light, 1840.

Alexander, Shana. *Anyone's Daughter.* New York: Viking Press, 1979.

American Medical Association Committee on Human Sexuality. *Human Sexuality.* Chicago: American Medical Association, 1973.

Andelin, Aubrey P. *Man of Steel and Velvet.* Santa Barbara, Calif.: Pacific Press, 1972.

André le Chaplain. *The Art of Courtly Love.* Translated by John Jay Parry. New York: Columbia University Press, 1941.

Apuleius. *The Golden Ass.* Translated by Robert Graves. New York: Farrar, Straus & Giroux, 1979.

Ardrey, Robert. *The Territorial Imperative.* New York: Bantam Books, 1973.

Arendt, Hannah. *Antisemitism.* New York: Harcourt, Brace & World, 1968.

———. *Eichmann in Jerusalem: A Report on the Banality of Evil.* Rev. ed. New York: Penguin Books, 1977.

———. *Men in Dark Times.* New York: Harcourt, Brace & World, 1968.

———. *On Revolution.* New York: Viking Press, 1976.

Ariès, Philippe. *Western Attitudes Toward Death.* Translated by Patricia M. Ranum. Baltimore: Johns Hopkins Press, 1977.

Armstrong, Louise. *Kiss Daddy Goodnight.* New York: Hawthorn Books, 1978.

Artaud, Antonin. *Collected Works.* Vol. 1. Translated by Victor Corti. London: Calder & Boyars, 1968.

———. *Collected Works.* Vol. 2. Translated by Victor Corti. London: Calder & Boyars, 1971.

Ashley, Elizabeth. *Actress.* New York: M. Evans & Co., 1978.

Astell, Mary. *A Serious Proposal to the Ladies.* New York: Source Book Press, 1970.

Atkins, Thomas R., ed. *Sexuality in the Movies.* Bloomington: Indiana University Press, 1975.

Atkinson, Ti-Grace. *Amazon Odyssey.* New York: Links Books, 1974.

Atwood, Margaret. *Lady Oracle.* New York: Avon Books, 1978.

Bacall, Lauren. *Lauren Bacall By Myself.* New York: Alfred A. Knopf, 1978.
Bainbridge, John. *Garbo.* New York: Holt, Rinehart & Winston, 1971.
Baldwin, James, and Nikki Giovanni. *A Dialogue.* Philadelphia: J. B. Lippincott Co., 1973.
Balsdon, J. P. V. D. *Roman Women: Their History and Habits.* New York: John Day Co., 1963.
Balzac, Honoré de. *A Harlot High and Low.* Translated by Rayner Heppenstall. New York: Penguin Books, 1977.
———. *Lost Illusions.* Translated by Herbert J. Hunt. New York: Penguin Books, 1979.
Banks, Lynn Reid. *Path to the Silent Country: Charlotte Brontë's Years of Fame.* New York: Delacorte Press, 1978.
Barbach, Lonnie Garfield. *For Yourself: The Fulfillment of Female Sexuality.* Garden City, N.Y.: Doubleday & Co., Anchor Press, 1976.
Barker-Benfield, G. J. *The Horrors of the Half-Known Life.* New York: Harper & Row, Publishers, 1976.
Barr, Jennifer. *Within a Dark Wood: The Personal Story of a Rape Victim.* Garden City, N.Y.: Doubleday & Co., 1979.
Barreno, Maria Isabel; Maria Teresa Horta; and Maria Velho Da Costa. *The Three Marias: New Portuguese Letters.* Translated by Helen R. Lane. New York: Bantam Books, 1975.
Barrett, William. *The Illusion of Technique.* Garden City, N.Y.: Doubleday & Co., Anchor Press, 1978.
Barry, Kathleen. *Female Sexual Slavery.* Englewood Cliffs, N.J.: Prentice-Hall, 1979.
Bart, Benjamin F. *Flaubert.* Syracuse, N.Y.: Syracuse University Press, 1967.
Barthes, Roland. *A Lover's Discourse.* Translated by Richard Howard. New York: Hill & Wang, 1979.
———. *Roland Barthes.* Translated by Richard Howard. New York: Hill & Wang, 1977.
———. *Sade/Fourier/Loyola.* Translated by Richard Miller. New York: Hill & Wang, 1976.
Bataille, Georges. *Blue of Noon.* Translated by Harry Mathews. New York: Urizen Books, 1978.
———. *Death and Sensuality.* New York: Ballantine Books, 1969.
———. *Story of the Eye.* Translated by Joachim Neugroschel. New York: Urizen Books, 1977.
Baudelaire, Charles. *The Letters of Baudelaire.* Translated by Arthur

Symons. New York: Albert & Charles Boni, 1927.
Baum, Charlotte; Paula Hyman; and Sonya Michel. *The Jewish Woman in America*. New York: Dial Press, 1976.
Becker, Ernest. *The Revolution in Psychiatry*. London: Collier-Macmillan, 1964.
———. *The Structure of Evil*. New York: Free Press, 1976.
Bednarik, Karl. *The Male in Crisis*. Translated by Helen Sebba. New York: Alfred A. Knopf, 1970.
Beer, Patricia. *Reader, I Married Him*. New York: Barnes & Noble, 1979.
Bell, Alan P., and Martin S. Weinberg. *Homosexualities*. New York: Simon & Schuster, 1978.
Bell, Arthur. *Kings Don't Mean a Thing: The John Knight Murder Case*. New York: William Morrow & Co., 1978.
Bell, Clive. *Civilization*. New York: Harcourt, Brace & Co., 1928.
Benet, Mary Kathleen. *Writers in Love*. New York: Macmillan Publishing Co., 1977.
Bennett, H. S. *Six Medieval Men and Women*. Cambridge: Cambridge University Press, 1955.
Berg, A. Scott. *Max Perkins: Editor of Genius*. New York: E. P. Dutton & Co., 1978.
Bernanos, Georges. *Tradition of Freedom*. New York: Roy Publishers, 1950.
Berrigan, Daniel. *A Book of Parables*. New York: Seabury Press, 1977.
Bettelheim, Bruno. *Surviving and Other Essays*. New York: Alfred A. Knopf, 1979.
———. *Symbolic Wounds*. Glencoe, Ill.: Free Press, 1954.
———. *The Uses of Enchantment: The Meaning and Importance of Fairy Tales*. New York: Alfred A. Knopf, 1976.
Beyle, Marie-Henri [Stendhal]. *Love*. Translated by Gilbert and Suzanne Sale. Harmondsworth, England: Penguin Books, 1975.
Blanchot, Maurice. "Sade." In *Justine; Philosophy in the Bedroom; Eugénie de Franval, and Other Writings*, Donatien-Alphonse-François de Sade. Translated by Richard Seaver and Austryn Wainhouse, pp. 36–72. New York: Grove Press, 1966.
Blease, W. Lyon. *The Emancipation of English Women*. London: Constable & Co., 1910.
Bleuel, Hans Peter. *Sex and Society in Nazi Germany*. Edited by Heinrich Fraenkel. Translated by J. Maxwell Brownjohn. Philadelphia: J. B. Lippincott Co., 1973.
Block, Iwan. *Marquis de Sade: The Man and His Age*. Translated by James Bruce. Newark, N.J.: Julian Press, 1931.

Bode, Janet. *Fighting Back: How to Cope with the Medical, Emotional, and Legal Consequences of Rape*. New York: Macmillan Publishing Co., 1978.
Borges, Jorge Luis. *The Book of Sand*. Translated by Norman Thomas di Giovanni. New York: E. P. Dutton & Co., 1977.
Boserup, Ester. *Woman's Role in Economic Development*. New York: St. Martin's Press, 1970.
Bosworth, Patricia. *Montgomery Clift*. New York: Harcourt Brace Jovanovich, 1978.
Bousfield, Paul. *Sex and Civilization*. New York: E. P. Dutton & Co., 1925.
Brady, Katherine. *Father's Days: A True Story of Incest*. New York: Seaview Books, 1979.
Brain, James Lewton. *The Last Taboo: Sex and the Fear of Death*. Garden City, N.Y.: Doubleday & Co., Anchor Press, 1979.
Brando, Anna Kashfi, and E. P. Stein. *Brando for Breakfast*. New York: Crown Publishers, 1979.
Brandt, Paul [Hans Licht]. *Sexual Life in Ancient Greece*. Translated by J. H. Freese. New York: Barnes & Noble, 1963.
Breslin, Catherine. *The Mistress Condition*. New York: E. P. Dutton & Co., 1976.
Briffault, Robert. *The Mothers: The Matriarchal Theory of Social Origins*. New York: Macmillan Co., 1931.
Brøgger, Suzanne. *Deliver Us from Love*. Translated by Thomas Teal. New York: Delacorte Press, Seymour Lawrence, 1976.
Brontë, Anne. *The Tenant of Wildfell Hall*. Harmondsworth, England: Penguin Books, 1979.
Brown, E. K., and Leon Edel. *Willa Cather: A Critical Biography*. New York: Avon Books, 1980.
Brown, Norman O. *Love's Body*. New York: Random House, 1966.
Brown, Ronald. *Lasers: Tools of Modern Technology*. Garden City, N.Y.: Doubleday & Co., 1968.
Brownmiller, Susan. *Against Our Will: Men, Women and Rape*. New York: Simon & Schuster, 1975.
Bryant, Anita. *Amazing Grace*. Old Tappan, N.J.: Fleming H. Revell Co., 1971.
———. *The Anita Bryant Story*. Old Tappan, N.J.: Fleming H. Revell Co., 1977.
———. *Bless This House*. Old Tappan, N.J.: Fleming H. Revell Co., 1972.
———. *Mine Eyes Have Seen the Glory*. Old Tappan, N.J.: Fleming H. Revell Co., 1970.
Bugliosi, Vincent, and Ken Hurwitz. *Till Death Us Do Part*. New

York: W. W. Norton & Co., 1978.

Burkhart, Kathryn. *Women in Prison*. Garden City, N.Y.: Doubleday & Co., 1973.

Burne, Glenn S. *Remy de Gourmont: His Ideas and Influence in England and America*. Carbondale, Ill.: Southern Illinois University Press, 1963.

Burney, Fanny. *Evelina*. New York: W. W. Norton & Co., 1965.

Butters, John H. *Holography and Its Technology*. London: Peter Peregrinus, 1971.

Camus, Albert. *Lyrical and Critical Essays*. Edited by Philip Thody. Translated by Ellen Conroy Kennedy. New York: Random House, Vintage Books, 1970.

———. *The Rebel*. Translated by Anthony Bower. New York: Random House, Vintage Books, 1954.

Carden, Maren Lockwood. *The New Feminist Movement*. New York: Russell Sage Foundation, 1974.

Carpenter, Edward. *Love's Coming-of-Age*. New York: Mitchell Kennerley, 1911.

Carter, A. E. *Charles Baudelaire*. Boston: Twayne Publishers, 1977.

Carter, Angela. *The Sadeian Woman and the Ideology of Pornography*. New York: Pantheon Books, 1979.

Casanova, Giacomo. *History of My Life*. Vols. 11 and 12. Translated by Willard R. Trask. New York: Harcourt Brace Jovanovich, 1971.

Cassady, Carolyn. *Heart Beat: My Life with Jack and Neal*. New York: Pocket Books, 1976.

Castaneda, Carlos. *The Second Ring of Power*. New York: Simon & Schuster, 1977.

Catullus, C. Valerius. *The Carmina of Catullus*. Translated by Barriss Mills. West Lafayette, Ind.: Purdue University Press, 1965.

———. *Erotica*. Translated by Walter K. Kelly. London: Henry G. Bohn, 1854.

Cetynski, Karol [Ka-Tzetnik 135633]. *Piepel*. Translated by Moshe M. Kohn. London: Anthony Blond, 1961.

Chakotin, Serge. *The Rape of the Masses: The Psychology of Totalitarian Political Propaganda*. Translated by E. W. Dickes. New York: Alliance Book Corp., 1940.

Charnas, Suzy McKee. *Walk to the End of the World*. New York: Ballantine Books, 1977.

Chase-Riboud, Barbara. *Sally Hemings*. New York: Viking Press, 1979.

Chesler, Phyllis. *About Men*. New York: Simon & Schuster, 1978.

———. *Women and Madness*. Garden City, N.Y.: Doubleday & Co., 1972.
———, and Emily Jane Goodman. *Women, Money and Power*. New York: William Morrow & Co., 1976.
Chicago, Judy. *The Dinner Party*. Garden City, N.Y.: Doubleday & Co., Anchor Press, 1979.
———. *Through the Flower: My Struggle as a Woman Artist*. Garden City, N.Y.: Doubleday & Co., Anchor Books, 1977.
Children's Rights: Toward the Liberation of the Child. New York: Praeger Publishers, 1971.
Chodorow, Nancy. *The Reproduction of Motherhood*. Berkeley: University of California Press, 1978.
Christenson, Cornelia V. *Kinsey: A Biography*. Bloomington: Indiana University Press, 1971.
Cleaver, Eldridge. *Soul on Fire*. Waco, Tex.: Word Books, 1978.
Clemens, Samuel [Mark Twain]. *Letters from Earth*. Edited by Bernard de Voto. New York: Perennial Library Press, 1974.
Cleugh, James. *The First Masochist: A Biography of Leopold von Sacher-Masoch (1836–1895)*. London: Anthony Blond, 1967.
———. *The Marquis and the Chevalier*. London: Andrew Melrose, 1951.
Clifford, Deborah Pickman. *Mine Eyes Have Seen the Glory: A Biography of Julia Ward Howe*. Boston: Little, Brown & Co., 1979.
Cline, Victor B., ed. *Where Do You Draw the Line?* Provo, Utah: Brigham Young University Press, 1974.
Closs, August. *Medusa's Mirror: Studies in German Literature*. London: Cresset Press, 1957.
Clurman, Harold. *Ibsen*. New York: Macmillan Publishing Co., 1977.
Cole, William Graham. *Sex and Love in the Bible*. New York: Association Press, 1959.
Coles, Robert. *Eskimos, Chicanos, Indians*. Boston: Little, Brown & Co., 1977.
———, and Jane Hallowell Coles. *Women of Crisis*. New York: Delacorte Press, Seymour Lawrence, 1978.
Colette. *The Innocent Libertine*. Translated by Antonia White. New York: Farrar, Straus & Giroux, 1978.
———. *My Apprenticeships*. Translated by Helen Beauclerk. New York: Farrar, Straus & Giroux, 1978.
Condorcet, Marie Jean Antoine. *Condorcet: Selected Writings*. Edited by Keith Michael Baker. Indianapolis: Bobbs-Merrill Co., 1976.
Connell, Noreen, and Cassandra Wilson, eds. *Rape: The First Sourcebooks for Women*. New York: New American Library, 1974.

Cooke, Joanne; Charlotte Bunch-Weeks; and Robin Morgan, eds. *The New Women: An Anthology of Women's Liberation*. Greenwich, Conn.: Fawcett Publications, 1971.

Cooper, David. *The Death of the Family*. New York: Random House, Vintage Books, 1971.

Cooper, Elizabeth. *The Harim and the Purdah*. New York: Century Company, n.d.

Cordelier, Jeanne. *"The Life": Memoirs of a French Hooker*. Translated by Harry Mathews. New York: Viking Press, 1978.

Costa, Mariarosa Dalla, and Selma James. *The Power of Women and the Subversion of the Community*. Bristol, England: The Falling Wall Press, 1973.

Cott, Nancy F. *The Bonds of Womanhood: "Women's Sphere" in New England, 1780–1835*. New Haven: Yale University Press, 1977.

Crawford, Christina. *Mommie Dearest*. New York: William Morrow & Co., 1978.

Daly, Mary. *Beyond God the Father: Toward a Philosophy of Women's Liberation*. Boston: Beacon Press, 1974.

———. *Gyn/Ecology: The Metaethics of Radical Feminism*. Boston: Beacon Press, 1979.

Davidson, Sara. *Loose Change*. Garden City, N.Y.: Doubleday & Co., 1977.

Davies, Marion. *The Times We Had: Life with William Randolph Hearst*. Edited by Pamela Pfau and Kenneth S. Marx. New York: Ballantine Books, 1977.

Davis, Elizabeth Gould. *The First Sex*. Baltimore: Penguin Books, 1973.

Dawidowicz, Lucy S. *The War Against the Jews 1933–1945*. New York: Bantam Books, 1976.

Day, Beth. *Sexual Life Between Blacks and Whites*. London: Collins, 1974.

De Beauvoir, Simone. *The Coming of Age*. Translated by Patrick O'Brian. New York: Warner Paperback Library, 1973.

———. "Must We Burn Sade?" Translated by Annette Michelson. In *The 120 Days of Sodom and Other Writings*. Donatien-Alphonse-François de Sade. Translated by Austryn Wainhouse and Richard Seaver, pp. 3–64. New York: Grove Press, 1967.

———. *The Second Sex*. Translated by H. M. Parshley. New York: Bantam Books, 1970.

De Becker, J. E. *The Nightless City, or the History of the Yoshiwara Yūkwaku*. Rutland, Vt.: Charles E. Tuttle Co., 1971.

DeCrow, Karen. *Sexist Justice: How Legal Sexism Affects You*. New York: Random House, 1974.

Decter, Midge. *Liberal Parents, Radical Children*. New York: Coward, McCann & Geoghegan, 1975.

———. *The Liberated Woman and Other Americans*. New York: Coward, McCann & Geoghegan, 1971.

———. *The New Chastity and Other Arguments Against Women's Liberation*. New York: Berkley Medallion Books, 1973.

Defoe, Daniel. *Roxana or The Fortunate Mistress*. Cleveland: World Publishing Co., 1946.

Deforges, Régine. *Confessions of O*. Translated by Savine d'Estrée. New York: Viking Press, 1979.

De Francis, Vincent. *Protecting the Child Victim of Sex Crimes*. Denver: American Humane Association, 1969.

De Jesus, Carolina Maria. *Child of the Dark: The Diary of Carolina Maria de Jesus*. Translated by David St. Clair. New York: New American Library, 1962.

De Jonge, Alex. *Baudelaire: Prince of Clouds*. New York: Paddington Press, 1976.

De Koven, Anna. *Women in Cycles of Culture*. New York: G. P. Putnam's Sons, 1941.

Delaney, Janice; Mary Jane Lupton; and Emily Toth. *The Curse: A Cultural History of Menstruation*. New York: E. P. Dutton & Co., 1976.

Delbo, Charlotte. *None of Us Will Return*. Translated by John Githens. New York: Grove Press, 1968.

Deming, Barbara. *Prison Notes*. New York: Grossman Publishers, 1966.

———. *Revolution and Equilibrium*. New York: Grossman Publishers, 1971.

———. *Running Away from Myself: A Dream Portrait of America Drawn from the Films of the 40's*. New York: Grossman Publishers, 1969.

———. *We Cannot Live Without Our Lives*. New York: Grossman Publishers, 1974.

Dennett, R. E. *At the Back of the Black Man's Mind*. London: Frank Cass & Co., 1968.

Densmore, Emmet. *Sex Equality: A Solution of the Woman Problem*. New York: Funk & Wagnalls Co., n.d.

De Riencourt, Amaury. *Sex and Power in History*. New York: David McKay Co., 1974.

Des Pres, Terrence. *The Survivor: An Anatomy of Life in the Death Camps*. New York: Pocket Books, 1977.

Dickinson, Robert Latou, and Lura Beam. *A Thousand Marriages: A Medical Study of Sex Adjustment*. Westport, Conn.: Greenwood Press, 1970.

Didion, Joan. *The White Album*. New York: Pocket Books, 1980.
Diner, Helen. *Mothers and Amazons: The First Feminine History of Culture*. Garden City, N.Y.: Doubleday & Co., Anchor Press, 1973.
Dinnerstein, Dorothy. *The Mermaid and The Minotaur*. New York: Harper & Row, Publishers, 1976.
Dix, Tennille. *The Black Baron: The Strange Life of Gilles de Rais*. Indianapolis: Bobbs-Merrill Co., 1930.
Dodgson, Charles Lutwidge [Lewis Carroll]. *Alice's Adventures in Wonderland/Through the Looking-Glass/The Hunting of the Snark*. New York: Liveright, 1932.
Dostoevsky, Fydor. *The Insulted and the Injured*. Translated by Constance Garnett. New York: Macmillan Co., 1950.
Dostoievsky, Fedor Mikhailovich. *The Diary of a Writer*. Translated by Boris Brasol. New York: George Braziller, 1954.
Douglas, Ann. *The Feminization of American Culture*. New York: Avon Books, 1978.
Douglass, Frederick. *Frederick Douglass on Women's Rights*. Edited by Philip S. Foner. Westport, Conn.: Greenwood Press, 1976.
Dover, K. J. *Greek Homosexuality*. Cambridge: Harvard University Press, 1978.
Dreifus, Claudia. *Woman's Fate: Raps from a Feminist Consciousness-Raising Group*. New York: Bantam Books, 1973.
Duffy, Maureen. *The Passionate Shepherdess: Aphra Behn 1640–1689*. New York: Avon Books, 1979.
Dufournier, Denise. *Ravensbrück: The Women's Camp of Death*. Translated by F. W. McPherson. London: George Allen & Unwin, 1948.
Dworkin, Andrea. *Our Blood: Prophecies and Discourses on Sexual Politics*. New York: Harper & Row, Publishers, 1976.
———. *Woman Hating*. New York: E. P. Dutton & Co., 1974.
Edel, Leon. *Bloomsbury: A House of Lions*. New York: Avon Books, 1980.
———. *Henry James, The Master: 1901–1916*. New York: Avon Books, 1978.
Edwards, Anne. *Vivien Leigh*. New York: Pocket Books, 1978.
Ehrenreich, Barbara, and Deirdre English. *Complaints and Disorders: The Sexual Politics of Sickness*. Old Westbury, N.Y.: Feminist Press, 1973.
———. *For Her Own Good*. Garden City, N.Y.: Doubleday & Co., Anchor Press, 1978.
———. *Witches, Midwives, and Nurses*. Old Westbury, N.Y.:

Feminist Press, 1973.
Ehrlich, Paul R. *The Race Bomb*. New York: Ballantine Books, 1978.
Elliott, Grace Loucks. *Understanding the Adolescent Girl*. New York: Henry Holt & Co., 1930.
Elliott, Neil. *Sensuality in Scandinavia*. New York: Weybright & Talley, 1970.
Ellis, Havelock. *My Life*. Boston: Houghton Mifflin Co., 1939.
———. *On Life and Sex*. London: Wm. Heinemann, 1948.
———. *Sex and Marriage*. Westport, Conn.: Greenwood Press, Publishers, 1977.
———. *Studies in the Psychology of Sex*. Vol. 1. New York: Random House, 1936.
———. *Studies in the Psychology of Sex*. Vol. 2. New York: Random House, 1937.
Ellul, Jacques. *Propaganda: The Formation of Men's Attitudes*. Translated by Konrad Kellen and Jean Lerner. New York: Alfred A. Knopf, 1965.
Emecheta, Buchi. *The Bride Price*. New York: George Braziller, 1976.
———. *The Slave Girl*. New York: George Braziller, 1977.
Emerson, Gloria. *Winners and Losers*. New York: Random House, 1976.
Ephron, Nora. *Scribble, Scribble: Notes on the Media*. New York: Alfred A. Knopf, 1978.
Epstein, Cynthia Fuchs. *Woman's Place*. Berkeley: University of California Press, 1973.
Epstein, Helen. *Children of the Holocaust*. New York: G. P. Putnam's Sons, 1979.
Evans, Hilary. *Harlots, Whores and Hookers*. New York: Taplinger Publishing Co., 1979.
Exner, Judith. *My Story*. New York: Grove Press, 1977.
Fabre, Jean Henri. *The Wonders of Instinct*. Translated by Alexander Teixeira de Mattos and Bernard Miall. New York: Century Co., 1918.
Fallaci, Oriana. *Interview with History*. Translated by John Shepley. New York: Liveright, 1976.
———. *Letter to a Child Never Born*. Garden City, N.Y.: Doubleday & Co., Anchor Press, 1978.
Farley, Lin. *Sexual Shakedown: The Sexual Harassment of Women on the Job*. New York: McGraw-Hill Book Co., 1978.
Fasteau, Marc Feigen. *The Male Machine*. New York: McGraw-Hill Book Co., 1974.

Fedder, Ruth. *A Girl Grows Up*. New York: McGraw-Hill Book Co., 1939.

Fénelon, Fania, and Marcelle Routier. *Playing for Time*. Translated by Judith Landry. New York: Berkley Books, 1979.

Ferguson, John. *Utopias of the Classical World*. Ithaca, N.Y.: Cornell University Press, 1975.

Ferm, Robert L. *Jonathan Edwards the Younger: 1745–1801*. Grand Rapids, Mich.: Wm. B. Eerdmans Publishing Co., 1976.

Figes, Eva. *Patriarchal Attitudes*. Greenwich, Conn.: Fawcett Publications, 1971.

Finnegan, Frances. *Poverty and Prostitution*. Cambridge: Cambridge University Press, 1979.

Firestone, Shulamith. *The Dialectic of Sex*. New York: Bantam Books, 1972.

Fisher, Elizabeth. *Woman's Creation*. Garden City, N.Y.: Doubleday & Co., Anchor Press, 1979.

Flacelière, Robert. *A Literary History of Greece*. Translated by Douglas Garman. Chicago: Aldine Publishing Co., 1964.

Flanner, Janet. *Paris Was Yesterday: 1925–1939*. New York: Popular Library, 1972.

Flaubert, Gustave. *Letters*. Translated by J. M. Cohen. London: George Weidenfeld & Nicolson, 1950.

———. *Salammbo*. Translated by A. J. Krailscheimer. New York: Penguin Books, 1977.

———. *Sentimental Education*. Translated by Robert Baldick. Harmondsworth, England: Penguin Books, 1974.

———. *The Temptation of St. Anthony*. Translated by Lafcadio Hearn. New York: Alice Harriman Co., 1910.

Flexner, Eleanor. *Century of Struggle*. New York: Atheneum Publishers, 1973.

———. *Mary Wollstonecraft*. Baltimore: Penguin Books, 1973.

Fontaine, Joan. *No Bed of Roses*. New York: William Morrow & Co., 1978.

Forest, Eva. *From a Spanish Prison*. New York: Random House, Moon Books, 1975.

Foster, Jeannette. *Sex Variant Women in Literature*. Baltimore: Diana Press, 1975.

Foucault, Michel. *Discipline and Punish: The Birth of the Prison*. Translated by Alan Sheridan. New York: Random House, Vintage Books, 1979.

———. *The History of Sexuality*. Translated by Robert Hurley. New York: Pantheon Books, 1978.

Fowles, John. *The Collector.* New York: Dell Publishing Co., 1979.

Fowlie, Wallace. *Climate of Violence: The French Literary Tradition from Baudelaire to the Present.* New York: Macmillan Co., 1967.

Francke, Linda Bird. *The Ambivalence of Abortion.* New York: Random House, 1978.

Frank, Anne. *The Diary of a Young Girl.* New York: Pocket Books, 1972.

Frankfort, Ellen. *Vaginal Politics.* New York: Bantam Books, 1973.

———. *The Voice: Life at* The Village Voice. New York: William Morrow & Co., 1976.

———, and Frances Kissling. *Rosie: The Investigation of a Wrongful Death.* New York: Dial Press, 1979.

Frankl, George. *The Failure of the Sexual Revolution.* London: Kahn & Averill, 1974.

Freeman, Lucy. *Too Deep for Tears.* New York: E. P. Dutton & Co., Hawthorn Books, 1980.

Freire, Paulo. *Pedagogy of the Oppressed.* Translated by Myra Bergman Ramos. New York: Seabury Press, 1973.

French Institute of Public Opinion. *Patterns of Sex and Love: A Study of the French Woman and Her Morals.* Translated by Lowell Bair. New York: Crown Publishers, 1961.

Freud, Sigmund. *Character and Culture.* Edited by Philip Rieff. New York: Collier Books, 1963.

———. *The Freud/Jung Letters: The Correspondence Between Sigmund Freud and C. G. Jung.* Edited by William McGuire. Translated by Ralph Manheim and R. F. C. Hull. Princeton, N.J.: Princeton University Press, 1974.

———. *The Standard Edition of the Complete Psychological Works of Sigmund Freud.* Edited and translated by James Strachey and Anna Freud. Vols. 4, 5, 6, 9, 10, 13, 17, 19, 21, 23. London: Hogarth Press and Institute of Psycho-Analysis, 1953–1968.

———. *Three Essays on the Theory of Sexuality.* Edited by James Strachey. New York: Basic Books, Publishers, 1962.

Friday, Nancy. *My Mother/My Self.* New York: Delacorte Press, 1977.

Friedan, Betty. *It Changed My Life: Writings on the Women's Movement.* New York: Random House, 1976.

Fritz, Leah. *Dreamers and Dealers: An Intimate Appraisal of the Women's Movement.* Boston: Beacon Press, 1980.

———. *Thinking Like a Woman.* Rifton, N.Y.: Win Books, 1975.

Fryer, Judith. *The Faces of Eve: Women in the Nineteenth Century American Novel.* New York: Oxford University Press, 1976.

Fuchs, Estelle. *The Second Season: Life, Love and Sex—Women in the Middle Years.* Garden City, N.Y.: Doubleday & Co., Anchor Press, 1977.

Fuller, Margaret. *Woman in the Nineteenth Century.* New York: W. W. Norton & Co., 1971.

Fürer-Haimendorf, Christoph von. *Morals and Merit: A Study of Values and Social Controls in South Asian Society.* London: Weidenfeld & Nicolson, 1967.

Gage, Matilda Joslyn. *Woman, Church and State.* New York: Arno Press, 1972.

Galbraith, John Kenneth. *The Nature of Mass Poverty.* Cambridge: Harvard University Press, 1979.

Gamio, Manuel. *The Life Story of the Mexican Immigrant.* New York: Dover Publications, 1971.

———. *Mexican Immigration to the United States.* Chicago: University of Chicago Press, 1930.

Gardiner, Harold C. *Catholic Viewpoint on Censorship.* Garden City, N.Y.: Hanover House, 1958.

Gardner, John. *The Life and Times of Chaucer.* New York: Random House, Vintage Books, 1978.

———. *On Moral Fiction.* New York: Basic Books, 1978.

Garson, Barbara. *All the Livelong Day: The Meaning and Demeaning of Routine Work.* Garden City, N.Y.: Doubleday & Co., 1975.

Gattégno, Jean. *Lewis Carroll: Fragments of a Looking-Glass.* Translated by Rosemary Sheed. New York: Thomas Y. Crowell Co., 1974.

Gautier, Théophile. *Mademoiselle de Maupin.* New York: Ives Washburn, 1929.

Gavron, Hannah. *The Captive Wife: Conflicts of Housebound Mothers.* London: Routledge & Kegan Paul, 1966.

Gay, Peter. *Freud, Jews and Other Germans: Masters and Victims in Modernist Culture.* New York: Oxford University Press, 1978.

Gear, Norman. *The Divine Demon: A Portrait of the Marquis de Sade.* London: Frederick Muller, 1963.

Gebhard, Paul H., John H. Gagnon, Wardell B. Pomeroy, and Cornelia V. Christenson. *Sex Offenders: An Analysis of Types.* New York: Harper & Row, Publishers, and Paul B. Hoeber, 1965.

Geismar, Maxwell. *Henry James and the Jacobites.* Boston: Houghton Mifflin Co., 1963.

Gennep, Arnold van. *The Rites of Passage.* Translated by Monika B. Vizedom and Gabrielle L. Caffee. Chicago: University of Chicago Press, 1972.

Gerassi, John. *The Boys of Boise*. New York: Macmillan Co., 1966.
Gerson, Menachem. *Family, Women, and Socialization in the Kibbutz*. Lexington, Mass.: Lexington Books, 1978.
Gibson, Gifford Guy, and Mary Jo Risher. *By Her Own Admission*. Garden City, N.Y.: Doubleday & Co., 1977.
Gibson, Jessie E. *On Being a Girl*. New York: Macmillan Co., 1927.
Gide, André. *Corydon*. New York: Farrar, Straus and Co., 1950.
Giffin, Frederick C., ed. *Woman as Revolutionary*. New York: New American Library, 1973.
Gilder, George. *Sexual Suicide*. New York: Quadrangle, 1973.
Gilman, Charlotte Perkins. *Herland*. New York: Pantheon Books, 1979.
———. *The Home: Its Work and Influence*. Urbana: University of Illinois Press, 1972.
———. *The Living of Charlotte Perkins Gilman: An Autobiography*. New York: Harper & Row, Publishers, 1975.
———. *Women and Economics*. New York: Harper & Row, Publishers, 1966.
Gilman, Richard. *Decadence: The Strange Life of an Epithet*. New York: Farrar, Straus & Giroux, 1980.
Ginder, Richard. *Binding with Briars*. Englewood Cliffs, N.J.: Prentice-Hall, 1975.
Girard, René. *Violence and the Sacred*. Translated by Patrick Gregory. Baltimore: Johns Hopkins Press, 1979.
Gissing, George. *The Odd Women*. New York: W. W. Norton & Co., 1977.
Gittelson, Natalie. *Dominus*. New York: Farrar, Straus & Giroux, 1978.
Glasgow, Maude. *Problems of Sex*. Boston. Christopher Publishing House, 1949.
Glazer, Nathan. *Affirmative Discrimination: Ethnic Inequality and Public Policy*. New York: Basic Books, 1975.
Goebbels, Joseph. *Final Entries 1945: The Diaries of Joseph Goebbels*. Edited by Hugh Trevor-Roper. Translated by Richard Barry. New York: G. P. Putnam's Sons, 1978.
Goering, Emmy. *My Life with Goering*. London: David Bruce & Watson, 1972.
Goethe, Johann Wolfgang von. *Elective Affinities*. Translated by R. J. Hollingdale. New York: Penguin Books, 1978.
———. *The Sufferings of Young Werther*. Translated by Bayard Quincy Morgan. New York: Frederick Ungar Publishing Co., 1957.

Goffman, Erving. *Relations in Public.* New York: Harper & Row, Publishers, 1972.

Goldberg, Steven. *The Inevitability of Patriarchy.* New York: William Morrow & Co., 1973.

Goldman, Emma. *Red Emma Speaks: Selected Writings and Speeches.* Edited by Alix Kates Shulman. New York: Random House, Vintage Books, 1972.

———. *The Traffic in Women and Other Essays on Feminism.* New York: Times Change Press, 1970.

Goldstein, Jeffrey H. *Aggression and Crimes of Violence.* New York: Oxford University Press, 1975.

Goldstein, Michael J.; Harold S. Kant; and John J. Hartman. *Pornography and Sexual Deviance.* Berkeley: University of California Press, 1974.

Gombrowicz, Witold. *Ferdydurke.* Translated by Eric Mosbacher. *Pornografia.* Translated by Alastair Hamilton. *Cosmos.* Translated by Eric Mosbacher. New York: Grove Press, 1978.

Goncourt, Edmond and Jules de. *The Woman of the Eighteenth Century.* Translated by Jacques Le Clercq and Ralph Roeder. New York: Minton, Balch & Co., 1927.

Gordimer, Nadine. *The Late Bourgeois World.* New York: Viking Press, 1966.

Gorer, Geoffrey. *The Life and Ideas of the Marquis de Sade.* London: Peter Owen, 1953.

Gorky, Maxim. *My Childhood.* Translated by Ronald Wilks. Harmondsworth, England: Penguin Books, 1978.

Gosse, Edmund. *The Life of Algernon Charles Swinburne.* New York: Macmillan Co., 1917.

Gould, Lois. *Not Responsible for Personal Articles.* New York: Random House, 1978.

Gourmont, Remy de. *Decadence and Other Essays on the Culture of Ideas.* Translated by William Aspenwall Bradley. London: Grant Richards, 1942.

———. *Dream of a Woman.* Translated by Lewis Galantiere. New York: Boni & Liveright, 1927.

———. *Philosophic Nights in Paris.* Translated by Isaac Goldberg. Boston: John W. Luce & Co., 1920.

Grass, Günter. *The Flounder.* New York: Fawcett Crest, 1979.

Gray, Madeline. *Margaret Sanger.* New York: Richard Marek Publishers, 1978.

Green, Martin. *The von Richthofen Sisters: The Triumphant and the Tragic Modes of Love.* New York: Basic Books, 1974.

Greene, Gerald and Caroline. *S–M: The Last Taboo.* New York: Grove Press, 1974.
Gribble, Francis. *Madame de Staël and Her Lovers.* New York: James Pott & Co., 1907.
Grier, Barbara. *Lesbiana.* Reno, Nev.: Naiad Press, 1976.
———, and Coletta Reid, eds. *The Lavender Herring: Lesbian Essays from The Ladder.* Baltimore: Diana Press, 1976.
———. *Lesbian Lives: Biographies of Women from The Ladder.* Baltimore: Diana Press, 1976.
Griffin, Susan. *Rape: The Power of Consciousness.* New York: Harper & Row, Publishers, 1979.
———. *Woman and Nature: The Roaring Inside Her.* New York: Harper & Row, Publishers, 1978.
Grimké, Sarah M. *Letters on the Equality of the Sexes and the Condition of Woman.* New York: Source Book Press, 1970.
Grosskurth, Phyllis. *Havelock Ellis.* New York: Alfred A. Knopf, 1980.
———. *The Woeful Victorian: A Biography of John Addington Symonds.* New York: Holt, Rinehart & Winston, 1964.
Grossman, Leonid. *Dostoevsky.* Translated by Mary Mackler. Indianapolis: Bobbs-Merrill Co., 1975.
Group for the Advancement of Psychiatry. *The Right to Abortion: A Psychiatric View.* New York: Charles Scribner's Sons, 1970.
Guyon, René. *Sexual Freedom.* Translated by Eden and Cedar Paul. New York: Alfred A. Knopf, 1958.
Hagen, Richard. *The Bio-Sexual Factor.* Garden City, N.Y.: Doubleday & Co., 1979.
Hale, Beatrice Forbes-Robertson. *What's Wrong with Our Girls?* New York: Frederick A. Stokes Co., 1923.
Hammer, Signe. *Daughters and Mothers, Mothers and Daughters.* New York: Quadrangle, The New York Times Co., 1975.
———, ed. *Women: Body and Culture.* New York: Harper & Row, Publishers, 1975.
Hardwick, Elizabeth. *Seduction and Betrayal: Women and Literature.* New York: Random House, 1974.
Hardy, Thomas. *Jude the Obscure.* New York: New American Library, 1961.
———. *The Well-Beloved.* London: Macmillan London, 1978.
Harris, Frank. *Oscar Wilde.* London: Constable & Co., 1938.
Harris, Janet. *The Prime of Ms. America: The American Woman at 40.* New York: New American Library, 1976.
Harris, Marvin. *Cannibals and Kings: The Origins of Cultures.* New

York: Random House, Vintage Books, 1977.
———. *Cows, Pigs, Wars, and Witches: The Riddles of Culture.* New York: Random House, Vintage Books, 1978.
———. *Cultural Materialism: The Struggle for a Science of Culture.* New York: Random House, 1979.
Hartman, Mary, and Lois W. Banner, eds. *Clio's Consciousness Raised.* New York: Harper & Row, Publishers, 1974.
Hawthorne, Nathaniel. *The Blithedale Romance.* New York: W. W. Norton & Co., 1958.
Hayman, Ronald. *De Sade: A Critical Biography.* New York: Thomas Y. Crowell Co., 1978.
Hayward, Brooke. *Haywire.* New York: Alfred A. Knopf, 1977.
Heavens, O. S. *Lasers.* New York: Charles Scribner's Sons, 1971.
Heiber, Helmut. *Goebbels.* Translated by John K. Dickinson. New York: Hawthorn Books, 1972.
Heilbrun, Carolyn G. *Toward a Recognition of Androgyny.* New York: Alfred A. Knopf, 1973.
Heller, Joseph. *Good as Gold.* New York: Simon & Schuster, 1979.
Hemingway, Mary Welsh. *How It Was.* New York: Alfred A. Knopf, 1976.
Hemmings, F. W. J. *The Life and Times of Emile Zola.* New York: Charles Scribner's Sons, 1977.
Hennessey, Caroline. *The Strategy of Sexual Struggle.* New York: Lancer Books, 1971.
Hennig, Margaret, and Anne Jardim. *The Managerial Woman.* Garden City, N.Y.: Doubleday & Co., Anchor Press, 1977.
Henry, Joan. *Women in Prison.* London: White Lion Publishers, 1973.
Hericourt, Jenny P. D'. *A Woman's Philosophy of Woman; or Woman Affranchised.* New York: Carleton, Publisher, 1864.
Hernton, Calvin C. *Sex and Racism in America.* New York: Grove Press, 1978.
Herold, J. Christopher. *Mistress to an Age: A Life of Madame de Staël.* New York: Harmony Books, 1979.
Herr, Michael. *Dispatches.* New York: Alfred A. Knopf, 1977.
Hersh, Blanche Glassman. *The Slavery of Sex.* Urbana: University of Illinois Press, 1978.
Heymann, C. David. *Ezra Pound: The Last Rower, a Political Profile.* New York: Viking Press, 1976.
Higham, Charles. *Marlene.* New York: Pocket Books, 1979.
Hinton, William. *Fanshen: A Documentary of Revolution in a Chinese Village.* New York: Random House, Vintage Books, 1966.

Hirschfeld, Magnus. *Sexual Anomalies*. New York: Emerson Books, 1956.

Hite, Shere. *The Hite Report*. New York: Macmillan Publishing Co., 1976.

———. *Sexual Honesty: By Women, for Women*. New York: Warner Paperback Library, 1974.

Hitler, Adolf. *Mein Kampf*. Translated by Ralph Manheim. Boston: Houghton Mifflin Co., 1962.

Hocquenghem, Guy. *Homosexual Desire*. Translated by Daniella Dangoor. London: Allison & Busby, 1978.

Hodann, Max. *History of Modern Morals*. Translated by Stella Browne. London: Wm. Heinemann, 1937.

Holbrook, David, ed. *The Case Against Pornography*. Open Court, Ill.: Library Press, 1973.

Hollander, Anne. *Seeing Through Clothes*. New York: Avon Books, 1980.

Holleran, Andrew. *Dancer from the Dance*. New York: Bantam Books, 1979.

Horn, Pamela. *The Victorian Country Child*. Kineton, England: Roundwood Press, 1974.

Horos, Carol V. *Rape*. New Canaan, Conn.: Tobey Publishing Co., 1974.

Howard, Jane. *Families*. New York: Simon & Schuster, 1978.

Howard, Maureen. *Facts of Life*. New York: Penguin Books, 1980.

Howe, Louise Kapp. *Pink Collar Workers*. New York: G. P. Putnam's Sons, 1977.

Hughes, Pennethorne. *Witchcraft*. Harmondsworth, England: Penguin Books, 1971.

Hunt, Morton M. *The Natural History of Love*. New York: Alfred A. Knopf, 1959.

Huysmans, J. K. *Against Nature*. Translated by Robert Baldick. New York: Penguin Books, 1979.

———. *Là-Bas*. Translated by Keene Wallace. New York: Dover Publications, 1972.

Hyde, H. Montgomery. *A History of Pornography*. New York: Farrar, Straus & Giroux, 1965.

Hyslop, Lois Boe, ed. *Baudelaire as a Love Poet and Other Essays*. University Park: Pennsylvania State University Press, 1969.

Inglis, Ruth. *Sins of the Fathers*. New York: St. Martin's Press, 1978.

Iovetz-Tereshchenko, N. M. *Friendship—Love in Adolescence*. London: George Allen & Unwin, 1936.

Irving, John. *The World According to Garp*. New York: Pocket Books, 1979.

Ivinskaya, Olga. *A Captive of Time*. Translated by Max Hayward. Garden City, N.Y.: Doubleday & Co., 1978.
Janeway, Elizabeth. *Between Myth and Morning: Women Awakening*. New York: William Morrow & Co., 1974.
Jay, Karla, and Allen Young, eds. *After You're Out*. New York: Links Books, 1975.
———. *The Gay Report*. New York: Summit Books, 1979.
———, eds. *Out of the Closets: Voices of Gay Liberation*. New York: Douglas, 1972.
Jenness, Linda, ed. *Feminism and Socialism*. New York: Pathfinder Press, 1972.
Jerome, Judson, *Families of Eden: Communes and the New Anarchism*. New York: Seabury Press, 1974.
Johnston, Jill. *Gullibles Travels*. New York: Links Books, 1974.
———. *Lesbian Nation: The Feminist Solution*. New York: Simon & Schuster, 1973.
Jones, Ann. *Women Who Kill*. New York: Holt, Rinehart, & Winston, 1980.
Jones, Ernest. *Life and Work of Sigmund Freud*. Abridged. Edited by Lionel Trilling and Steven Marcus. New York: Basic Books, 1961.
Kalstone, David. *Five Temperaments*. New York: Oxford University Press, 1977.
Kanter, Rosabeth Moss. *Commitment and Community: Communes and Utopias in Sociological Perspective*. Cambridge: Harvard University Press, 1973.
Kardiner, Abram. *Sex and Morality*. Indianapolis: Bobbs-Merrill Co., 1954.
Karlen, Arno. *Sexuality and Homosexuality*. New York: W. W. Norton & Co., 1971.
Karst, Georg M. *The Beasts of the Earth*. Translated by Emil Lengyel. New York: Albert Unger, 1942.
Kaye, Harvey E. *Male Survival: Masculinity Without Myth*. New York: Grosset & Dunlap, 1974.
Keats, John. "Ode on a Grecian Urn." In *John Keats and Percy Bysshe Shelley: Complete Poetical Works*. New York: Modern Library, n.d.
Kemble, Frances Anne. *Journal of a Residence on a Georgian Plantation in 1838–1839*. New York: New American Library, 1975.
Kempe, Ruth S., and C. Henry Kempe. *Child Abuse*. Cambridge: Harvard University Press, 1978.
Kendall, Elaine. *The Upper Hand: The Truth about American Men*. Boston: Little, Brown & Co., 1965.

Kern, Stephen. *Anatomy and Destiny: A Cultural History of the Human Body*. Indianapolis: Bobbs-Merrill Co., 1975.

Kessler, Suzanne J., and Wendy McKenna. *Gender*. New York: John Wiley & Sons, 1978.

Key, Ellen. *Love and Marriage*. Translated by Arthur G. Chater. New York: G. P. Putnam's Sons, 1911.

Keyes, Evelyn. *Scarlett O'Hara's Younger Sister*. Secaucus, N.J.: Lyle Stuart, 1977.

Kindleberger, Charles P. *Power and Money*. New York: Basic Books, 1970.

King, Richard. *The Party of Eros*. Chapel Hill: University of North Carolina Press, 1972.

Kinsey, Alfred C.; Wardell B. Pomeroy; and Clyde E. Martin. *Sexual Behavior in the Human Male*. Philadelphia: W. B. Saunders Co., 1948.

———, and Paul H. Gebhard. *Sexual Behavior in the Human Female*. Philadelphia: W. B. Saunders Co., 1953.

Kirkendall, Lester A., and Robert N. Whitehurst, eds. *The New Sexual Revolution*. New York: Donald W. Brown, 1971.

Kirkpatrick, Clifford. *Nazi Germany: Its Women and Family Life*. Indianapolis: Bobbs-Merrill Co., 1938.

Klein, Carole. *Aline*. New York: Warner Books, 1980.

Klein, Melanie. *Our Adult World*. New York: Basic Books, 1963.

Klossowski, Pierre. "Nature as Destructive Principle." Translated by Joseph H. McMahon. In *The 120 Days of Sodom and Other Writings*. Donatien-Alphonse-François de Sade. Translated by Austryn Wainhouse and Richard Seaver, pp. 65–86. New York: Grove Press, 1967.

Kneeland, George J. *Commercialized Prostitution in New York City*. New York: Century Co., 1913.

Kocourek, Albert, and John H. Wigmore, eds. *Evolution of Law: Select Readings on the Origin and Development of Legal Institutions*. Vol. 2 of *Primitive and Ancient Legal Institutions*. Boston: Little, Brown & Co., 1915.

Koestler, Arthur. *The Trail of the Dinosaur and Other Essays*. New York: Macmillan Co., 1955.

Kolbenschlag, Madonna. *Kiss Sleeping Beauty Good-Bye*. Garden City, N.Y.: Doubleday & Co., 1979.

Kollontai, Alexandra. *The Autobiography of a Sexually Emancipated Communist Woman*. Translated by Salvator Attanasio. New York: Herder & Herder, 1971.

Komarovsky, Mirra. *Dilemmas of Masculinity: A Study of College*

Youth. New York: W. W. Norton & Co., 1976.

Kopay, David, and Perry Deane Young. *The David Kopay Story*. New York: Arbor House Publishing Co., 1977.

Korngold, Ralph. *Robespierre and the Fourth Estate*. New York: Modern Age Books, 1941.

Kraditor, Aileen. *The Ideas of the Woman Suffrage Movement 1890–1929*. Garden City, N.Y.: Doubleday & Co., Anchor Books, 1971.

———, ed. *Up from the Pedestal: Selected Writings in the History of American Feminism*. Chicago: Quadrangle Books, 1968.

Krafft-Ebing, Richard Freiherr von. *Psychopathia Sexualis*. Translated by Harry E. Wedeck. New York: G. P. Putnam's Sons, 1965.

Kramer, Jane. *The Last Cowboy*. New York: Harper & Row Publishers, 1977.

Kramer, Larry. *Faggots*. New York: Warner Books, 1979.

Kreps, Juanita. *Sex in the Marketplace: American Women at Work*. Baltimore: Johns Hopkins Press, 1974.

———. *Women and the American Economy: A Look to the 1980s*. Englewood Cliffs, N.J.: Prentice-Hall, 1976.

Kronenberger, Louis. *Oscar Wilde*. Boston: Little, Brown & Co., 1976.

Kronhausen, Phyllis and Eberhard. *Erotic Fantasies*. New York: Grove Press, 1969.

———. *Sex Histories of American College Men*. New York: Ballantine Books, 1960.

Laclos, Pierre-Ambroise-François Choderlos de. *Les Liaisons Dangereuses*. Translated by P. W. K. Stone. New York: Penguin Books, 1979.

Laing, R. D. *The Facts of Life*. New York: Pantheon Books, 1976.

———. *The Politics of the Family and Other Essays*. New York: Pantheon Books, 1969.

———. *Self and Others*. New York: Penguin Books, 1978.

Landes, Ruth. *The City of Women*. New York: Macmillan Co., 1947.

Lane, Margaret. *Frances Wright and the "Great Experiment."* Totowa, N.J.: Rowman & Littlefield, 1972.

Lang, Andrew. *The Secret of the Totem*. New York: Ams Press, 1970.

Langer, Lawrence L. *The Age of Atrocity*. Boston: Beacon Press, 1978.

Lasch, Christopher. *The Culture of Narcissism*. New York: Warner Books, 1979.

Laubscher, B. J. F. *Sex, Custom and Psychopathology: A Study of South*

African Pagan Natives. New York: Robert M. McBride & Co., 1938.
Lautréamont, Le Comte de. *Maldoror.* Translated by Alexis Lykiard. New York: Thomas Y. Crowell Co., 1973.
Lawrence, D. H. *Sex, Literature and Censorship.* Edited by Harry T. Moore. New York: Twayne Publishers, 1953.
Lawrence, Frieda. *Not I, But the Wind.* London: Wm. Heinemann, 1935.
Lawrence, T. E. *The Letters of T. E. Lawrence.* Edited by David Garnett. Garden City, N.Y.: Doubleday, Doran & Co., 1939.
———. *The Mint.* London: Johnathan Cape, 1955.
———. *Seven Pillars of Wisdom.* New York: Penguin Books, 1962.
Layish, Aharon. *Women and Islamic Law in a Non-Muslim State.* New York: John Wiley & Sons, 1975.
Lazarre, Jane. *The Mother Knot.* New York: McGraw-Hill Book Co., 1976.
Leakey, Richard E., and Roger Lewin. *People of the Lake.* Garden City, N.Y.: Doubleday & Co., Anchor Press, 1978.
Lebowitz, Fran. *Metropolitan Life.* New York: Fawcett Crest, 1978.
Lee, Vera. *The Reign of Women in Eighteenth-Century France.* Cambridge, Mass.: Schenkman Publishing Co., 1975.
Lefkowitz, Mary R., and Maureen B. Fant, eds. *Women in Greece and Rome.* Toronto: Samuel-Stevens, 1977.
Le Gallienne, Eva. *With a Quiet Heart.* New York: Viking Press, 1953.
Lély, Gilbert. *The Marquis de Sade.* Translated by Alec Brown. London: Elek Books, 1961.
Lennig, Walter. *Portrait of De Sade.* Translated by Sarah Twohig. New York: Herder & Herder, 1971.
Lerner, Gerda, ed. *Black Women in White America.* New York: Random House, Vintage Books, 1973.
Lerner, Max. *Ideas are Weapons: The History and Uses of Ideas.* New York: Viking Press, 1940.
Lessing, Doris. *A Small Personal Voice.* New York: Random House, Vintage Books, 1975.
Lévi-Strauss, Claude. *Totemism.* Translated by Rodney Needham. Boston: Beacon Press, 1963.
Lévy, Bernard-Henri. *Barbarism with a Human Face.* New York: Harper & Row, Publishers, 1979.
Levy, Howard S. *Japanese Sex Crimes in Modern Times.* Taipei: Chinese Association for Folklore, 1975.

Lewis, Oscar. *The Children of Sanchez.* New York: Random House, Vintage Books, 1963.

———. *Five Families.* New York: Basic Books, 1975.

Leyland, Winston, ed. *Gay Sunshine Interviews.* San Francisco: Gay Sunshine Press, 1978.

Lichtenstein, Grace. *Desperado.* New York: Dial Press, 1977.

Lind, Earl. *Autobiography of an Androgyne.* New York: Arno Press, 1975.

———. *The Female-Impersonators.* New York: Arno Press, 1975.

Lloyd, Robin. *For Money or Love: Boy Prostitution in America.* New York: Vanguard Press, 1976.

Longford, Elizabeth. *Byron.* Boston: Little, Brown & Co., 1976.

Longford Committee Investigating Pornography. *Pornography: The Longford Report.* London: Coronet Books, 1972.

Lorenz, Konrad. *Behind the Mirror: A Search for a Natural History of Human Knowledge.* Translated by Ronald Taylor. New York: Harcourt Brace Jovanovich, 1977.

Lottman, Herbert R. *Albert Camus.* Garden City, N.Y.: Doubleday & Co., 1979.

Lourie, Richard. *Letters to the Future: An Approach to Sinyavsky-Tertz.* Ithaca, N.Y.: Cornell University Press, 1975.

Lovelace, Linda, and Mike McGrady. *Ordeal.* Secaucus, N.J.: Citadel Press, 1980.

Ludovici, Anthony M. *Woman.* London: Constable & Co., 1926.

Lundberg, Ferdinand, and Marynia F. Farnham. *Modern Woman: The Lost Sex.* New York: Harper & Brothers, Publishers, 1947.

Macadams, Cynthia. *Emergence.* New York: Chelsea House Publishers, 1977.

McBride, Angela Barron. *A Married Feminist.* New York: Harper & Row, Publishers, 1976.

McGovern, William Montgomery. *From Luther to Hitler: The History of Fascist-Nazi Political Philosophy.* Boston: Houghton Mifflin Co., 1941.

Mack, John E. *A Prince of Our Disorder: The Life of T. E. Lawrence.* Boston: Little, Brown & Co., 1976.

MacKinnon, Catharine A. *Sexual Harassment of Working Women.* New Haven: Yale University Press, 1979.

McNeill, Elizabeth. *Nine and a Half Weeks.* New York: Berkley Publishing Corp., 1979.

MacPherson, Myra. *The Power Lovers.* New York: Ballantine Books, 1975.

Mahler, Margaret S.; Fred Pine; and Anni Bergman. *The Psychologi-*

cal Birth of the Human Infant. New York: Basic Books, 1975.
Mailer, Norman. *Cannibals and Christians.* New York: Dial Press, 1966.
———. *Genius and Lust: A Journey Through the Major Writings of Henry Miller.* New York: Grove Press, 1976.
———. *Marilyn: A Biography.* New York: Grosset & Dunlap, 1973.
———. *The Prisoner of Sex.* Boston: Little, Brown & Co., 1971.
Maisch, Herbert. *Incest.* Translated by Colin Bearne. New York: Stein & Day, 1972.
Malinowski, Bronislaw. *Crime and Custom in Savage Society.* New York: Harcourt, Brace & Co., 1926.
Mallow, Alex, and Leon Chabot. *Laser Safety Handbook.* New York: Van Nostrand Reinhold Co., 1978.
Mandelstam, Nadezhda. *Hope Against Hope.* Translated by Max Hayward. New York: Atheneum Publishers, 1978.
Manvell, Roger, and Heinrich Fraenkel. *Himmler.* New York: G. P. Putnam's Sons, 1965.
Marchand, Henry L. *Sex Life in France.* New York: Panurge Press, 1935.
Marcus, Steven. *The Other Victorians.* New York: Basic Books, 1966.
Marcuse, Herbert. *An Essay on Liberation.* Boston: Beacon Press, 1969.
———. *Negations.* Boston: Beacon Press, 1968.
Mare, Margaret, and Alicia C. Percival. *Victorian Best-seller: The World of Charlotte M. Yonge.* London: George G. Harrap & Co.; New York: Chanticleer Press, 1949.
Márquez, Gabriel García. *Innocent Eréndira and Other Stories.* Translated by Gregory Rabassa. New York: Harper & Row, Publishers, 1979.
Marshall, Donald S., and Robert C. Suggs, eds. *Human Sexual Behavior.* New York: Basic Books, 1971.
Marshall, Samuel L., ed. *Laser Technology and Applications.* New York: McGraw-Hill Book Co., 1968.
Masters, William H., and Virginia E. Johnson. *Homosexuality in Perspective.* Boston: Little, Brown & Co., 1979.
———. *Human Sexual Inadequacy.* Boston: Little, Brown & Co., 1970.
———. *The Pleasure Bond.* New York: Bantam Books, 1976.
Mathiez, Albert. *The Fall of Robespierre.* New York: Alfred A. Knopf, 1927.
Maupassant, Guy de. *A Woman's Heart.* Translated by Ernest Boyd. New York: Alfred A. Knopf, 1926.

———. *A Woman's Life*. Translated by H. N. P. Sloman. New York: Penguin Books, 1977.
May, Gita. *Madame Roland and the Age of Revolution*. New York: Columbia University Press, 1970.
Mead, Margaret. *Male and Female*. New York: New American Library, 1962.
———, and James Baldwin. *A Rap on Race*. New York: Dell Publishing Co., Delta Books, 1972.
Meijer, M. J. *Marriage Law and Policy in the Chinese People's Republic*. Hong Kong: Hong Kong University Press, 1971.
Melville, Herman. *Moby Dick*. New York: Random House, 1930.
———. *Typee*. New York: Dodd, Mead & Co., 1923.
Mencken, H. L. *In Defense of Women*. Garden City, N.Y.: Garden City Publishing Co., 1922.
Merriam, Eve. *After Nora Slammed the Door*. Cleveland: World Publishing Co., 1964.
Michelet, Jules. *History of the French Revolution*. Edited by Gordon Wright. Translated by Charles Cocks. Chicago: University of Chicago Press, 1967.
Mill, John Stuart. *Essays on Politics and Culture*. Edited by Gertrude Himmelfarb. Garden City, N.Y.: Doubleday & Co., 1962.
———. *The Letters of John Stuart Mill*. Vol. 2. Edited by Hugh S. R. Elliot. London: Longmans, Green and Co., 1910.
Miller, Casey, and Kate Swift. *Words and Women*. Garden City, N.Y.: Doubleday & Co., Anchor Press, 1977.
Miller, Jean Baker. *Toward a New Psychology of Women*. Boston: Beacon Press, 1976.
Miller, Nathan. *The Child in Primitive Society*. New York: Brentano's Publishers, 1928.
Millett, Kate. *Sexual Politics*. New York: Avon Books, 1971.
———. *The Basement: Meditations on a Human Sacrifice*. New York: Simon & Schuster, 1979.
———. *The Prostitution Papers*. New York: Avon Books, 1973.
Mishima, Yukio. *Madame de Sade*. Translated by Donald Keene. New York: Grove Press, 1967.
Mitchell, Hannah. *The Hard Way Up*. London: Virago, 1977.
Mitchell, Juliet. *Woman's Estate*. New York: Random House, Vintage Books, 1973.
Mitford, Jessica. *Kind and Usual Punishment: The Prison Business*. New York: Alfred A. Knopf, 1973.
Mitscherlich, Alexander. *Doctors of Infamy: The Story of the Nazi Medical Crimes*. New York: Henry Schuman, 1949.

Modell, Arnold H. *Object Love and Reality*. New York: International Universities Press, 1968.

Moers, Ellen. *The Dandy: Brummell to Beerbohm*. New York: Viking Press, 1960.

———. *Literary Women: The Great Writers*. Garden City, N.Y.: Doubleday & Co., 1976.

Mohr, James C. *Abortion in America*. New York: Oxford University Press, 1979.

Money, John. *Love and Love Sickness*. Baltimore: Johns Hopkins Press, 1980.

———, and Herman Musaph, eds. *Handbook of Sexology*. Amsterdam: Elsevier/North-Holland Biomedical Press, 1977.

Montagu, Ashley. *The Nature of Human Aggression*. Oxford: Oxford University Press, 1978.

Montgomery, James Stuart. *The Incredible Casanova*. Garden City, N.Y.: Doubleday & Co., 1950.

Moody, Anne. *Coming of Age in Mississippi*. New York: Dell Publishing Co., 1979.

Moore, Katharine. *Victorian Wives*. London: Allison & Busby, 1974.

Moravia, Alberto. *The Fetish*. Translated by Angus Davidson. New York: Manor Books, 1973.

———. *The Woman of Rome*. Translated by Lydia Holland. New York: Manor Books, 1974.

Morgan, Elaine. *The Descent of Woman*. New York: Bantam Books, 1973.

Morgan, Lewis H. *Ancient Society*. Chicago: Charles H. Kerr & Co., 1877.

Morgan, Marabel. *The Total Woman*. New York: Pocket Books, 1975.

Morgan, Robin. *Going Too Far*. New York: Random House, 1977.

———. "The Network of the Imaginary Mother." In *Lady of the Beasts: Poems*. New York: Random House, 1976, pp. 61–88.

———, ed. *Sisterhood Is Powerful*. New York: Random House, 1970.

Morse, J. Mitchell. *Prejudice and Literature*. Philadelphia: Temple University Press, 1976.

Müller, Filip. *Eyewitness Auschwitz*. Translated by Susanne Flatauer. New York: Stein & Day, 1979.

Murdoch, Iris. *Henry and Cato*. New York: Viking Press, 1977.

Nash, Mary. *The Provoked Wife: The Life and Times of Susannah Cibber*. Boston: Little, Brown & Co., 1977.

Naumann, Bernd. *Auschwitz*. Translated by Jean Steinberg. New York: Frederick A. Praeger, Publishers, 1966.

Nehrich, Richard B., Jr.; Glenn I. Voran; and Norman F. Dessel. *Atomic Light: Lasers—What They Are and How They Work.* New York: Sterling Publishing Co., 1967.

Neruda, Pablo. *Memoirs.* Translated by Hardie St. Martin. New York: Penguin Books, 1978.

Nicole, Christopher. *The Secret Memoirs of Lord Byron.* Philadelphia: J. B. Lippincott Co., 1978.

Nin, Anaïs. *Delta of Venus.* New York: Harcourt Brace Jovanovich, 1977.

———. *In Favor of the Sensitive Man and Other Essays.* New York: Harcourt Brace Jovanovich, 1976.

———. *Little Birds.* New York: Harcourt Brace Jovanovich, 1979.

———. *The Novel of the Future.* New York: Macmillan Publishing Co., Collier Books, 1976.

Noakes, Jeremy, and Geoffrey Pridham, eds. *Documents on Nazism 1919–1945.* New York: Viking Press, 1975.

Noonan, John T., Jr., ed. *The Morality of Abortion.* Cambridge: Harvard University Press, 1970.

North, Maurice. *The Outer Fringe of Sex.* London: Odyssey Press, 1970.

Nyström-Hamilton, Louise. *Ellen Key: Her Life and Work.* Translated by A. E. B. Fries. New York: G. P. Putnam's Sons, 1913.

Oakley, Ann. *Sex, Gender and Society.* New York: Harper & Row, Colophon Books, 1972.

———. *The Sociology of Housework.* New York: Pantheon Books, 1974.

———. *Woman's Work: The Housewife, Past and Present.* New York: Random House, Vintage Books, 1976.

O'Donnell, Thomas J. *The Confessions of T. E. Lawrence.* Athens, Ohio: Ohio University Press, 1979.

O'Faolain, Julia, and Lauro Martines, eds. *Not in God's Image: Women in History from the Greeks to the Victorians.* New York: Harper & Row, Torchbooks, 1973.

O'Neill, Nena. *The Marriage Premise.* New York: M. Evans & Co., 1977.

Oppenheimer, Martin. *The Urban Guerrilla.* Chicago: Quadrangle Books, 1970.

Owings, Chloe. *Women Police.* New York: Frederick H. Hitchcock, 1925.

Packard, Vance. *The Sexual Wilderness.* New York: David McKay Co., 1968.

Pankhurst, Emmeline. *My Own Story*. New York: Hearst's International Library Co., 1914.

Pankhurst, Sylvia. *The Suffragette Movement*. London: Virago, 1978.

Parker, Gail, ed. *The Oven Birds: American Women on Womanhood 1820–1920*. Garden City, N.Y.: Doubleday & Co., Anchor Books, 1972.

Patai, Raphael. *Sex and Family in the Bible and the Middle East*. Garden City, N.Y.: Doubleday & Co., 1959.

Paulhan, Jean. "The Marquis de Sade and His Accomplice." In *Justine; Philosophy in the Bedroom; Eugénie de Franval, and Other Writings*. Donatien-Alphonse-François de Sade. Translated by Richard Seaver and Austryn Wainhouse, pp. 3–36. New York: Grove Press, 1966.

Paz, Octavio. *The Labyrinth of Solitude*. Translated by Lysander Kemp. New York: Grove Press, 1961.

———. *The Other Mexico: Critique of the Pyramid*. Translated by Lysander Kemp. New York: Grove Press, 1972.

Peck, Mary Gray. *Carrie Chapman Catt: A Biography*. New York: H. W. Wilson Co., 1944.

Peckham, Morse. *Art and Pornography: An Experiment in Explanation*. New York: Basic Books, 1969.

Peters, H. F. *Zarathustra's Sister: The Case of Elisabeth and Friedrich Nietzsche*. New York: Crown Publishers, 1977.

Petronius, Arbiter. *The Satyricon*. Translated by J. M. Mitchell. London: George Routledge & Sons, 1923.

Pietropinto, Anthony, and Jacqueline Simenauer. *Husbands and Wives: A Nationwide Survey of Marriage*. New York: Times Books, 1979.

Pinzer, Maimie. *The Maimie Papers*. Edited by Ruth Rosen and Sue Davidson. Old Westbury, N.Y.: Feminist Press in cooperation with Schlesinger Library of Radcliffe College, 1977.

Poe, Edgar Allan. *Literary Criticism of Edgar Allan Poe*. Edited by Robert L. Hough. Lincoln: University of Nebraska Press, 1965.

———. *Tales of Mystery and Imagination*. N.p.: Spencer Press, 1936.

Pomeroy, Wardell B. *Dr. Kinsey and the Institute for Sex Research*. New York: Harper & Row, Publishers, 1972.

Portugés, Paul. *The Visionary Poetics of Allen Ginsberg*. Santa Barbara, Calif.: Ross-Erikson, Publishers, 1978.

Praz, Mario. *The Romantic Agony*. Translated by Angus Davidson. London: Oxford University Press, 1954.

President's Commission on Obscenity and Pornography. *The Report of the Commission on Obscenity and Pornography*. New York: Random House, 1970.

Price, Richard. *Ladies' Man*. New York: Bantam Books, 1979.

Putnam, Emily James. *The Lady*. Chicago: University of Chicago Press, 1970.

Raley, Patricia E. *Making Love: How to Be Your Own Sex Therapist*. Photographs by Alan Winston. New York: Dial Press, 1976.

Rauschning, Anna. *No Retreat*. New York: Bobbs-Merrill Co., 1942.

Ray, Gordon N. *H. G. Wells and Rebecca West*. New Haven: Yale University Press, 1974.

Raymond, Janice G. *The Transsexual Empire: The Making of the She-Male*. Boston: Beacon Press, 1979.

Ready, John F. *Effects of High-Power Laser Radiation*. New York: Academic Press, 1971.

Reckless, Walter C. *Vice in Chicago*. Montclair, N.J.: Patterson Smith, 1969.

Reed, Evelyn. *Problems of Women's Liberation*. New York: Pathfinder Press, 1972.

———. *Woman's Evolution*. New York: Pathfinder Press, 1975.

Reich, Wilhelm. *The Mass Psychology of Fascism*. Translated by Vincent R. Carfagno. New York: Farrar, Straus & Giroux, 1970.

———. *The Sexual Revolution*. Translated by Theodore P. Wolfe. New York: Farrar, Straus & Giroux, 1970.

Reid, John. *The Best Little Boy in the World*. New York: G. P. Putnam's Sons, 1973.

Reik, Theodor. *Of Love and Lust*. New York: Farrar, Straus & Co., 1957.

Reimann, Viktor. *Goebbels: The Man Who Created Hitler*. Translated by Stephen Wendt. Garden City, N.Y.: Doubleday & Co., 1976.

Reiss, Curt. *Joseph Goebbels*. Garden City, N.Y.: Doubleday & Co., 1948.

Restif de la Bretonne, Nicolas-Anne Edmé. *The Corrupted Ones*. Translated by Alan Hull Walton. London: Neville Spearman, 1967.

Revel, Jean-François. *The Totalitarian Temptation*. Translated by David Hapgood. Garden City, N.Y.: Doubleday & Co., 1977.

Rich, Adrienne. *Of Woman Born: Motherhood as Experience and Institution*. New York: W. W. Norton & Co., 1976.

———. "Twenty-one Love Poems," I. In *The Dream of a Common Language*. New York: W. W. Norton & Co., 1978.

Richardson, Joanna. *Stendhal.* New York: Coward, McCann & Geoghegan, 1974.
Rimbaud, Arthur. "A Season in Hell." In *A Season in Hell and The Drunken Boat.* Bilingual ed. Translated by Louise Varèse, pp. 2–89. Norfolk, Conn.: New Directions Books, 1961.
Rist, Ray C., ed. *The Pornography Controversy: Changing Moral Standards in American Life.* New Brunswick, N.J.: Transaction Books, 1975.
Roe, Clifford G. *Panders and Their White Slaves.* New York: Fleming H. Revell Co., 1910.
Roland, Marie-Jeanne Phlipon. *The Private Memoirs of Madame Roland.* Edited by Edward Gilpin Johnson. Chicago: A. C. McClurg & Co., 1901.
Rorvik, David M. *In His Image: The Cloning of a Man.* Philadelphia: J. B. Lippincott Co., 1978.
Rose, Al. *Storyville, New Orleans.* University, Ala.: The University of Alabama Press, 1974.
Rosen, Harold, ed. *Abortion in America.* Boston: Beacon Press, 1967.
Rosner, Fred. *Sex Ethics in the Writings of Moses Maimonides.* New York: Bloch Publishing Co., 1974.
Ross, Susan C. *The Rights of Women: The Basic ACLU Guide to a Woman's Rights.* New York: Avon Books, 1973.
Rossi, Alice S., ed. *The Feminist Papers: From Adams to de Beauvoir.* New York: Bantam Books, 1974.
Rossi, William A. *The Sex Life of the Foot and Shoe.* New York: Ballantine Books, 1978.
Rousseau, Jean-Jacques. *The Confessions.* Translated by J. M. Cohen. New York: Penguin Books, 1979.
———. *Émile.* Translated by Barbara Foxley. London: Dent, Everyman's Library, 1963.
Rowbotham, Sheila. *Hidden from History.* London: Pluto Press, 1974.
———. *Woman's Consciousness, Man's World.* Baltimore: Penguin Books, 1973.
———. *Women, Resistance, and Revolution.* New York: Random House, Vintage Books, 1974.
———, and Jeffrey Weeks. *Socialism and the New Life: The Personal and Sexual Politics of Edward Carpenter and Havelock Ellis.* London: Pluto Press, 1977.
Rowe, William Woodin. *Dostoevsky: Child and Man in His Works.*

New York: New York University Press, 1968.
Rubin, Lillian Breslow. *Worlds of Pain.* New York: Basic Books, 1976.
Rugoff, Milton. *Prudery and Passion: Sexuality in Victorian America.* New York: G. P. Putnam's Sons, 1971.
Rukeyser, Muriel. *The Traces of Thomas Hariot.* New York: Random House, 1971.
Rushdoony, Rousas J. *The Politics of Pornography.* New Rochelle, N.Y.: Arlington House Publishers, 1974.
Ruskin, John. *Sesame and Lilies.* Philadelphia: Rodgers Co., 1871.
Russell, Diana E. H., and Nicole Van de Ven, eds. *Crimes Against Women: Proceedings of the International Tribunal.* Millbrae, Calif.: Les Femmes Publishing, 1976.
Sade, Donatien-Alphonse-François de. *Adelaide of Brunswick.* Translated by Hobart Ryland. Washington, D.C.: Scarecrow Press, 1954.
———. *Crimes of Passion.* Edited and translated by Wade Baskin. New York: Philosophical Library, 1965.
———. *Juliette.* Translated by Austryn Wainhouse. New York: Grove Press, 1976.
———. *Juliette or, Vice Amply Rewarded.* Abridged. Translated by Pieralessandro Casavini. New York: Lancer Books, 1965.
——— *Justine; Philosophy in the Bedroom; Eugénie de Franval, and Other Writings.* Translated by Richard Seaver and Austryn Wainhouse. New York: Grove Press, 1966.
———. *The 120 Days of Sodom and Other Writings.* Translated by Austryn Wainhouse and Richard Seaver. New York: Grove Press, 1967.
———. *Selected Letters.* Edited by Margaret Crosland. Translated by W. J. Strachan. New York: October House, 1966.
Salisbury, Charlotte Y. *China Diary.* New York: Walker & Co., 1973.
Sand, George. *Indiana.* Translated by George Burnham Ives. Chicago: Cassandra Editions, 1978.
———. *My Life.* Edited and translated by Dan Hofstadter. New York: Harper & Row, Publishers, 1979.
Sandford, Jeremy. *Prostitutes.* London: Abacus, 1977.
Sanger, Margaret. *Margaret Sanger: An Autobiography.* New York: Dover Publications, 1971.
Sanger, William W. *The History of Prostitution.* New York: Medical Publishing Co., 1906.

Santini, Rosemarie. *The Secret Fire: A New View of Women and Passion.* Chicago: Playboy Press, 1976.

Sarotte, Georges-Michel. *Like a Brother, Like a Lover.* Translated by Richard Miller. Garden City, N.Y.: Doubleday & Co., Anchor Press, 1978.

Sarton, May. *Kinds of Love.* New York: W. W. Norton & Co., 1980.

Sartre, Jean-Paul. *Anti-Semite and Jew.* Translated by George J. Becker. New York: Schocken Books, 1970.

Sarvis, Betty, and Hyman Rodman. *The Abortion Controversy.* New York: Columbia University Press, 1974.

Saxton, Martha. *Louisa May: A Modern Biography of Louisa May Alcott.* Boston: Houghton Mifflin Co., 1977.

Schapiro, Leonard. *Totalitarianism.* New York: Praeger Publishers, 1972.

Schlafly, Phyllis. *The Power of the Positive Woman.* New Rochelle, N.Y.: Arlington House Publishers, 1977.

Schneir, Miriam, ed. *Feminism: The Essential Historical Writings.* New York: Random House, Vintage Books, 1972.

Schor, Lynda. *True Love and Real Romance.* New York: Coward, McCann & Geoghegan, 1979.

Schreiner, Olive. *Woman and Labour.* London: Virago, 1978.

Schulder, Diane, and Florynce Kennedy. *Abortion Rap.* New York: McGraw-Hill Book Co., 1971.

Scott, Hilda. *Does Socialism Liberate Women?* Boston: Beacon Press, 1974.

Scott, Walter. *The Lives of the Novelists.* New York: E. P. Dutton & Co., 1928.

Sebald, Hans. *Momism: The Silent Disease of America.* Chicago: Nelson-Hall Co., 1976.

Selzer, Michael. *Terrorist Chic.* New York: Hawthorn Books, 1979.

Sexton, Anne. *Anne Sexton: A Self-Portrait in Letters.* Edited by Linda Gray Sexton and Lois Ames. Boston: Houghton Mifflin Co., 1977.

Sharif, Omar, and Marie-Thérèse Guinchard. *The Eternal Male: My Own Story.* Translated by Martin Sokolinsky. Garden City, N.Y.: Doubleday & Co., 1977.

Shaw, Bernard. *The Intelligent Woman's Guide to Socialism and Capitalism.* New York: Brentano's Publishers, 1928.

Sheehy, Gail. *Passages.* New York: E. P. Dutton & Co., 1976.

Sherfey, Mary Jane. *The Nature and Evolution of Female Sexuality.* New York: Random House, Vintage Books, 1973.

Shiloh, Ailon, ed. *Studies in Human Sexual Behavior: The American Scene*. Springfield, Ill.: Charles C. Thomas Publisher, 1970.
Showalter, Elaine. *A Literature of Their Own: British Women Novelists from Brontë to Lessing*. Princeton, N.J.: Princeton University Press, 1977.
Sidel, Ruth. *Women and Child Care in China*. New York: Hill & Wang, 1972.
Signoret, Simone. *Nostalgia Isn't What It Used to Be*. New York: Penguin Books, 1978.
Simmons, Ernest J. *Chekhov*. Chicago: University of Chicago Press, 1970.
Sklar, Anna. *Runaway Wives*. New York: Coward, McCann & Geoghegan, 1976.
Sklar, Dusty. *God and Beasts: The Nazis and the Occult*. New York: Thomas Y. Crowell Co., 1977.
Slater, Philip. *Footholds*. New York: E. P. Dutton & Co., 1977.
———. *The Glory of Hera: Greek Mythology and the Greek Family*. Boston: Beacon Press, 1968.
Smith, Liz. *The Mother Book*. Garden City, N.Y.: Doubleday & Co., 1978.
Snodgrass, Jon, ed. *For Men Against Sexism*. Albion, Calif.: Times Change Press, 1977.
Sochen, June. *The New Woman: Feminism in Greenwich Village, 1910–1920*. New York: Quadrangle Books, 1972.
Solanis, Valerie. *SCUM Manifesto*. New York: Olympia Press, 1970.
Sontag, Susan. *Illness as Metaphor*. New York: Random House, Vintage Books, 1979.
———. *On Photography*. New York: Farrar, Straus and Giroux, 1977.
———. *Styles of Radical Will*. New York: Dell Publishing Co., Delta Books, 1970.
Spence, Jonathan D. *The Death of Woman Wang*. New York: Penguin Books, 1979.
Spruill, Julia Cherry. *Women's Life and Work in the Southern Colonies*. New York: W. W. Norton & Co., 1972.
Stade, George. *Confessions of a Lady-Killer*. New York: W. W. Norton & Co., 1979.
Staël-Holstein, Anne Louise Germain Necker. *Corinne*. Translated by Isabel Hill. New York: A. L. Burt, Publisher, n.d.
Stanton, Elizabeth Cady, and the Revising Committee. *The Woman's Bible*. Seattle: Coalition Task Force on Women and Religion, 1975.

Stapleton, Ruth Carter. *The Gift of Inner Healing*. Waco, Tex.: Word Books, Publisher, 1976.

Starkie, Enid. *Flaubert: The Making of the Master*. London: Weidenfeld & Nicolson, 1967.

Stein, George H., ed. *Hitler*. Englewood Cliffs, N.J.: Prentice-Hall, 1968.

Stein, Gertrude. *Writings and Lectures 1909–1945*. Edited by Patricia Meyerowitz. Baltimore: Penguin Books, 1971.

Stein, Martha L. *Lovers, Friends, Slaves*. New York: Berkley Medallion Books, 1975.

Steiner, George. *Language and Silence*. New York: Atheneum Publishers, 1977.

Steiner, Jean-François. *Treblinka*. Translated by Helen Weaver. New York: Simon & Schuster, 1967.

Steiner, Shari. *The Female Factor: A Study of Women in Five Western European Countries*. New York: G. P. Putnam's Sons, 1977.

Steinmann, Anne, and David J. Fox. *The Male Dilemma: How to Survive the Sexual Revolution*. New York: Jason Aronson, 1974.

Stekel, Wilhelm. *Sadism and Masochism*. Vol. 1. Translated by Louise Brink. New York: Liveright Publishing Corp., 1953.

Stern, Susan. *With the Weathermen: The Personal Journal of a Revolutionary Woman*. Garden City, N.Y.: Doubleday & Co., 1975.

Stewart, Desmond. *T. E. Lawrence*. New York: Harper & Row, Publishers, 1977.

Stoker, Bram. *Dracula*. New York: Dell Publishing Co., 1978.

Stoller, Robert J. *Sex and Gender*. New York: Science House, 1968.

———. *Sexual Excitement: Dynamics of Erotic Life*. New York: Pantheon Books, 1979.

Stoltenberg, John. "Eroticism and Violence in the Father-Son Relationship." In *For Men Against Sexism*, edited by Jon Snodgrass, pp. 97–109. Albion, Calif.: Times Change Press, 1977.

———. "Refusing to Be a Man." In *For Men Against Sexism*, edited by Jon Snodgrass, pp. 36–41. Albion, Calif.: Times Change Press, 1977.

———. "Toward Gender Justice." In *For Men Against Sexism*, edited by Jon Snodgrass, pp. 74–83. Albion, Calif.: Times Change Press, 1977.

Stone, Merlin. *When God Was a Woman*. New York: Dial Press, 1976.

Storr, Anthony. *Sexual Deviation*. Harmondsworth, England: Penguin Books, 1964.

Strindberg, August. *Inferno and From an Occult Diary*. Translated by Mary Sandbach. New York: Penguin Books, 1979.

Strouse, Jean, ed. *Women and Analysis*. New York: Grossman Publishers, 1974.

Styron, William. *Sophie's Choice*. New York: Bantam Books, 1980.

Swinburne, Algernon Charles. *Lesbia Brandon*. Edited by Randolph Hughes. London: Falcon Press, 1952.

———. *Love's Cross-currents*. New York: Harper & Brothers, Publishers, 1905.

Swithenbank, Michael. *Ashanti Fetish Houses*. Accra: Ghana Universities Press, 1969.

Symonds, John Addington. *In the Key of Blue and Other Prose Essays*. London: Elkin Mathews, 1896.

———. *A Problem in Modern Ethics Being an Inquiry into the Phenomenon of Sexual Inversion*. London, 1896.

Symons, Arthur. *The Art of Aubrey Beardsley*. New York: Boni & Liveright, 1918.

Szasz, Thomas. *The Manufacture of Madness*. New York: Dell Publishing Co., Delta Books, 1970.

———. *Schizophrenia: The Sacred Symbol of Psychiatry*. New York: Basic Books, 1976.

Talese, Gay. *Thy Neighbor's Wife*. Garden City, N.Y.: Doubleday & Co., 1980.

Tanner, Leslie B., ed. *Voices from Women's Liberation*. New York: New American Library, 1971.

Tavris, Carol, and Susan Sadd. *The Redbook Report on Female Sexuality*. New York: Delacorte Press, 1977.

Tawney, R. H. *Equality*. London: Unwin Books, 1964.

Tennov, Dorothy. *Psychotherapy: The Hazardous Cure*. Garden City, N.Y.: Doubleday & Co., Anchor Press, 1976.

Thérèse of Lisieux. *The Autobiography of St. Thérèse of Lisieux: The Story of a Soul*. Translated by John Beevers. Garden City, N.Y.: Doubleday & Co., Image Books, 1957.

Thibaudet, Albert. *French Literature from 1795 to Our Era*. Translated by Charles Lam Markmann. New York: Funk & Wagnalls, 1967.

Thomas, Donald. *The Marquis de Sade*. Boston: Little, Brown & Co., 1976.

Thomas, Piri. *Down These Mean Streets*. New York: Random House, Vintage Books, 1974.

Tiger, Lionel, and Joseph Shepher. *Women in the Kibbutz*. New

York: Harcourt Brace Jovanovich, 1975.
Tillich, Hannah. *From Time to Time*. Briarcliff Manor, N.Y.: Stein & Day, 1974.
Todd, John. *Woman's Rights*. Dodge, Mary A. [Hamilton, Gail]. *Woman's Wrongs*. New York: Arno Press, 1972.
Toplin, Robert Brent. *Unchallenged Violence*. Westport, Conn.: Greenwood Press, 1975.
Trilling, Diana. *We Must March My Darlings*. New York: Harcourt Brace Jovanovich, 1978.
Tripp, C. A. *The Homosexual Matrix*. New York: New American Library, 1976.
Tripp, Maggie, ed. *Woman in the Year 2000*. New York: Arbor House, 1974.
Troyat, Henry. *Firebrand: The Life of Dostoevsky*. New York: Roy Publishers, 1946.
Tucker, Anne, ed. *The Woman's Eye*. New York: Alfred A. Knopf, 1973.
Turnbull, Colin M. *The Forest People: A Study of the Pygmies of the Congo*. New York: Simon & Schuster, 1961.
———. *The Mountain People*. New York: Simon & Schuster, 1972.
Turquet-Milnes, G. *The Influence of Baudelaire in France and England*. London: Constable and Company, 1913.
Tyler, Anne. *Earthly Possessions*. New York: Alfred A. Knopf, 1977.
Ullerstam, Lars. *The Erotic Minorities*. Translated by Anselm Hollo. London: Calder & Boyars, 1967.
Velde, Theodore H. Van de. *Ideal Marriage*. Translated by Stella Browne. New York: Covici, Friede Publishers, 1930.
Vetālpañcavimšati. *Vikram and the Vampire*. Translated by Richard F. Burton. New York: Dover Publications, 1969.
Vidal, Gore. *The City and the Pillar*. New York: New American Library, 1965.
———. *Homage to Daniel Shays: Collected Essays 1952–1972*. New York: Random House, Vintage Books, 1973.
———. *Kalki*. New York: Random House, 1978.
———. *Matters of Fact and of Fiction: Essays 1973–1976*. New York: Random House, Vintage Books, 1978.
———. *Myron*. New York: Ballantine Books, 1975.
Vilar, Esther. *The Manipulated Man*. New York: Farrar, Straus and Giroux, 1972.
Vittorini, Elio. *Women of Messina*. Translated by Frances Frenaye and Frances Keene. New York: New Directions Books, 1973.

Wald, Karen. *Children of Che.* Palo Alto, Calif.: Ramparts Press, 1978.

Wallace, Irving. *The Nympho and Other Maniacs.* New York: Simon & Schuster, 1971.

Wallace, Michele. *Black Macho and the Myth of the Superwoman.* New York: Dial Press, 1979.

Wallas, Ada. *Before the Bluestockings.* London: George Allen & Unwin, 1929.

Warrior, Betsy, and Lisa Leghorn. *Houseworker's Handbook.* Cambridge, Mass.: Woman's Center, 1975.

Weil, Simone. *The Need for Roots.* New York: Harper & Row, Colophon Books, 1971.

———. *Waiting for God.* Translated by Emma Craufurd. New York: Harper & Row, Publishers, 1973.

Weininger, Otto. *Sex and Character.* New York: G. P. Putnam's Sons, 1975.

Weintraub, Stanley. *Beardsley.* New York: George Braziller, 1967.

Weiss, Peter. *The Persecution and Assassination of Jean-Paul Marat As Performed by the Inmates of the Asylum of Charenton Under the Direction of the Marquis de Sade.* Translated by Geoffrey Skelton. New York: Atheneum Publishers, 1967.

Wells, H. G. *The Invisible Man; The War of the Worlds; A Dream of Armageddon.* London: T. Fisher Unwin, 1924.

Wharton, Edith. *Madame de Treymes and Others.* New York: Charles Scribner's Sons, 1970.

———. *Summer.* New York: Harper & Row, Publishers, 1980.

White, Edmund. *Nocturnes for the King of Naples.* New York: Penguin Books, 1980.

———. *States of Desire.* New York: E. P. Dutton & Co., 1980.

Wilde, Oscar. *Intentions and The Soul of Man.* London: Methuen & Co., 1908.

Wilkerson, Albert E., ed. *The Rights of Children: Emergent Concepts in Law and Society.* Philadelphia: Temple University Press, 1973.

Willard, Elizabeth Osgood Goodrich. *Sexology as the Philosophy of Life.* Buffalo, N.Y.: Heritage Press, 1974.

Wilson, Edmund. *The Bit Between My Teeth: A Literary Chronicle of 1950–1965.* New York: Farrar, Straus & Giroux, 1965.

———. *The Wound and the Bow: Seven Studies in Literature.* New York: Farrar, Straus & Giroux, 1978.

Wilson, Edward O. *On Human Nature.* New York: Bantam Books, 1979.

———. *Sociobiology: The New Synthesis.* Cambridge: Harvard University Press, Belknap Press, 1975.
Winwar, Frances. *The Saint and the Devil: Joan of Arc and Gilles de Rais.* New York: Harper & Brothers, Publishers, 1948.
Wolfenden, John. *Report of the Committee on Homosexual Offences and Prostitution.* London: Her Majesty's Stationery Office, 1957.
———. *The Wolfenden Report: Report of the Committee on Homosexual Offenses and Prostitution.* New York: Stein & Day, 1963.
Wolff, Charlotte. *Love Between Women.* New York: Harper & Row, Colophon Books, 1972.
Wolff, Geoffrey. *Black Sun.* New York: Random House, 1976.
Wollstonecraft, Mary. *Letters Written During a Short Residence in Sweden, Norway, and Denmark.* Lincoln: University of Nebraska Press, 1976.
———. *Thoughts on the Education of Daughters.* New York: Garland Publishing, 1974.
———. *A Vindication of the Rights of Woman.* New York: W W. Norton & Co., 1967.
Woodhull, Victoria Claflin. *The Victoria Woodhull Reader.* Edited by Madeleine B. Sterm. Weston, Mass.: M & S Press, 1974.
———, and Tennessee C. Claflin. *The Human Body The Temple of God.* London, 1890.
Woodward, Bob, and Scott Armstrong. *The Brethren.* New York: Simon & Schuster, 1979.
Woodward, Helen Beal. *The Bold Women.* New York: Farrar, Straus and Young, 1953.
Woolf, Virginia. *The Common Reader.* New York: Harcourt, Brace & World, 1953.
———. *The Diary of Virginia Woolf: Volume II, 1920–1924.* Edited by Anne Olivier Bell. New York: Harcourt Brace Jovanovich, 1978.
———. *The Pargiters: The Novel–Essay Portion of THE YEARS.* Edited by Mitchell A. Leaska. New York: New York Public Library & Readex Books, 1977.
———. *A Room of One's Own.* New York: Harcourt, Brace & World, 1957.
———. *Three Guineas.* New York: Harcourt, Brace & World, 1966.
"Y." *The Autobiography of an Englishman.* London: Paul Elek, 1975.
Yarmolinsky, Avram. *Dostoevsky: A Life.* New York: Harcourt, Brace & Co., 1934.
Young, Tracy. *Women Who Love Women.* New York: Pocket Books, 1977.

Articles, Interviews, Pamphlets, Papers, Periodicals

Adams, Virginia. "Getting at the Heart of Jealous Love." *Psychology Today*, May 1980, p. 38.

Aegis, Winter/Spring 1980.

Alexander, et al. v. Yale University 459 F. Supp. 1 (D. Conn. 1977).

Altman, Dennis. "Interview with Gore Vidal." *Christopher Street*, January 1978, pp. 4–10.

American Journal of Obstetrics and Gynecology 135, no. 6 (November 15, 1979), and no. 7 (December 1, 1979).

Arkes, Hadley. "Marching Through Skokie." *National Review*, May 12, 1978, pp. 588–93.

Bachy, Victor. "Danish 'Permissiveness' Revisited." *Journal of Communication* 26, no. 1 (Winter 1976): 40–43.

Barry, Kathy. "The Real Patricia Hearst Story: 'What I Couldn't Say Until Now.'" *Redbook*, October 1978, p. 112.

Behr, Edward. "Perils of Polanski." *Newsweek*, May 14, 1979, p. 125.

Benz, Hamilton. "The Lady Reveals All." *Museum* 1, no. 1 (March–April 1980): 74–77.

Berger, Alan. "The Porn Wars Heat Up: Is Censorship an Option?" *The Real Paper*, July 14, 1979, p. 14.

Biskind, Peter. "Larry Flynt Rises Up Angry." *Seven Days*, February 24, 1978, pp. 25–27.

Blachford, Gregg. "Looking at Pornography: Erotica and the Socialist Morality." *Radical America*, January–February 1979, pp. 7–18.

Blasius, Mark. "Interview: Guy Hocquenghem." *Christopher Street*, April 1980, pp. 36–45.

Bode, Ken. "On the Seamy Side of the Street." *Politics Today*, May–June 1978, p. 26.

Bronski, Michael. "What Does Soft Core Porn Really Mean to the Gay Male?" *Gay Community News*, January 28, 1978, pp. 6–7.

Brownmiller, Susan. "Rashomon in Maryland." *Esquire*, May 1968, p. 130.

Bruno v. Codd, 407 N.Y.S. 2d 165 (App. Div. 1978, appeal docketed, August 8, 1978).

Cady, Barbara. "Playgirl Interview: Larry Flynt." *Playgirl*, March 1978, p. 43.

Califia, Pat. "The New Puritans." *The Advocate*, April 17, 1980, pp. 14–18.

Chasseguet-Smirgel, Janine. "Reflexions on the Connections Between Perversion and Sadism." Translated by Jacqueline Pollock. *International Journal of Psycho-Analysis* 59 (1978): 27–35.

Clark, Jil. "Circulating Information." Interview with Allen Young. *Gay Community News*, May 12, 1979, pp. 8–9.

———. "Interview: Robin Morgan." *Gay Community News*, January 20, 1979, pp. 11–13.

Coleman, Kate. "Souled Out." *New West*, May 19, 1980, pp. 17–27.

Contemporary Ob/Gyn 13, no. 6 (June 1979), and 14, no. 3 (September 1979), no. 4 (October 1979), and no. 6 (December 1979).

Corea, Gena. "The Caesarean Epidemic." *Mother Jones*, July 1980, p. 28.

———. Interview with Dr. Herbert Ratner, September 20, 1979. Unpublished.

———. "'Scientific' Obstetrics Attacks the Home Birth Movement." Unpublished ms.

Court, John H. "Pornography and Sex-Crimes: Further Evidence on an Old Controversy." Mimeographed. Bedford Park: The Flinders University of South Australia.

DeMott, Benjamin. "The Pro-Incest Lobby." *Psychology Today*, March 1980, p. 11.

Denneny, Michael. "Anatomy of a Love Affair." *Christopher Street*, February 1978, pp. 2–32.

———. "Blue Moves: Conversations with a Male Porn Dancer." *Christopher Street*, February 1980, pp. 26–35.

Dodgson, Charles Lutwidge [Lewis Carroll]. Photographs, edited by David Ray. *New Letters*, Fall 1978.

Donnerstein, Edward. "Pornography and Violence Against Women: Experimental Studies." Mimeographed. Madison: University of Wisconsin.

———. "Pornography Commission Revisited: Aggressive-Erotica and Violence Against Women." Mimeographed. Madison: University of Wisconsin.

Dudar, Helen. "America Discovers Child Pornography." *Ms.*, August 1977, p. 45.

Duncan, Carol. "The Esthetics of Power in Modern Erotic Art." *Heresies*, January 1977, pp. 46–50.

Duncan, Lois. "Can This Marriage Be Saved?" *Ladies' Home Journal*, January 1980, p. 6.

Dunn, Angela Fox. "The Dark Side of Erotic Fantasy." *Human Behavior* 7, no. 11 (November 1978): 18–23.

Dworkin, Andrea. "The Bruise That Doesn't Heal." *Mother Jones*, July 1978, pp. 31–36.

———. "The Lie." *New Women's Times*, November 9, 1979, pp. 6–7.

———. "Phallic Imperialism—Why Economic Recovery Will Not Work for Us." *Ms.*, December 1976, pp. 101–4.

———. "Pornography and Grief." *New Women's Times*, December 1978, pp. 8–9.

———. "Pornography: The New Terrorism." *The Body Politic*, August 1978, pp. 11–12.

———. "The Power of Words." *Gay Community News*, May 27, 1978, pp. 14–15.

———. "Safety, Shelter, Rules, Form, Love—The Promise of the Ultra-Right." *Ms.*, June 1979, p. 62.

———. *Why So-Called Radical Men Love and Need Pornography*. Pamphlet. East Palo Alto, Calif.: Frog in the Well, 1978.

Echols, Alice. "Neo-Separatism." December 23, 1978. Mimeographed.

Ellis, John. "Photography/Pornography/Art/Pornography." *Screen*, Spring 1980, pp. 81–108.

Ephron, Nora. "Women." *Esquire*, February 1973, p. 14.

"Espansion of the Marital Rape Exemption." *National Center on Women and Family Law Newsletter*, July 1980, p. 3.

Fag Rag, no. 26.

Fallaci, Oriana. "An Interview with Khomeini." *The New York Times Magazine*, October 7, 1979, pp. 29–31.

The Family Planning Council of Western Massachusetts, Inc., News, January 1, 1978.

Forer, Lois G. "Rape Is an Expression of Hatred." Letter, *The New York Times*, February 7, 1979.

Gelbert, Bruce Michael. "Coming Out 'S' in Print." *Fag Rag*, Fall 1978, pp. 7–8.

Gelles, Richard J. "Violence and Pregnancy: A Note on the Extent of the Problem and Needed Services." *The Family Coordinator* 24, no. 1 (January 1975): 81–86.

Gengle, Dean. "Scripture from the Book of Krassner." *The Advocate*. March 22, 1978, pp. 22–25.

Gilman, Richard. "Position Paper." *The New York Times Book Review*, July 29, 1979, p. 10.

Goldstein, Richard. "Some Parting Shots." *The Village Voice*, August 13, 1979, p. 44.

Greer, Philip, and Myron Kandel. "Road to Videotape Market Is Paved with Pornography." *New York Post*, May 29, 1979.

Griffin, Susan. "On Pornography." *Chrysalis*, no. 4, pp. 15–17.

Guidelines for Equal Treatment of the Sexes in McGraw-Hill Book Company Publications. Pamphlet.

Hagberg, Karen. "Collective Thinking: Karen Hagberg Comments." *The Empty Closet*, July–August 1977, p. 3.

Hannon, Gerald. "Devices and Desires." *The Body Politic*, November 1979, pp. 32–34.

Haskell, Molly. "Rape in the Movies: Update on an Ancient War." *The Village Voice*, October 8, 1979, p. 1.

Hentoff, Nat. "The New Legions of Erotic Decency." *Inquiry*, December 10, 1979, pp. 5–7.

Heresies: Third World Women 2, no. 4, issue 8 (1979).

Hinckle, Warren. "Why Eldridge Cleaver Is a Wife-Beater." *San Francisco Chronicle*, May 13, 1980.

Horn, Richard. "The Lighter Side of Laser." *The New York Times Magazine*, pt. 2, September 30, 1979, pp. 96–104.

Jay, Karla. "Pot, Porn, and the Politics of Pleasure." Mimeographed.

Johnston, Gordon. "Tyranny of the Penis." *Christopher Street*, March 1980, pp. 40–47.

Johnston, Jill. "A Few Rude Generalizations on Behalf of Enslavement and Other Remembrances of the '70s." *The Village Voice*, February 18, 1980, p. 31.

Jong, Erica. "You Have to Be Liberated to Laugh." *Playboy*, April 1980, p. 154.

"Journal Mothers Testify to Cruelty in Maternity Wards." *Ladies' Home Journal*, December 1958, p. 58.

Keen, Sam. "A Voyeur in Plato's Cave." *Psychology Today*, February 1980, pp. 85–101.

Keshishian, John M. "An Anatomy of a Burmese Beauty Secret." *National Geographic*, June 1979, pp. 798–801.

Kitzinger, Sheila. "Some Mothers' Experiences of Induced Labour," report of The National Childbirth Trust. Mimeographed. London: October 1975.

Klein, Jeffrey. "Born Again Porn." *Mother Jones*, February–March 1978, p. 12.

Kleinberg, Seymour. "Alienated Affections: Friendships Between Gay Men and Straight Women." *Christopher Street*, October–November 1979, pp. 26–40.

Kornbluth, Jesse. "The Education of Christie Hefner." *Savvy*, March 1980, pp. 15–22.

Kostash, Myrna. "Power and Control: A Feminist View of Pornography." *This Magazine*, July–August 1978, pp. 4–7.

Kristol, Irving. "The Shadow of the Marquis." *Encounter*, February 1957, pp. 3–5.

"L.A. Murder 'Targets'—500 Girls." *San Francisco Chronicle*, February 16, 1980.

Lauritsen, John. "Dangerous Trends in Feminism: Disruptions, Censorship, Bigotry." Mimeographed.

Lerner, Max. "Playboy: An American Revolution of Morality." *New York Post*, January 10, 1979.

Levering, Robert. "TV on Trial." *The San Francisco Bay Guardian*, August 3, 1978, pp. 5–8.

Lindsey, Robert. "Sex Films Find Big Market in Home Video." *The New York Times*, April 5, 1979.

Lorde, Audre. *Uses of the Erotic: The Erotic as Power*. Pamphlet, 1978.

"The 'Madonnas' Turn On Their Pimps." *Newsweek*, July 7, 1980, pp. 70–71.

Malamuth, Neil M. "Erotica, Aggression and Perceived Appropriateness." Paper presented at the 86th Annual Convention of the American Psychological Association, September 1, 1978. Mimeographed.

———. "Rape Fantasies as a Function of Repeated Exposure to Sexual Violence." Paper presented at the Second National Conference on the Evaluation and Treatment of Sexual Aggressives, May 1979. Mimeographed.

———, and James V. P. Check. "Penile Tumescence and Perceptual Responses to Rape as a Function of Victim's Perceived Reactions." Paper presented at the annual meeting of the Canadian Psychological Association, June 1979. Mimeographed.

———; Seymour Feshbach; and Yoram Jaffe. "Sexual Arousal and Aggression: Recent Experiments and Theoretical Issues." *Journal of Social Issues* 33, no. 2 (1977): 110–33.

———; Scott Haber; and Seymour Feshbach. "Testing Hypotheses Regarding Rape: Exposure to Sexual Violence, Sex Differences, and the 'Normality' of Rapists." Winnipeg: University of Manitoba; Los Angeles: University of California. Mimeographed.

———; Maggie Heim; and Seymour Feshbach. "Sexual Responsiveness of College Students to Rape Depictions: Inhibitory and Disinhibitory Effects." Winnipeg: University of Manitoba; Los Angeles: University of California. Mimeographed.

———, and Barry Spinner. "A Longitudinal Content Analysis of Sexual Violence in the Best-Selling Erotica Magazines." Winnipeg: University of Manitoba. Mimeographed.

The Marriage Law of the People's Republic of China. Peking: Foreign Language Press, 1973.

Mead, Margaret. "Women and the 'New' Pornography." *Redbook,* February 1976, pp. 29–32.

Miles, Angela. "The Politics of Feminist Radicalism: A Study in Integrative Feminism," Ph.D. dissertation, University of Toronto, 1979.

Miller, Marilyn G., and Janet S. McCoy. *Domestic Violence in Oregon: Preliminary Findings.* Salem, Oreg.: Governor's Commission for Women, 1979.

Mitzel, John. "Boston/Boise: Pederasty in the Athens of America?" Edited by James M. Saslow. *Gaysweek,* February 27, 1978, pp. 12–13.

Money, John. "Bisexual, Homosexual, and Heterosexual: Society, Law, and Medicine." *Journal of Homosexuality* 2, no. 3 (Spring 1977): 229–33.

———. "Imagery in Sexual Hang-Ups." *The Humanist,* March–April 1978. Reprint.

———. "List of Inclusion or Displacement Paraphilias; Hypophilias, Male and Female," 1976. Mimeographed.

———. "Sex, Love, and Commitment." *Journal of Sex and Marital Therapy* 2, no. 4 (Winter 1976): 273–76.

———. "Statement on Antidiscrimination Regarding Sexual Orientation." *Journal of Homosexuality* 2, no. 2 (Winter 1976–77): 159–60.

Morgan, Robin. "How to Run the Pornographers Out of Town (and Preserve the First Amendment)." *Ms.,* November 1978, p. 55.

Morgan, Ted. "United States Versus the Princes of Porn." *The New York Times Magazine,* March 6, 1977, p. 16.

Moss, Leland. "In Pursuit of Pornography." *Gaysweek,* January 30, 1978, p. 23.

Munk, Erika. "A Case of Sexual Abuse." *The Village Voice,* October 22, 1979, p. 1.

Ob. Gyn. News 14, no. 19 (October 1, 1979), no. 20 (October 15, 1979), no. 21 (November 1, 1979), no. 23 (December 1, 1979), no. 24 (December 15, 1979); 15, no. 5 (March 1, 1980), no. 6 (March 15, 1980), no. 7 (April 1, 1980), no. 8 (April 15, 1980), no. 9 (May 1, 1980).

Pankhurst, Christabel, "The Government and White Slavery." Pamphlet reprinted from *The Suffragette,* April 18, April 25, 1913.

Peary, Gerald. "Woman in Porn." *Take One,* September 1978, pp. 28–32.

"Playboy Gives First Amendment Awards." *The National Law Journal*, July 14, 1980, p. 35.

Pliner, Roberta. "Fag-hags, Friends or Fellow-travelers?" *Christopher Street*, October–November 1979, pp. 16–25.

Poett, James. "Deep Peep." *The Village Voice*, May 1, 1978, p. 1.

Polskin, Howard. "Pornography Unleashed." *Panorama*, July 1980, pp. 34–39.

Popert, Ken. "Towards a Theory of Fistfucking." *The Body Politic*, March 1980, p. 22.

Prescott, James W. "Is There a Cure for Violence?" *Penthouse Forum*, September 1977, pp. 33–39.

"Preying on Playgrounds: The Sexploitation of Children in Pornography and Prostitution." *Pepperdine Law Review* 5 (1978): 809–46.

Reavis, Dick. "Town Without Pity." *Texas Monthly*, May 1980, p. 140.

Rechy, John. *The New Censorship and Repression*. Reprint by the Lambda Book Club. N.d.

Reed, David. "Repression and Exaggeration: The Art of Tom of Finland." *Christopher Street*, April 1980, pp. 16–21.

Reed, Rex. "'Cruising' sickens, insults, and distorts." *Daily News*, February 15, 1980.

Reeves, Tom. "In Defense of Boy Love." *Gay Community News*, December 24, 1977, p. 5.

Rembar, Charles. "Obscenity—Forget It." *The Atlantic*, May 1977, pp. 37–41.

Rohrbaugh, Joanna Bunker. "Femininity on the Line." *Psychology Today*, August 1979, pp. 30–42.

Rubin, Gayle. "Sexual Politics, the New Right, and the Sexual Fringe." *The Leaping Lesbian*, February 1978, pp. 9–13.

Russell, Diana E. H. "On Pornography." *Chrysalis*, no. 4, pp. 11–15.

Safire, William. "A 'Bum Rap' for Thevis?" *The Springfield* (Mass.) *Morning Union*, June 16, 1978, p. 18.

Satchell, Michael. "The Big Business of Selling Smut." *Parade*, August 19, 1979, pp. 4–5.

"Schedule of Course on Human Sexuality." Piscataway, N.J.: College of Medicine and Dentistry of New Jersey Rutgers Medical School, 1978, 1979. Mimeographed.

Schwartz, Toby. "Larry Flynt's Media Empire: Will the Porn King Save the Counterculture?" *Valley Advocate*, February 22, 1978, pp. 12–13.

Shultz, Gladys Denny. "Journal Mothers Report on Cruelty in Maternity Wards." *Ladies' Home Journal*, May 1958, p. 44.

"The Skin-Book Boom: What Have They Done to the Girl Next Door?" *Esquire*, November 1976, pp. 91–99.

Smith, Don D. "The Social Content of Pornography." *Journal of Communication* 26, no. 1 (Winter 1976): 16–24.

Smith, Howard, and Lin Harris, "Orgasmology and More." *The Village Voice*, November 12–18, 1980, p. 28.

Smith, Marjorie M. "'Violent Pornography' and the Women's Movement." *The Civil Liberties Review*, Januarv–February 1978, pp. 50–53.

Stambolian, George. "Interview with a Masochist." *Christopher Street*, July–August 1980, pp. 16–22.

Steinem, Gloria. "Erotica and Pornography: A Clear and Present Difference." *Ms.*, November 1978, p. 53.

———. "Linda Lovelace's 'Ordeal.'" *Ms.*, May 1980, pp. 72–77.

———. "Pornography: Not Sex But the Obscene Use of Power." *Ms.*, August 1977, cover, pp. 43–44.

Thurman, Judith. "What Is 'The Real Thing' for a Porn Star?" *Ms.*, March 1976, pp. 37–39.

United States Department of Health, Education, and Welfare. *Advance Data*, no. 9 (August 10, 1977).

Van Gelder, Lindsy. "Anita Bryant on the March: The Lessons of Dade County." *Ms.*, September 1977, p. 75.

Veasey, Jack. "Sex as Big Business: Inside Skin Mags." *Philadelphia Gay News*, February 1978, p. 20.

Walker, Chris. "Potentially Beneficial Aspects of Pornography." *Fag Rag*, no. 25 (Spring 1979), pp. 8–10.

Woods, Laurie. "Litigation on Behalf of Battered Women." *Women's Rights Law Reporter* 5, no. 1 (Fall 1978): 7–33.

Women's Institute for Freedom of the Press. "The First Annual Conference on Planning a National and International Communications System for Women: A Report." Delivered April 7–8, 1979.

Yoakum, Robert. "The Great *Hustler* Debate." *Columbia Journalism Review* 16, no. 1 (May–June 1977): 53–58.

———. "'An Obscene, Lewd, Lascivious, Indecent, Filthy, and Vile Tabloid Entitled *Screw*.'" *Columbia Journalism Review* 15, no. 6 (March–April 1977): 38.

Young, Ian. "A Nosegay for Jamie." *The Gay Clone*. New York: Hunter College, 1980, pp. 14–15.

Index